Tests and Assessments in

Tests and Assessments in Counseling provides students with current information on assessment tools and techniques through detailed case scenarios and vignettes. Going beyond basic information about a multitude of assessments, the authors focus on the use of instruments in individual cases to allow readers to more fully grasp the integral relationship between tests and assessment data and the counseling process. Chapters guide students through choosing the most effective assessment tool, successfully administering the assessment, and making meaningful and useful results of the data with the client. Test questions are also included at the end of each chapter.

Bill McHenry, PhD, NCC, LPC, has coauthored/edited six books, dozens of peer-reviewed journal articles, and several book chapters in the field of counseling. He has presented at international, national, regional, and state professional counseling organizations. Dr. McHenry has been a counselor educator for fifteen years and has taught courses on tests and assessments throughout his teaching career.

Kathryn C. MacCluskie, EdD, is a professor of counseling at Cleveland State University. She has authored/coauthored five books in the areas of clinical skill development, use of test data in clinical assessment, and becoming an effective counselor. Dr. MacCluskie has taught assessment courses for many years in the field of counselor education.

Jim McHenry, EdD, NCC, CRC, LPC, has coauthored/edited five textbooks and numerous professional counseling journal articles. He is a professor emeritus and has taught nearly every course offered in a counseling program. His 32-year career as a counselor and counselor educator includes working as a school counselor, mental health counselor, and rehabilitation counseling consultant. Dr. McHenry has taught appraisal techniques regularly throughout his career.

Tests and Assessments in Counseling

A Case by Case Exploration

Edited by
Bill McHenry,
Kathryn C. MacCluskie, and
Jim McHenry

Routledge
Taylor & Francis Group

NEW YORK AND LONDON

First published 2018
by Routledge
711 Third Avenue, New York, NY 10017

and by Routledge
2 Park Square, Milton Park, Abingdon, Oxon, OX14 4RN

Routledge is an imprint of the Taylor & Francis Group, an informa business

Library of Congress Cataloging-in-Publication Data
A catalog record for this book has been requested

ISBN: 978-1-138-22867-2 (hbk)
ISBN: 978-1-138-22870-2 (pbk)
ISBN: 978-1-315-27953-4 (ebk)

Typeset in Bembo
by Apex CoVantage, LLC

Contents

About the Authors/Editors

Bill McHenry, PhD, NCC, LPC, is chair and associate professor in the counseling program at St. Edward's University. He has been a counselor educator for over 15 years and worked as a counselor with carried clientele ranging across the spectrum of ages and psychological issues. Bill has taught assessment courses at the graduate level throughout his career to students focusing on school, mental health, college, and marriage and family counseling.

Kathryn C. MacCluskie, EdD, is a professor of counselor education at Cleveland State University. She has worked in a variety of positions in clinical settings including the Federal Bureau of Prisons, community mental centers, and private practice. She has been teaching assessment skills to students since 1994.

Jim McHenry, EdD, NCC, LPC, CRC, is professor emeritus, Edinboro University of Pennsylvania. He was a public school teacher (5 years), a guidance counselor (3 years), and a professor of counselor education (32 years). Both NBCC certified (retired) and CRC certified (retired), he directed for many years both a CORE accredited graduate rehabilitation counseling program and a university program for disadvantaged college students, sometimes concurrently. He has authored and coauthored numerous journal articles and five books.

Contributing Authors

Jonathan D. Brown, MS, is a second-year PhD student studying counselor education and supervision in the Penfield College of Mercer University. He has a history of working with adolescents and youth in the psychiatric residential setting, young adults overcoming substance abuse, and state Vocational Rehabilitation. Jonathan currently works as a graduate fellow to assist with the functions and running of the Center for the Study of Narrative at Mercer University. His current areas of interest include narrative therapy, technology in counseling, rehabilitation counseling, social justice advocacy, and working with adolescents and young adults.

Stephanie S.J. Drcar, PhD, is an assistant professor of counselor education at Cleveland State University. She has worked with community and university populations and enjoys being a part of the growth process of both clients and students. Her research focuses on women's experiences of marginalization and she enjoys the continual process of growth in her multicultural competency as she teaches and learns alongside her students.

Trigg A. Even, PhD, LPC–S, NCC, is a counselor educator, counselor supervisor, and private practitioner specializing in counseling with children, adolescents, and their families. Dr. Even has also served direct service and administrative roles in adolescent residential treatment, community not-for-profit, and K-12 public education settings. He regularly consults on school-based mental health practices, counselor professional development, and counselor ethics.

Enobong J. Inyang, PhD, LPC–S, NCC, is a counselor educator and supervisor with about 15 years of clinical experience in the therapeutic community, specializing in substance abuse and sex offender treatment and reentry issues. Dr. Inyang has served as coordinator of Substance Abuse Treatment Program, program administrator of Sex Offender Rehabilitation and Reentry Program, and a consultant for a non-profit agency on the Federal Fatherhood Initiative.

Robin Leichtman, PhD, LPC, serves as a clinician working with children, adolescents, young adults, and adults. She is an adjunct professor at Cleveland State University facilitating master-level students' progress toward becoming clinicians as well as supporting individuals during their master-level practicum and doctoral internship at the agency where she works. Her clinical areas of expertise include psychological evaluations, assessment use for counselors, ADHD, anxiety, and depression. She is certified as a Gestalt psychotherapist by the training faculty of the Gestalt Institute of Cleveland.

Suneetha B. Manyam, PhD, LPC, CPCS, NCC, is an associate professor with 11+ years of teaching, 10 years of clinical, and 11+ years of research experience in the counseling and human development fields. She is a licensed professional counselor with national counselor certification. She coauthored and administered federal grants from the Counseling Department at Mercer University and from India. Currently, she is serving as a project director for Mercer University's $956 K Rehabilitation Service Administrative Grant. Her research and andragogical interests include marital adjustment, acculturation and multicultural issues, anxiety and stress management through meditation, PTSD and military families, and research methods in counseling. Dr. Manyam is an expert at qualitative, quantitative, and mixed methodologies who regularly presents at national and international conferences. She has several scientific publications in peer-reviewed journals and serves on the editorial board for two leading counseling journals. She teaches research and statistics I and II, research design, life span development, practicum, internship, and multicultural counseling courses in clinical mental health counseling, school counseling, rehabilitation counseling, and counselor education and supervision programs.

Ellen C. Melton, PhD, LPC–S, has served as a psychology instructor and counselor educator for over 13 years and continues to enjoy teaching full-time. She has a private practice in which she focuses on women in transition, providing low-cost counseling in the community where she lives, and is currently on the board of a local non-profit organization. She also supervises counseling interns and conducts board-certified trainings for counseling and marriage and family therapy supervisors.

Teri Ann Sartor, PhD, LPC–S, NCC, CHST is a counselor educator at Lamar University, counselor supervisor, and private practitioner who specializes in counseling child and adolescent populations. Dr. Sartor has served in both direct service and administrative roles in residential and community not-for profit organizations. She regularly consults with community agencies and professional counselors on clinical mental health issues, counselor supervision, and counselor ethics. Dr. Sartor is also an editor for the book *Ethical and Legal Issues in Counseling Children and Adolescents.*

Debra A. Tkac, MA, PCC–S, is an adjunct instructor of counselor education at Cleveland State University, teaching counseling practicum and internship courses. She has worked as a clinician and supervisor in community mental health settings for over 25 years and works in a private practice setting. Her clinical work includes therapy with children, adolescents, adults, and families experiencing trauma and chronic mental health issues.

Tyler Wilkinson, PhD, LPC, NCC, ACS, is an assistant professor and is the coordinator of the Clinical Mental Health Counseling Program at Mercer University. He has taught assessment courses to graduate counseling students throughout his academic career. Dr. Wilkinson has clinical experience in a myriad of settings including inpatient behavioral health and private practice. His clinical experience includes working with individuals, families, and couples.

Melanie A. Williams, MA, LPC, has more than 13 years of experience in public schools as a teacher, elementary school counselor, crisis counselor, high school graduation coach, and advanced academics specialist. She regularly provides presentations and workshops to school staff and parents on topics pertaining to social emotional needs of children and adolescents, achievement, behavior interventions, school transitions, and instructional differentiation. She currently works as the gifted and talented assessment specialist for a school district of 25,000 students.

Acknowledgments

I (Bill) would like to start by thanking my co-editors/authors and each of the wonderful contributing authors on this book. Without your knowledge, skills, and ability to communicate the depth of using tests and assessments in the counseling process, this book would not have been possible. To Kathie, I say thank you so much for making this dream come to fruition. When we first discussed the content and focus of the book, it was as if we were reading from the same script. I am so glad to have worked with you on this project and hope we have other stuff to offer the field together in the future. To dad, once again I am reminded of how lucky I am to have a father with such immense and vast knowledge of the field of counseling. I love writing with you and suspect we have several more books to offer to the field of counseling in the coming years. Sharpen your pencil, dad!

It is with great joy that we once again publish with the wonderful folks at Routledge. To our exceptional editor, Anna, your gifts of support, advice, time management, and friendship are not missed on me. I cannot thank you enough for all you have done for our projects, and especially this book. You are a writer's dream. To the rest of the Routledge team, you never treated this book as just another project, but rather, made sure we had all the necessary support throughout the process. Thank you so much for your professionalism and guidance. You made this book a better product and we are forever thankful for that. Thank you goes especially to my lovely wife Missy and our four wonderful children, Meghan, Billy, Katie, and Shane!

From my (Kathie) perspective on this project, my deepest thanks go to Jim McHenry, one of my very first mentors in graduate school. As is evidenced by this book, he was a wonderful role model, and collaborating with him and Bill has been a profoundly satisfying experience. I also wish to acknowledge all our collaborating authors who so willingly joined our team to create a book that is going to be of great help to struggling assessment students! My husband David, dad Jim, and sons David and Alex are always there with unfailing encouragement and support that make my projects actually get finished. Finally, thanks to our editors and production staff at Routledge for their support and their spirit of collaboration, so deeply appreciated!

First, I (Jim) give thanks to both Kathie and Bill, each of whom are exceptional counselor educators who continue to play significant roles in the field. Second, a sincere thanks to the other contributors to the book. The breadth of information they have collectively added to this volume makes a valuable addition to any professional's tool bag. Third, I thank the many other competent professionals who I have worked with during my career. I'll let Drs. Salene Cowher and Ernst Auerbacher stand for those many individuals who have shared their insights with me over the years. And finally, I thank my bride of 56 years, Paula Rae McHenry, for pointing me in the right direction all those years.

Preface

This book is the combination of a number of forces and experts, and represents what we hope is another step forward in the field of tests and assessments. For years, we have each taught assessment classes at the graduate level and failed to find what we wanted, or at times needed, in the typical textbooks. Specifically, we found texts to be highly effective at listing and describing a litany of varied appraisal tools across the major domains (e.g., career, personality, etc.). We found as teachers that our students needed much more depth and clarity on individual assessment tools rather than a broad overview of numerous instruments. This is not just our opinion, but in actuality, how it really works in the world of counseling.

We have found in our clinical experiences—which range across schools, universities, mental health agencies, rehabilitation settings, and private practice—that *the vast majority* of counselors learn several instruments and then they stick with them. This is an important observation and realization. Over the course of a career, a counselor cannot become masterful with 20 or 30 tests and assessments. But with practice, counselors *can* learn to be highly effective with certain instruments. This, then, should be your task as a reader, clinician, and professional. Develop a high degree of proficiency with several instruments that are useful for the populations you serve.

In each of the settings we served, "they" had their favorite assessments and tests for the population they served. We quickly and readily learned these tools and how the results could be effective in the counseling process. At times, however, we observed overuse of assessments. For example, one of us worked in a college counseling center. The standard operating procedure was to have each new client fill out the following paperwork before they met with the assessment specialist: the Beck Depression Inventory (BDI), the Millon Clinical Multiaxial Inventory (MCMI), and the standard intake form for the agency. What could be the harm?

First, it seemed rather odd that no matter what the client's presenting problem was, the BDI was administered. We wonder what it was like for a client to arrive, a student, 18 years old, homesick, and anxious about mid-terms to be handed an assessment asking them about suicidal thoughts? We also wonder about the message to all clients: "before we speak with you, you must be tested for mental health issues." Our experience is that in some settings, this message may run counter to the intended impact of the services provided. We believe counselors should listen closely to their clients before deciding to administer a test or assessment.

Batteries of instruments are, in many cases, an excellent way to more deeply understand the client's issue(s), personality, temperament, etc. Multiple measures used in a battery can illuminate more than just one test. But the timing matters, the philosophy of testing matters. As we will address in the pages and chapters that follow, understanding the case as best as possible and THEN using multiple instruments to further the process is the advisable way to approach our work.

Why we wrote/edited this book? Having taught so many sections of assessment classes, and spoken with other counselor educators across the country regarding their style of teaching such a course, we found that, in almost every program, the course itself was geared toward students developing proficiency and skill in administering, scoring, and then helping the client interpret the results. We agree with this approach to teaching this topic. Depth in understanding a few assessments and tests is critical in developing the necessary professional skills to effectively and ethically use instruments throughout a counselor's career.

Once a therapist acquires the skills associated with test and assessments, he or she can generalize this awareness and knowledge (e.g., norming, reliability, validity, the normal curve, etc.) to other instruments. But acquisition of mastery of an instrument takes time, practice, experience, mentoring, and additional training. Appraisal of individual clients using formal assessment tools is scientific; it is also artistic and intuitive.

1 Introduction

Bill McHenry

Introduction

Humans are the most complex, dynamic, and sophisticated creatures in the universe. Consequently, assessing, appraising, attempting to measure ourselves is an incredibly complex task (Camara, 2014), a task so daunting that the tools, techniques and processes our field has developed over the past hundred-or-so years, as valuable as they might presently be, only begin to give us a glimpse into the world of the client.

Imperfect as they are, however, if used in conjunction with other salient pieces of information, such tools can greatly aid counselor-client progress (Hood & Johnson, 2007). Unfortunately, ineffectively utilized assessment can impede the counseling process and result in negative client outcomes (Anastasi & Urbina, 1997).

Assessment—which includes both formal and informal tests, instruments, observations, self-reports, etc.—requires expert knowledge of the tools, techniques and standards by which an individual's results are being measured/compared (Drummond & Jones, 2010). (Please note carefully the use of the phrase "an individual's results" in the last sentence). *All assessment* is individual based. *n=1*. Period. Even in cases in which we are administering group tests/assessments, as we will present later in this book, the actual *assessment* still takes place at the individual level.

Certainly then, it follows that no matter what instrumentation we are utilizing, the data belong to the person with whom we are working. This book is framed with that basic construct at its core.

Data

One of the assessments we will cover in a later chapter is a very widely used inventory, Holland's Self-Directed Search (SDS). The SDS provides a quick self-report of skills, interests and aptitudes of the client that can then be used to help the client identify job clusters he/she might want to consider. Clients are asked to self-report their likes and dislikes in relation to a number of prompts such as "practice a musical instrument." Then they are asked to attest to things that they do well or competently (e.g., "I can repair furniture"). They are also asked to self-rate on a scale from 7–1 (high to low) in six domains (e.g., "clerical ability") (Dozier, Sampson, & Reardon, 2015).

One of your authors was part of a project that encouraged local Latino high school students to consider attending college. The program provided college-based experiences and included the SDS as a part of a battery of assessments to aid students in their possible choice of majors. Master's-level counseling students were used to proctor and score the SDS. Although the SDS is self-scorable, in this particular case we decided to use several instruments and then try to combine the results for the students to acquire an even greater understanding of self. When one of the master's students was scoring the SDS for one of the participants, something very peculiar was noticed.

One particular participant had indicated that he had no interest in anything on the SDS and possessed no skills/abilities/aptitudes. Considering the data in hand, with no other data yet, the counseling student consulted with me on how to proceed. Her hypotheses ranged from "maybe he's depressed and suicidal" to "maybe he didn't understand, he is ESL." She then guessed that even though each of the participants had been offered English or Spanish versions of the instrument (he had chosen English), possibly he had not understood the prompts. She then returned to other data she had observed. Since he had presented very quiet and reserved, her lean went back to depression. Finally, she offered a developmentally based guess, suggesting that since he was at a stage of non-compliance as a teen, maybe he was just presenting as defiant and resistant.

Of course, the most important thing to do in this case was to sit and talk with the participant to hear his perspective on how he answered the SDS. The counseling student was encouraged to do this and learned quite a bit from the process. In this case, it was very easy to assume that the data received through the SDS was inaccurate and there must be a reason he completed it incorrectly. The truth turned out to be far more compelling than our conjecture and assumptions were.

When asked to help her understand his answers on the SDS, the young man politely and clearly stated that he was going to be a professional soccer player. Exhibiting no braggadocio, he reported that he was the best player on his school team, and had already received offers in his home country to join *a professional team*. He further stated that he had no other interests in working at anything but being a soccer player. He also allowed that he was "ok" at some of the things on the SDS, but when compared to how good he was at soccer, he was "bad" at them. We find it very interesting that, from *his* perspective, his *worldview*, he had filled out the SDS as accurately as possible. However, for our understanding and clarification, we felt more data and discussion was needed to really do justice to these results. Thus, we will encourage you throughout the book to use more than one data source for assessment purposes. Multi-method assessment provides a much more 3D view of the client. In almost all cases, more data is better.

A second important lesson from this case is that results of *any* assessment should be corroborated as best possible with the client (Bram, 2015). As we will discuss throughout the remaining chapters, consensus building with the client is critical in helping him/her make meaning from results. For example, when considering the SDS, if a client scored very high on the *artistic* and very low on the *conventional*, results delivered in a format that was regimented, directive and orderly (e.g., a list of occupations they might consider) might not fit well with the client's overall way of looking at the world. Rather an approach that used some forms of artistic representation of the results might be better received (e.g., a mosaic word art representation of the results).

Returning to the case described so far, the counseling student was still a bit perplexed as to what to do with the SDS results. She was also interested to find out why he chose to attend this event when he had no real desire to attend college. His response was that he wanted to be with his friends. As the day went on, it became clear that had a strong social interest and was well respected by his peers. So what to do with the results?

The student was encouraged to retake the assessment, this time from the perspective of ranking and rating his skills without comparing them to his soccer ability and interest. He was also encouraged to think about the results as a good tool to consider when he eventually retired from soccer and as possible hobbies. He followed the new instructions, leading to a significant change in the results.

In hindsight, what could the counselor have done differently? Of course, she could have done more preparation upfront. She could have sat with each of the participants and had an introductory "session" to get to know them better. Unfortunately, time constraints are always a pressing issue for counselors. In this case, the most important thing that happened in the end was that the counselor and client went over the results and then reassessed under better circumstances (his view of the questions and prompts being different).

There will always be variables that mitigate the certainty of test and assessment results (Chiu, 2014). Any of the hypotheses this counseling student forwarded could have been true. A deeply depressed person might not have any interests and he/she may hold a life view that he or she is incapable of achieving many things. In the case presented previously, however, James Marcia's developmental theory might suggest that this client most likely had foreclosed on his identity and, thus, any other career options (Marcia, 1980).

The Testing Conditions

Sophisticated assessments can shed great amounts of light onto an individual's personality, can determine a client's level of development, and can even detect whether or not a client is being honest, genuine and real in his or her responses, etc. Under ideal conditions, test error can be minimal and the results of the process can hold a high degree of validity. For most tests and assessments, optimal conditions are similar and should be common sense.

Testing should take place in an environment free of obstructions (visual, auditory, mechanical, internal noise, etc.). If you are proctoring an IQ test to a student, and there is a terribly loud thunderstorm with heavy rain hitting the metal roof of the building you are in, and, if the student happens to have PTSD, it would be readily recognized that the results may not detect the student's true IQ. So, in this case, do we turn around and retest the student the next day or maybe a couple of days later? Hopefully not. In many tests, especially instruments that call for the client to demonstrate knowledge and/or learning, for up to two weeks after the assessment, the brain is still actively attempting to solve the problems from the test. Therefore, we would expect that if we immediately retest this student, the test score would actually go from being lowered (due to the impact of the loud noise during the first examination) to elevated (due to prior test knowledge) (Drummond & Jones, 2010; Hood & Johnson, 2007).

Ideal environmental conditions (low noise pollution, limited visual stimulation, etc.) are very important in the testing process. However, another significant variable that will determine the degree of validity of results lays within the client. Factors that may influence (minimally or greatly) test results include mood, current state of health, recent sleep pattern, medications and diet. Such influences are rarely optimized to allow for peak performance during a test. However, awareness on the part of the counselor and client as to the potential implications of internal and external factors on the test results is important (Bram, 2015). One way we like to consider assessment results is to remember that the results are based on all of the possible influences on the client during that one particular time in that one particular place while they were in that one particular state. This doesn't mean that results are typically not reliable. In actuality, many good instruments have high levels of reliability (consistency).

Meaning-Making

In many cases, counselors and clients are best served when they allow time to consider the results, what the results mean for the client, and how the data might be used to help the client move forward on a topic or issue. This is an extremely important part of the process that requires professional skill on the part of the counselor to help the client fit what may be new information into his or her personal world (Wong, 2015).

When it comes to helping a client make meaning from assessment results, the clinician becomes a very important variable as well. Consider the case example that follows. In this case, how might the variability across different styles by clinicians impact the way the results are conferred, shared, communicated, described, and, in the end, how the counselor will help the client make meaning from the data?

Case Example: The Case of John

John, 58, a Caucasian male, is coming to counseling for help with dealing with what he describes as an "overbearing" boss. Dealing with his new boss, John experiences anxiety, frustration and uncertainty, and has been considering, reconsidering and considering again, "*What is wrong with me?*"

He has been administered the following instruments (with the associated outcomes/ results/assessment data):

Myers-Briggs Personality Type Indicator (MBTI). The ISFJ code provided through the MBTI indicates several significant characteristics that the counselors attend to. Specifically, John may have personality characteristics that lead him to *complain and feel resentful and unappreciated while he struggles to actually assert his needs*. Interestingly, this personality type also may lead a counselor to understand that John has a tendency to *hold a rigid outlook on hierarchy, structure, and procedures*. Further characteristics of this personality type include being *practical, realistic, concrete, and specific*.

Coping Responses Inventory (CRI). Results from this instrument allow a client to better understand his way of dealing/coping with a challenging life stressor. There are eight scales that help determine the style being used by the client in a particular scenario. Of the eight scales, four are identified as being *approach* styles (meaning that the client is moving toward the problem cognitively and/or behaviorally). The remaining four scales identify coping responses that a client may use to *avoid* the life issue. The scales are not identified as being isolated and often it is discovered that a client uses both *approach* and *avoidance* responses.

John's results indicate that he scored highest on the following scales: *Seeking Guidance and Support (SG)* and *Emotional Discharge (ED)*. The SG function allows him to seek counseling, talk to friends and family about the issue, and specifically includes *behavioral strategies that have the client gather more information about the problem through discussing it with others seeking guidance, support and new information*. The ED response specifically allows John to *disperse some of the energy associated with the issue by expressing his emotions to others*.

Now consider two counselors, and their unique perspectives, approaches and theoretical underpinnings.

Counselor #1 is a cognitive-behavioral therapist. She specifically uses Rational-Emotive Behavioral Therapy (REBT) in her approach.

Counselor #2 is a Narrative Therapist. He also incorporates Solution-Focused Brief Therapy into his counseling style.

Both counselors share the results factually with the client. They report the data in a similar manner. The client reacts negatively to the results. John responds by saying the following: "Are there any other tests you can give me? These don't seem right." Then after a pause, he continues: "I've been at this company for over 30 years, and really never had any problems with my boss. It sounds to me like you are now saying I have always had these problems of avoiding emotions and stuff."

Each of these counselors has a specific dominant theory base from which she or he operates in focusing on the client's responses and reactions. These theories, and their unique theoretical lens, in turn then affect the counselor's responses back to the client (Shapiro, 2012).

Counselor #1 may respond by challenging the client to consider what beliefs he has that may be preventing him from even hearing the results. She may want to challenge the client (gently or firmly) to help him understand how his emotionally discharged reaction to the results seems to corroborate them. Not a bad therapeutic approach. Perhaps, from it, she may be able to help him come to better understand himself and how the new boss's presence surfaces certain reactions from him (that are both rational and sometimes irrational).

Counselor #2 may approach the client's responses from a perspective of asking him to share a story or example of when he struggled with the decision of a boss, or didn't like how the boss was coming across, but handled it well. This counselor, using his particular theory base, can focus on the exceptions to the dominant story (and the client's reaction to the feedback) while surfacing unique moments when the client used a different response approach.

One really important aspect to this case example is the fact that the client had an immediate, strong response to the results. This can happen, especially when the feedback provided runs counter to the client's self-image, self-concept. A useful model to help explain the inherent risk in providing feedback that is new to a client through the assessment process is found in Johari's Window (see Figure 1.1).

The theory behind Johari's window is straightforward. In essence, there are four different areas in which information about self can be placed. In part, these areas are determined by the awareness an individual has of self. For example, "known to self" and "not known to self" are descriptors (adjectives used to describe the individual). Things that are "known to self" may include the client's awareness that they are "helpful" to others. An example of a descriptor that may not be known to self might be (perhaps for someone with low self-esteem) that they are "intelligent." But the theory and use of the Johari window goes much further than just things known or not known about self (Luft, 1969).

There are two other categories that help shed light onto the awareness of an individual. These are items "known to others" and "not known to others." The same examples may fit this category as well ("others" may experience and know a client to be "helpful" but not know them to be "intelligent"). When we combine the four categories, it can be readily understood that there are four window panes through which a client's understanding of self and "others'" awareness of the client can be determined (Luft & Ingham, 1955).

For example, the "arena" pane of glass contains those things that are readily open and transparent about the client. The 11th grader who aces the SAT and who has a 4.0 is observed by her teachers as being highly intelligent and has the internal knowledge that she is smart. In counseling, some of the most important work that can be done is to help the client "move" items from the other three panes into the "arena."

A client who is "nervous" and "shy" may know that internally, but prefer not for others to see that side of himself. Therefore, he may try to keep that part of himself in the "façade" area—out of the awareness of others. Certainly this decision to not let others see his shyness and/or nervousness may fall under the guise of a façade, or unauthentic self.

	Known to Self	Not Known to Self
Known to Others	Arena	Blind Spot
Not Known to Others	Façade	Unknown

Figure 1.1 Johari's Window

The "blind spot" area provides exemplars of an individual that are known to others, but that the client is not aware of. For example, a client may not realize she is "controlling." While those around her are keenly aware of her tendency to be in control of many if not all of the things around her, she may be oblivious to this style and approach.

Finally, the "unknown" pane houses those attributes and tendencies by the client that are unknown to both the client and the rest of the world. In this area, the counselor may help the client come to know new things about self (either positive or negative); for example, a predisposition to drugs and alcohol or a certain mental health disorder.

How might this information connect to the use of tests and assessments in the counseling process? *Of course, assessing clients is an act of discovery.* An attempt to better come to know the client through formal measurements allowing deeper awareness of the issue being assessed (e.g., intelligence testing, career interests, level of depression, etc.). Therefore, if the assessment data is valid, the client *should* get results that add to his or her understanding of self and place in the world (Gregory, 2013).

But here is the potential issue: *what if the results are directly opposed to what the client knows about himself?* In the previous example, where two counselors delivered results in the same exact way to the client, he responded by attacking the data because it did not fit his worldview of self, identity and what was *known to him, about him.* So, here we see the incredibly important value of anchoring the feedback that the client receives in a way that is akin to his or her pre-conceived notions. Effective counselors help the client make room for new information to move from the *blind spot, façade* and *unknown* panes into the *arena.* Then it can become meaningful and useful. As you read this book, each of the chapter authors will provide clear examples of how to incorporate feedback in a meaningful way that holistically incorporates the previous views of the client.

History of Tests and Assessments—The Past, the Present and the Future

Inherent in the development of any field are moments in time that serve to describe the building efforts, from one individual or group to another. The tests and assessments we have today, some of which have their origins in the early days of testing, have come a long way. As will be discussed in Chapter 2, psychometric principles of test/assessment creation, norming and administration have become a true science unto themselves. But to understand how we got to our current place of measurement, it is important to understand what events transitioned our field from fledgling observations to true scientific measures.

Francis Galton (1822–1911) is considered to be one of the first architects of scientific measurement through psychological testing. His seminal work was an attempt to understand intelligence through the use of testing that measured reaction time and physical strength. Of course, today we can quickly see the flawed logic, the poorly crafted correlation and causation between two unalike issues (reaction time = intelligence). In his time, however, his efforts were truly groundbreaking. The formalized attempt to measure individual levels of intelligence across people was an important first step in the development of our field (Gregory, 2013).

Cattell (1860–1944), a student of Galton, though limited by his resources and the previous knowledge of human intellect, human physiology and the like, was able to articulate and promote the belief that psychology, as a field, could not progress without the investigation of tests and measurements proctored and categorized across a large number of participants (Cattell, 1890). This was another major step forward for the field of psychology, and later the field of counseling. Generally, Cattell is credited with being the pioneering agent for the modern IQ tests. In 1890, Cattell ushered in the term "mental test" to describe his work with college students. Following up on the work of his mentor, Cattell continued to try to ascertain level of intelligence through the assessment of physiological reaction times (strength, speed, sensitivity to pain, etc.). Anastasi and Urbina (1997) suggested that Cattell was convinced that the precision of reaction times and physiological reaction measurement was most likely the very best measures of intelligence humans could hope for. In essence, he considered the study of the seemingly far more complex constructs (e.g., memory, math skills, reading comprehension, etc.) to be far beyond the grasp of psychological measurement.

Stop and Consider

History allows us to look back with knowledge and awareness that is well beyond the grasp of those living in the times we are studying. In this case, we can look back on Galton and Cattell and chuckle, wonder about and perhaps even think, "What were they thinking?": reaction time and muscle strength = level of intelligence? Not only were they wrong, but in today's world they would be considered as being discriminatory in their views. In considering Cattell's premise that tasks such as computing math problems and comprehending the written words on a page would forever be beyond our scope of knowledge seems to be completely wrong. We can, to a fairly high level of accuracy, determine such things. So we posit four questions for you to consider:

Upon what fallacies or false assumptions are some of our current tests and assessments built?
What may be ahead in the world of tests and assessments?
Might we develop a saliva or blood test that takes moments to administer and provides 99% accurate results on IQ level?
Could we end up developing a brain scan that clearly and specifically describes an individual's personality?

After Galton and Cattell started the major movement toward formal psychological tests, the watershed moment in the field was the development of what we know of now as an IQ test by Binet and Simon. In an effort to assess the comprehension and reasoning ability in children and adults, they devised an instrument that relied more heavily on verbal content (as opposed to focusing significantly on sensations and perceptions). Problematically, however, early versions of this test did not have a clear way of objectifying results. In further iterations of the test, specifically by Lawrence Terman (from Stanford), the scales of the test became solidified and the concept of intelligence quotient or IQ score was provided (IQ = mental age/chronological age) (Gregory, 2013).

Up to this point in the history of tests and assessments, a lot of focus had been on individual testing and results. World War I provided the impetus for the development of formalized attempts at group testing. During this time, the Army Alpha and Army Beta were developed. The goal was the efficient and effective classification of the million-plus recruits entering the military. Such a test would allow for key decisions to be aided through scientific data, such as: assignments of duties, tracking for leadership roles, rationale for early discharge or rejection from military service. Two forms of the test were developed. The Army Alpha was the standard exam while the Beta was developed to provide test results for recruits who were unable to read or were ESL.

The Army Alpha and Beta were revised several times then released to the public and truly ushered in the era of group testing. In some ways, the world became more aware of the idea of measuring intelligence and defining a person's level of intelligence through an exam. What could go wrong? In the era of the popularization of the assembly line for automobiles, technological devices and manufacturing of products, group testing seemed to be a natural progression and fit with the world. In essence, the psychometric principles that uphold reliable and valid results were not developed to the point where the results of these tests were truly useful. By the 1930s, the testing movement was coming under serious fire by skeptics who, rightfully, pointed out the severe limitations in results (Anastasi & Urbina, 1997).

Up to this point, attempts have been made to successfully determine the intelligence of an individual through speed, strength, and the formation of group tests such as the Army Alpha and Beta, verbal comprehension and mathematical skills. The tests being developed to measure such constructs were (compared to today) unsophisticated, and had quite a bit of statistical error in them. Of course, things develop over time, cars have come a long way, planes have improved dramatically, etc. The next major step in the testing movement wasn't as much initially with the testing itself, but rather a rudimentary question of, "What should we be trying to measure?" What was intelligence? What should we be trying to assess to determine an individual's level, degree or associated score in relation to others? Researchers and pioneers such as L.L. Thurston, T.L. Kelley and Charles Spearman reimagined intelligence as aptitude across multiple areas (e.g., verbal comprehension, mathematical reasoning, spatial relations, mechanical skills, etc.). These constructs became known as *traits*. And through statistical analysis of the interplay and overlap across traits, using factor analysis, test results moved from one definitive score (e.g., IQ = 100) to a myriad of subtest scores for each trait (e.g., Full Scale IQ = 100; verbal reasoning = 110; mathematical/numerical = 85; spatial visualization = 94, etc.) (Gregory, 2013). Clearly, the differentiation across traits was a huge step forward for testing, as was the use of factor analysis to investigate and determine the inter-relationships between and among traits.

Measuring intelligence and then aptitude were not the only early forms of testing. Parallel paths were emerging in schools for the development of *achievement* tests and psychologists were also trying to better understand ways to assess and determine personality characteristics through formal measures.

In schools, measuring student achievement started early with the advent of E.L. Thorndike's rating scales (Drummond & Jones, 2010). He tried to detect achievement through formal measures of handwriting quality, written composition construction, spelling, mathematical computation and reasoning. While the early intelligence and aptitude tests were intended to measure an individual's inherent ability to think, reason and comprehend, Thorndike and those who followed were interested in determining the degree to which an individual student had actually comprehended the lessons provided in their schooling. That same line of demarcation exists today between achievement and aptitude/intelligence tests.

The Stanford Achievement Test, developed by Truman Kelley, Giles Ruch and Lewis Terman introduced the use of group standardization to testing in schools (Drummond & Jones, 2010). Group norming of tests was a critical step in the evolution of what we refer to today as norm-referenced tests. These instruments allow for the understanding of differences across different domains being assessed (e.g., history, mathematics, science, etc.) to compare both individual student results (to see how they are doing compared to peers across the norm group) as well as to determine effectiveness at the class and school levels.

Stop and Consider

Group testing can be a good way for a school to determine if the lessons are being taught and absorbed by the students. If the achievement test is sound psychometrically, we might assume that you can simply compare the results of one school to another to determine how effective the instruction is and how well the students are grasping the material. Makes sense. Except for the missing piece, which is the actual level of aptitude/intelligence for both schools. If school A has an average IQ of 100 and school B is at 115, we might (and should) expect the students in school B to be better able to pick up the lessons.

But those are Full Scale IQ averages. What if we consider the subscales as well?

Might we find even more areas of difference that might suggest that expectations for the schools to score similar on achievement testing is both illogical and irrational?

Further, of course, we might consider socioeconomic factors in each educational district as an even better measure of readiness to learn across both school populations in question.

Personality tests, one of the most important assessment tools for a counselor, emerged initially through the use of the technique known as *free association*. In this approach, the examiner would provide the individual with a word and ask him or her to respond with the first word that came to mind (Anastasi & Urbina, 1997). Though an inexact scientific approach, in this kernel, we recognize the attempts by clinicians and researchers to devise ways to formally assess personality.

There are many personality instruments on the market currently, and they all owe their roots back to the work by Woodworth during World War I. Just as other scientists were trying to help classify military recruits in the area of intelligence, Woodworth was trying to help ascertain which men should be excluded from the military due to significant psychological issues (Drummond & Jones, 2010).

Woodworth devised a self-report assessment through which he tried to separate out only those individuals who were currently exhibiting severe mental health issues. By no means was he trying to ascertain personality type; rather his approach was binary (yes or no for service). Crude as it was, this marked an early attempt to diagnose psychological impairment at the individual level.

During the 1920s, energy in the field of tests and assessments began to focus on *projective* means to assess personality. Among these instruments were the Rorschach Ink Blot Test and the Goodenough Draw-a-Man test. Projective assessments, in general terms, called for the client to "project" their personality onto a basic stimulus (e.g., ink blots or self-drawn pictures). Attempts were made to categorize the projection of the client into personality traits and temperaments (Anastasi & Urbina, 1997). While projectives are still in use today (e.g., ink blots, sand tray, early recollections), their use has become less quantifiable and more useful as a tool for clinical work (Yan & Chen, 2011).

Stop and Consider

One form of projective is the "house-tree-person." This assessment called for the client to draw a house, a tree and a person. It was hypothesized that depending on what features are drawn, meaningful extrapolation of not only personality but major issues in life could be recognized by the clinician in the drawings. For example, if a client drew a tree that had a knot in it, the symbolism such a drawing represented was that the client had a deep dark secret, most likely that they had been abused. While that may have been true in some cases, from a reliability and validity standing, can the field really believe this to be true of the majority of knots drawn by clients in trees?

What other factors may lead a client to draw a knot in a tree? Artistic talent and an eye for details? The client grew up with a tree in their yard that had a knot in it?

Projective techniques such as these can be very useful in understanding holistically how a client understands himself, his place in the world and those around him. But as a field, we have not, as of yet, been able to associate certain images or projections with specific psychological conditions or personality types.

The history of testing allows us to understand some of the pre-cursers to where we are today as a field. Importantly, and hopefully, readers will recognize that any and all tests and assessments are built upon our best awareness of constructs being measured and psychometric properties of testing. Granted, this is an inexact science. However, as we have progressed from the beginnings of the field, we have developed means by which we can much more fully test and assess the construct we are intending to measure. In this, we are confident in our results.

What Follows

This book has been written from a clinician's perspective. Our goal is to fill the gap in the current literature in making meaningful use of tests and assessments. Most counselors learn to provide feedback and test/assessment results in ways that work with their clients. This takes years of practice and attention to the nuances of testing. Our primary goal is to help readers to envision ways to effectively report results to clients and then *work more effectively with the client in making such results meaningful and useful*. The following chapters were developed to provide depth with certain assessments and tests associated with specific cases.

However, before we get to the cases and clinical implications of tests and assessment data with clients, we must take time to cover, review, re-review or introduce the concepts on which our field currently relies to assure the tests and assessments we use are being developed and used as they are intended.

Chapter 2

In Chapter 2, Kathryn MacCluskie covers the basic and advanced topics associated with psychometric properties of tests and assessments as well as measurement concepts. Included in this chapter will be issues of test construction, including validity, reliability, norming and test error.

Chapter 3

In Chapter 3, Dr. Ellen Melton addresses the ethical and legal aspects to using tests and assessments. Inherent in this chapter are issues such as ethical use of results, test manufacturers' guidelines for proctoring and interpreting results, and ethical dilemmas faced by clinicians with tests and assessments. Additionally, areas such as supervision, consultation and data management will be covered.

Chapter 4

In Chapter 4, Robin Leichtman and Kathryn MacCluskie cover the use of Mental Status Examinations and Intake Assessments. These basic skills associated with the effective work of a counselor can illuminate client cases while developing the groundwork for the work to follow.

The remaining chapters of the book will focus directly on a topical area (e.g., career assessments, suicidal assessment) with the major focus being on the clinical use of assessment results. We have invited experts in the associated field to provide the case analyses and information pertinent to the use of assessment results. The chapters that follow explore in depth the following topics: *career assessments and personality inventories, tests and assessments in substance abuse counseling, assessment of psychological conditions, using tests and assessments to inform your work with children and adolescents, intelligence testing, tests and assessments in rehabilitation counseling, suicidal ideation assessment, testing in K-12 schools and group testing.*

In each of Chapters 5–12, the instruments/tests/assessments being used will be introduced with the associated strengths and weaknesses. Further, the author(s) provide readers with the ideal populations the instruments have been developed for and what the typical referral questions/issues are that are associated with the use of the instruments. Specialized training needed for the instruments as well as ethical considerations will also be addressed.

Following the general overview of the instruments, a case will be presented that includes the referral issues, current and historical circumstances, a clear description of the client, and any other pertinent information for the case. The goal will be to allow readers to fully understand the case as it is presented, the instruments being used and the results/results-sharing process.

Results will be presented from each of the instruments being employed in the case with descriptions of qualitative and quantitative data as it pertains to the case and the instruments. Following a discussion of the data, the chapter author will then provide readers with an understanding of how they would provide feedback to the client on the results and work with them to make meaning from said results. Emphasis will be placed upon the actual feedback process, including how the counselor may frame the results and work with the client's reactions.

Generalizability

We have chosen this format for the book because we believe in several major guiding factors related to tests and assessments in counseling. Simply put, they are as follows:

1. There is an ever-growing list of good tests and assessments in our field.
2. No counselor can master all, or even many, of the tests and assessments we have at our disposal.
3. Counselors are smart and capable of transferring knowledge from one assessment or test to others, once they have learned the skills needed.
4. Assessment and testing are not separate from the counseling process but rather may provide a cornerstone to all the work we do with clients (in some cases formal assessments; in other cases, informal observations).
5. Many of the tests and assessments on today's market have additional trainings associated with them. No book can ever make a counselor an expert on any one particular test or assessment.
6. Finally, with all of the above points in mind, we intend for this book to:

    a. Introduce the concepts of tests and assessments from a psychometric, ethical, professional and pragmatic view; and
    b. Provide you with depth and understanding of different cases across the landscape of counseling to envision how test and assessment results can be used to forward the counseling process and therefore help the client.

There is both a science and an art to the process of administering, scoring, interpreting, and making effective clinical use of tests and assessments. As a current or future counselor, we sincerely hope that you find value in this book and use it to enhance your ability to serve your clients.

Test Your Knowledge:

1. If you are proctoring a test, and something happens that causes a negative impact on the results (e.g., disruption of some type), you should:
   a. Retest the client immediately
   b. Add points to the final score to balance out the disruption
   c. Wait at least two days and then retest
   d. None of the above

2. The goal of tests and assessments should be to make the client aware of:
   a. Only those things that are not known to self
   b. Only those things not known to others
   c. Only those things that are not known to self and others
   d. All of the above

3. Francis Galton tried to measure intelligence using which of the following?
   a. Physical strength
   b. Reaction time
   c. Both A and B
   d. None of the above

4. In the late 1800s, which theorist was credited with ushering in the dawn of the IQ test era?
   a. Binet
   b. Cattell
   c. Galton
   d. Spearman

5. The development of achievement tests is credited to:
   a. Thorndike
   b. Binet
   c. Spearman
   d. Cattell

6. The house-tree-person projective technique is considered by many to be:
   a. Definitive
   b. Without any true reliability or validity
   c. An assessment approach that should be used with caution in determining the "meaning" of symbolism
   d. None of the above

7. Johari's window allows that some assessment results might be:
   a. Previously known to the client
   b. Previously known to the counselor/others about the client
   c. Not previously known to the client or anyone else
   d. All of the above are correct

8. Assessment includes all of the following:
    a.   Formal measures such as test and assessment instruments
    b.   Informal data such as self-reports and observations
    c.   Both A and B are correct
    d.   Neither A nor B are correct

9. When it comes to the client making meaning from the assessment results, the role of the counselor is dictated in part by:
    a.   Their theoretical background
    b.   Their ability to work with the client in fitting the new information into their existing worldview
    c.   Their understanding of the instrument(s)
    d.   All of the above are correct

10. What test(s) ushered in the group testing movement?
    a.   Intelligence
    b.   Ability
    c.   Achievement
    d.   Army Alpha and Beta

Discussion Questions/Prompts:

1.   What preexisting beliefs do you have about the utility of test and assessment data?
2.   How do imagine testing and assessment techniques will change in the next 20 years?
3.   What factors may lead to such changes?
4.   When you consider your own personal experience with tests and assessments, what worked effectively to help you make meaning from the results?
5.   How will you handle situations when the environmental conditions have a negative impact on the test results?

2 Measurement Concepts

Kathryn C. MacCluskie

This chapter is intended to serve as a conceptual review of some basic measurement concepts. Readers are referred to Whiston (2012) for more comprehensive information related to test development and standardization. While a thorough discussion of test development will not be provided, we will focus on several related concepts and ideas that are essential to truly grasp and understand assessment results. Thus, the purpose of this chapter is to present some definitions and explanations of commonly used assessment terms that represent the conceptual foundation underneath the information yielded by tests and instruments, regardless of the domain being assessed. Standardized psychological and educational assessment relies upon foundational caveats and assumptions that enable test users to generate hypotheses. Sound test construction and standardized test administration can allow a user to arrive at conclusions that are empirically grounded and, in many cases, bring a reasonable degree of confidence about the actual results.

The most logical place to begin is to review the concepts of *constructs* and *construct validity*. Thorndike (1997) made the apt observation that assessment is never measuring a person, it is attempting to measure some attribute or dimension of that individual. Those attributes might include height, weight, handedness, intelligence, or mechanical aptitude. Regardless of the attribute, there needs to be some agreement among observers about first how to *define* that attribute, and then secondarily how to *measure* it. In the fields of psychology and education, much of the work of helping people is based on a series of related constructs. There has historically been a great deal of discourse and competing views about psychological constructs such as intelligence, academic aptitude, and personality. Those disagreements usually center around two themes: 1) what constitutes that particular construct or whether a construct can or should exist, and 2) what behavioral indicators reflect particular components of it. For example, you might be aware of the controversy of "high-stakes testing." The high-stakes controversy focuses on educators or clinicians making decisions about test takers, where the decisions being made have long-term implications for test takers despite some indication that the tests themselves may be biased or flawed.

One thing that differentiates psychological assessment from more biologically based assessments is that the very identification of a characteristic, or construct, is vulnerable to bias and interpretation. In medical tests such as blood type or pregnancy, laboratory tests give a definitive answer about the presence or absence of some condition. In contrast, the fields of psychology and counseling are "soft sciences," meaning that we intuit presence or absence of some construct based on a person's behavior, but there is no physical measurement to prove the existence of that construct. While we might refer to a person as "extroverted," there is no location in the human body to measure it—we infer "extroversion" on the basis of a person's behavior. Much of the work done in counseling and psychology is based on ideas or theories about individual characteristics that don't necessarily correspond to concrete evidence. Examples of commonly accepted constructs in psychology include intelligence and personality.

Many of the characteristics we attempt to assess through standardized assessment are ones that occur on a continuum, with varying degrees of presence in different types of contexts or environments. Consider your own level of tolerance for frustration . . . chances are that you are more able to tolerate frustration in some situations than you are in others. This makes the process of assessing even trickier because not only is human behavior notoriously hard to predict, it also changes with context and myriad other factors and variables. The majority of human characteristics under current discussion are seen as features of someone's personhood mainly by comparing that person to other similar people. We only are aware that a 3rd grade child is "tall" if we see him or her standing in a group of other 3rd graders. A person's level of "extroversion" is more meaningful if we compare his or her behavior to other individuals. Many "constructs" in the fields of counseling and psychology are models that are essentially socially constructed aspects of perceiving and defining individuals. We are able to comprehend relative degrees of a characteristic in a person because we use as a basis for comparison other persons with whom we have had contact. This is an important, foundational concept that will be of great value as you move forward in this text to the other chapters that cover instruments developed to assess specific aspects of psychological functioning.

Perhaps another of the most basic and foundational caveats in the specialty area of assessment is the idea that psychological assessment, like any other quantitative form of empirical inquiry, rests entirely on probability. We are attempting to make a reasonable *guess* about past, present, or future manifestations of some behaviors, attributes, or symptoms on the basis of likelihood that some other characteristic has been, is, or will be present. Note that the word "guess" is italicized. Even when a particular set of results seems compelling and definitive, a small possibility always exists that the observed results could be an anomaly and not reflective of the "true" scores. This is the same concept used in research and corresponding statistics; when a research finding is significant at the .001 level, it means that there is an extremely small, but present, possibility of obtaining different results if the study was done again.

MacCluskie, Welfel, and Toman (2002) identified occasions on which standardized test data could be of use:

* Generating a differential diagnosis in order to provide the best help
* Identifying the scope and extent of an individual's psychopathology related to a comparison group
* Identifying an individual's strengths and resilience
* Assisting in the counseling process for career development, special needs program inclusion, identifying barriers to growth through counseling
* Establishing a baseline for assessing an individual's growth on some dimension

One question students often ask about assessment is, what information are we obtaining that could not be acquired by conducting good interviews? The answer is, maybe not much. However, what testing *does* potentially afford us is supplemental information about other aspects of understanding the client's concerns, such as the relative severity of his or her distress, the typicality or atypicality of the particular concerns or symptoms, the prognosis, and what factors might improve the prognosis.

Tests typically are developed when the need for an instrument becomes apparent. For example, Alfred Binet is considered by some to have been a pioneer in intellectual assessment by having developed standardized procedures for identifying students in need of special education services in the early 1900s (www.verywell.com/history-of-intelligence-testing-2795581).

Similarly, the MMPI (Minnesota Multiphasic Personality Inventory) was developed in the 1930s as a means of assessing patients presenting with a broad range of psychopathology.

I will present an applied example of how a need arises, and then an instrument is developed and utilized in response. Within that example I will talk conceptually about validity, reliability, norms, and error.

Test Development

Suppose a local school district is experiencing a great deal of turnover with crossing guards. Crossing guards are very important for helping children who are not accompanied by an adult to stay safe on their way to and from school. The school officials are striving to assemble a stable group of employees who will remain in their jobs in order to reduce training time and also reduce the disruption of always being understaffed. Understaffed intersections are a big safety concern and having reliable adults to help small children cross busy streets is essential to the community.

One way to initiate solving this recruitment and turnover problem is to first consider the difference between persistent, versus non-persistent, crossing guards. Then we might start examining in closer detail the characteristics of people who have successfully maintained their crossing guard job for some extended period of time (we decide to choose a minimum employment of at least two years). We might even conduct some research by locating some crossing guards who have maintained their employment, demonstrating "success," and then interview them in the hope of identifying some common themes or characteristics that appear to be related to them staying on the job.

Perhaps after interviewing all the crossing guards who meet our interview selection criteria, we notice that a common theme among them is that they all have had their own children and grandchildren, and they all have been living in the community for at least 12 years. We notice further that 80% of them are retired; the other 20% never worked outside their homes before the crossing guard job. We begin hypothesizing that there is a high degree of relationship between having personal history with childcare and crossing guard success, and that being a longstanding member of a community also seems to be related. Note that we are not surmising that living in the community *causes* crossing guard employment longevity, but rather that they are correlated. When one is there, often the other is there as well.

So now we have a new construct, "crossing guard longevity." The operational definition of this construct is employment with that job title for at least two years. We have observed some characteristics of people who are high in "crossing guard longevity," and we need to further investigate whether or not our observed correlation is generalizable to other communities. One way we could further test this hypothesis would be to test the hypothesis by expanding to other school districts. We could also locate the individuals who left their crossing guard jobs in less than two months (i.e., those individuals with *low* crossing guard longevity). If our observed relationships between childcare, community membership, and job longevity are based on some real relationship, then the individuals who left their job early should demonstrate an absence of childcare history or community membership. Perhaps at the conclusion of our research, we conclude that there really is a construct called Crossing Guard Aptitude, which we are able to demonstrate has a high correlation with job longevity. Individuals who leave crossing guard jobs within two years of hire tend to demonstrate low scores on our Crossing Guard Aptitude Test, and individuals who maintain crossing guard employment demonstrate high scores on the Crossing Guard Aptitude Test.

The process of establishing this construct is very similar to the process test developers undergo, on a much larger scale. Commonly used constructs in psychology include intelligence, attitudes, personality traits, or emotional states such as depression or anxiety.

Instruments are developed that basically use numbers to describe the degree of presence of some characteristic; a condition that may correspond to a person's internal experience of that characteristic.

Once a construct has been empirically established to be observable with a reasonable degree of consistency, across individuals, settings, and time, we can consider what types of measurements would be the most accurate and precise tools for discerning that attribute. As test developers work to create such tools, they are striving to develop tools that are both valid and reliable. If an instrument is "valid," that means it is considered to measure the quality or attribute it purports to measure. If an instrument is reliable, that means the measurement itself will be stable (i.e., consistent) over time. One aspect of reliability (score stability) that can interfere with the stability is that changes in people naturally do happen over time. The process of human growth and development is continual throughout the lifespan, so the longer the period of time is from one testing to the next, the more likely it is that an observed score could change. Note, however, that if we are using norm-referenced, standardized scores, the entire group of individuals to whom the person is being compared will also have changed, so the derived score that reflects relative standing among age peers should remain fairly stable.

Validity

One synonym for validity is accuracy. Validity in psychological testing parlance basically means that there is a theory about a construct, and evidence exists to support that construct, and that those two factors justify the use of tests that appear to measure that construct. Refer to the Crossing Guard Aptitude Test. This same process applies in all the different categories and types of standardized psychological instruments.

The three broad categories of validity are construct validity, criterion validity, and content validity. Construct development and construct validity were discussed earlier in the chapter. Criterion validity means that there is evidence from other sources of data that the construct or the hypotheses about the construct are accurate. In our example about crossing guard turnover, if able to establish criterion-related validity, then we should see a high correlation between high scores on our test and high job longevity. There is also something called discriminant validity, meaning that if the construct is really describing an actual phenomenon, then presence of that phenomenon should have no correspondence with other attributes that seem unrelated. For example, if we are hypothesizing Crossing Guard Aptitude is a separate construct than "employee reliability," then as we are collecting test scores on those two instruments, we should observe no discernible correlation. In other words, scores on those two tests should be unrelated and we would expect the observed correlation to be close to 0. Just as a quick refresher on correlation coefficients, they range from -1.0, a perfect negative correlation to 0 to +1.0, a perfect positive correlation. A negative correlation between two variables means that as one variable goes up, another variable goes down. There is a negative correlation between years of education and incidence of illiteracy. A positive correlation means that as one variable increases in magnitude, the other variable also increases in magnitude. There is a positive correlation between years of education and median income. A correlation coefficient of +1.0 or -1.0 means that there is a 1:1 increase between the two variables.

Constructs vary in the degree to which they are accepted as "true" among psychologists and counselors. Temperament, personality characteristics, career interests, and memory are all examples of constructs that are widely accepted across many types of practitioners and academicians. There are other constructs that are more controversial or questioned; these include, for example, emotional intelligence, biological or psychological origins of homosexuality, and evolutionary psychology. There is often disagreement and controversy as researchers strive to define constructs; it is apparent in the types of discussions that appear in professional journals and at professional conferences as new constructs emerge in a discipline.

Reliability

A synonym for reliability is stability. The idea of reliability is basically that if a test does its job well, it should yield the same measurement consistently. When our car is "reliable" as rated by Consumer Reports, that means that every time we go to start it and drive it somewhere, it starts up and runs well and doesn't malfunction. If we have a good, "reliable," bathroom scale, then every time we step onto it, we should be observing very similar weight on the display. Of course, some qualities, such as body weight, change in small amounts over a short period of time, so if we were to step onto an accurate scale every hour on the hour, we might see minor fluctuations in our weight depending on how well we are hydrated, or whether we have recently eaten. When the measurement we are attempting to make is more difficult to do accurately, for example, distractibility in class for a 2nd grade child, the likelihood of error as a confounding factor in the measurement increases.

Fluctuations in any measurement are referred to as "error variance." The following formula describes the relationship between the observed score, the "true score," and the error, where "true score" is defined as the hypothetical actual amount of the attribute under investigation:

Observed Score = True Score + Error (there is a presumption of inherent error in the measurement).

Error refers to any factors that interfere with the "true score" manifesting during an evaluation. Error can come from any one of a number of sources, internal and external. Internal error refers to factors within the test taker, and might include the test taker being in physical discomfort (headache, hungry), forgetting to bring his or her reading glasses, or test anxiety. External sources of error variance include the tester making mistakes during test administration, poor lighting in the testing room, other problems with the test environment, and poorly written test items.

External sources of error, particularly those associated with test construction, can result in a test being unreliable, meaning that there is a broad fluctuation in scores from one time of testing to another. Every observed score on any test or instrument will carry some ratio of true score plus error variance. A good test, meaning one that is valid and reasonably reliable, is one whose format has minimized the contribution of error variance to an observed score. If you think about it, a test with high error variance is a waste of time because there is no way of knowing how far off we are with any given test score. Test-retest is a very useful way to establish stability over time, but in some types of tests it can be difficult to demonstrate. Rehearsal of a behavior (e.g., rapid simple addition and subtraction in one's head) sometimes results in improved efficiency. That's the whole basis of studying for a math test—becoming faster and more accurate. Unfortunately, though, in these types of skills that do respond to practice and rehearsal, it can be difficult to get valid test-retest data. For example, one measure of "intelligence" involves novel problem-solving skills; how quickly and accurately can a person solve a problem dissimilar to anything they have done before. Once a person is able to efficiently solve a novel problem, the problem is no longer novel, and so it becomes almost impossible to get another measurement on the time and speed of problem solution. Test developers try to circumvent this problem by creating alternate versions of the same stimulus items, at approximately the same level of difficulty, so that the possibility of practice effect is minimized.

There are several aspects of reliability of great importance as we consider whether we should rely on a given test score for valid information about a person. Test-retest, alternate forms, and split-half are all forms of reliability that developers can use to establish consistency over time. Here is a brief review of how each of those forms of reliability are established:

Test-retest—The test is administered to a group of test takers, there is a specified lapse of time, and then the same test is re-administered to the same test takers. A correlational coefficient is calculated for the two scores for each person.

Alternate forms—The authors develop two parallel versions of a test with closely similar test items, carefully accounting for item difficulty to keep them as similar as possible. The purpose of this form is to avoid practice effect or familiarity with tasks that are intended to be novel items for the test taker. Both forms are administered to each test taker, and the correlation coefficient is calculated for each person.

Split-half—In split-half reliability, an entire test is given to a test taker, and then the answers are divided up by odd and even numbered stimulus items. If the test is internally consistent, then the split-half correlation should be close to 1.0.

When a standardized instrument is developed and published by a testing company, it has already undergone extensive research and development to establish norms. The information about test development, establishment of validity and reliability, and the development of the norms and derived scores is provided in the technical manual for that instrument.

Norms

Psychological functioning, malfunctioning, and degree of absence or presence of particular characteristics are by necessity embedded in the sociocultural structure of a society. We identify "disturbed" behavior in part because it is behavior that is not commonly observed among others in the environment; it is atypical. Another aspect of "disturbed" behavior involves a person not meeting the *role demands* commonly placed upon someone of their age, gender, and ability status. These "role demands" are completely a function of our culture, what a group of people living in proximity agree constitutes "normal" and "abnormal" behavior. Once again we find that this book does not afford the space for a thorough discussion of social constructivism and the cultural relativity of psychological disturbance . . . the point is that we continually find ourselves in a position of needing to understand an individual's relative standing with some characteristic, in comparison to other, similar individuals. In the case of educational testing, it is very helpful to know how our own 3rd grade child is performing in math in comparison to all the other 3rd grade children in the classroom because the group performance is the basis for defining what is developmentally "typical." If our 3rd grader is struggling with certain math concepts, that struggle will become most apparent when he or she is no longer performing well on tests, or is showing some confusion and inability to solve math tasks the teacher is presenting to the classroom of learners.

One of the most helpful uses of standardized test data is to get a quantified sense of how a person is functioning in some realm in comparison to how other, similar individuals are functioning in that same realm. When we wish to conduct this type of a comparison, it is referred to as a "normative" comparison. Normative comparisons are especially useful when ascertaining whether an individual has special needs, or needs that go beyond what other individuals require, in order to perform some tasks. Note that "special" needs means only that the observed performance is atypical; it does not presume someone is particularly delayed or advanced, merely that their level of that attribute is not commonly seen among their peers.

The other way that norms can be useful is for a comparison of the relative strengths and weaknesses of an individual compared to other aspects of that same person. This type of comparison is called "ipsative." One great example of highly useful ipsative comparisons is in the area of career interests. The Strong Interest Inventory® yields a profile with levels of interest in each of six career interest categories, and being able to see the presence or interest level of each of those career categories in the context of the other five gives a counselor a basis for comparison when speaking with a client about where his or her highest level of interest lies. Yet another example of useful comparison is looking at a child's strengths and weaknesses in cognitive processing. Everyone has cognitive strengths and weaknesses; by using this type of a comparison in a cognitive ability test, it gives a user great information about the types of cognitive activity that come most easily to the person. It could also shed light on the ideal techniques or strategies to use those strengths in order to perform better in those areas that are a weakness. For example, taking math ability again, we might see a student who is very strong in verbal functioning but somewhat challenged in math reasoning. It could be possible to teach that student how to use her or his verbal skills as one mechanism for talking himself through a math problem solution.

We have been talking up to now about constructs, instrument development, and overall accuracy of both. We are moving away from reliability and validity, toward a brief review of statistical concepts. In standardized assessment, or in research design, when we have gathered a large number of raw scores, we must find strategies for describing that collection of scores. This brings us to the concepts of frequency distributions, measures of central tendency, and measures of dispersion. It will be easiest to communicate about these concepts if we are working from a concrete example.

Frequency Distributions

There are many occasions when we want information about what level of performance is "average" or "typical" for some subset of a population. For example, when we need to find out what a typical height is for children who are between 6 years and 6 years 6 months, we need to measure many youngsters who fall in that bandwidth of chronological age. This is our "norm group." We might travel to different regions or parts of the country to get the most inclusive and robust (or generalizable) sample possible. Our goal, in order to have the most accurate comparison, is to amass a subset of 6-year-olds that mirrors the distribution of all those kids in the country. Oftentimes test developers use data from the most recent US Census to construct a subset of the targeted population that is basically a miniature of the general population. The goal is to create a "stratified random sample," meaning that it is a carefully constructed group of individuals assembled in a group that roughly represents the US population. In order to identify "typical" scores, we need to take a tally of the frequency of occurrence of each raw score demonstrated by our test takers in the norming group. Standardizing an instrument is costly and time-consuming—developers are seeking to create an instrument that will be of use to many individuals in many regions.

Now imagine we have successfully traveled the country and obtained height measurements of hundreds of 6-year-olds. We have a massive volume of measurements and need some strategies for managing the data to make it useful. We have thus far assembled the measurements in Table 2.1.

We might begin by separating the scores between males and females and then graphing the scores. A graph we would then construct would show not only all the measurement scores that were observed, but also the frequency with which each measurement score was obtained. An abbreviated example of a possible frequency graph could look like Table 2.2.

If height, the measurement being assessed is "normally distributed," then the score frequency when graphed will be a "bell curve." Many characteristics of organisms in nature manifest in a bell curve, with typical measurements happening with the greatest frequency, and then showing diminishing frequency as higher and lower scores move out toward either

Table 2.1 Measurements Table

Subject No.	Gender	Measurement in inches
1	M	44
2	F	50
3	F	48
4	M	52
5	M	50.5
6	M	49
7	F	47

Table 2.2 Measurements Graph

Height	Number of Observed Cases
40	117
41	144
42	150
43	289
44	398
45	500
46	509
47	488

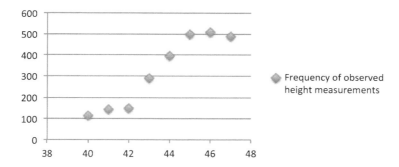

Figure 2.1 Frequency Graph

tail. Figure 2.1 offers you a visual of what the frequency distribution from this set of scores would look like if we were to plot it.

This bell curve enables us to have a quick, visual reference, regarding how any one particular 6-year-old's height compares to the general population of 6-year-olds. A bell curve, comprised of the frequency of observed raw scores, becomes a useful visual graphic for understanding normative, or atypical, levels of the attribute under study. The bell curve is literally the tool that we use for defining atypicality in the degree to which a person exhibits a characteristic or lack of that characteristic.

Measures of Central Tendency

This term "central tendency" is really just referring to most commonly observed measurements within a particular set of scores. If we are talking about the US population of 6- to

6.5-year-old children, there are many hundreds of thousands, and yet we need to find an efficient way to describe the huge set of scores we have obtained. One common way researchers and statisticians do this is by referring to particular characteristics of the data set. The goal is to reduce a very large number of scores to a much smaller, and yet highly descriptive, set of scores that enable us to comprehend the nature of the data we have gathered.

There are a number of different ways we can use a single or small number of scores as efficient yet accurate descriptors of our entire comprehensive set of scores. We might talk about the most frequently occurring raw score (the mode), or we could talk about the arithmetic average (the mean, the sum of all the measurements divided by the number of measurements), or the raw score that falls in the arithmetic middle (the median) of the highest and lowest observed score. These terms (mean, median, and mode) are all different methods for choosing a single score that best represents the entire collection of scores. A "normal distribution" of frequencies creates the shape of a bell curve if there are enough data points. In a normal distribution, the mean, median, and mode are all the same number. If a score distribution is skewed, meaning off center, the mean, median, and mode will all be different numbers. Part of what test developers strive for in development and standardization is to create stimulus items that yield a normal distribution of raw scores.

Measures of Dispersion

Returning to the frequency graph, and the bell curve, sometimes it's helpful to know the distance from the lowest observed measurement to the highest observed measurement. That distance is referred to as dispersion; how much measurements vary from one person to the next. Sometimes a characteristic will show very little variation across people, leading to a small range of scores. For example, on a midterm exam in a college class, if the instructor has taught well, and the students have prepared well for the exam, we would expect most scores to be close together, leading to a small range and a tight clumping of scores around the most commonly occurring one.

There are two types of dispersion index; one is the range, and the other is the variance and standard deviation.

Range

As described earlier in the chapter, the range is simply the distance between the lowest and highest observed score in a set of scores. A struggling student might be very upset to learn that his score on a history midterm exam was only 28 out of 50. However, if the range of observed scores for all the students was between 2 and 28, then from a *normative* perspective, a score of 28 would represent the top performance in the classroom. This is the difference between criterion-referenced scores and norm-referenced scores. A criterion-referenced score means the test user designates a minimum score as acceptable. If the teacher set a criterion-referenced requirement that students earn at least 70% of the possible points, then a raw score of 35 would be necessary to pass, and that score of 28 would be a failing score. If the teacher set a norm-referenced requirement that the top scoring 70% of students would pass the test while others would be considered failing, then that same score of 28 would be the top end of the subsequent 70% of observed scores.

Besides the range, which tells us the distance from lowest to highest score, there are other numbers that can tell us about the shape of the curve of that frequency distribution. Those indexes are the variance and the standard deviation. Referring back to the central tendency measures, we talked about the mean, median, and mode. In a perfectly symmetrical normal distribution (bell curve), all three of those are the same number. I'm going to explain how we would calculate standard deviation without the formula. As an exercise we might consider doing a brief standard deviation hand calculation. Consider the following set of test scores shown in Table 2.3.

If we want to know how a set of scores is arranged around the average score, we first calculate the arithmetic average. Adding the observed scores:

27
28
13
15
24
22
21
19
22
25

———

216

Then we would subtract each observed score from the average score.
216 / 10 = 21.6
The arithmetic mean of this score set is 21.6 (see Table 2.4).

Table 2.3 Range and Distribution

Student	Test Score
Bob	27
Mary	28
Jessica	13
Joe	15
Darius	24
Angel	22
Mariah	21
Alexander	19
David	22
Ron	25

Table 2.4 Mean

Test Score	Distance from the Mean	Distance Squared
27	27–21.6 = 5.4	29.16
28	28–21.6 = 6.4	40.96
13	13–21.6 = -8.6	73.96
15	15–21.6 = -6.6	43.56
24	24–21.6 = 2.4	5.76
22	22–21.6 = 0.4	0.16
21	21–21.6 = -0.6	0.36
19	19–21.6 = -2.6	6.76
22	22–21.6 = 0.4	0.16
25	25–21.6 = 3.4	11.56

Sum of distance squared: 212.4
divided by 10: 21.24
Variance is sum of distance squared divided by # of cases
212.4 / 10 = 21.24
Square root of the variance is the standard deviation
Square root: 4.6

If our math is correct, then there should be exactly the same number of scores above and below the average score. We could just add those up but since half the scores will be negative and the other half positive, we would end up with a sum of 0. To eliminate the negative scores, we can add a column in which we square all the difference scores since a negative number times itself becomes a positive number. Then we can add all those squared difference scores, and if we divide by the number of scores, it will give us the average difference score. To get the standard deviation, we have to "un-do" the squaring that we did back at the beginning. When we find the square root of the variance, we have arrived at the standard deviation.

The standard deviation is a very useful tool, especially when used in tandem with the mean. These two numbers tell us a great deal about the shape of the bell curve (also called the normal curve—see Figure 2.2 below) and also give us useful information about how any one individual's observed score compares to all the other test takers.

Standard Error of Measurement

We talked earlier in the chapter about reliability. A concept related to reliability, that integrates the ideas of normal distribution and also error variance, is the standard error of measurement. There is a method for using a reliability coefficient along with the standard deviation that enables us to calculate the standard error of measurement (SEM). The SEM can be thought of as the distribution of scores we would likely see if we could administer the same test to the same person many, many times without the person improving through practice effect. For example, going back to the 6-year-olds' heights, if we had the same child step up to the same

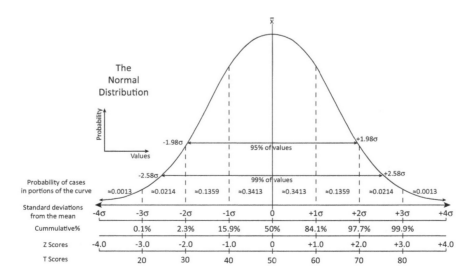

Figure 2.2 The Normal Curve

measuring stick many times, we would expect to see exactly the same measurement each time or if there was any variation in scores it would be miniscule. In contrast if we were able to administer the same history midterm test many times we might see a bit more variation in the scores one individual achieved. If we could create a graph of all the scores exhibited by that one individual, we could do a frequency analysis and construct a frequency distribution curve that would resemble a normal curve if we could give the test enough times. If we were to create that frequency distribution curve, and then did all the same calculations on that group of scores, we would end up with a mean and standard deviation for that score group. The standard deviation of that score group is the SEM. The SEM enables us to report scores and also to report the likelihood that the "true score" falls in that range.

Standardized Scores

Up to this point in the chapter, we have been discussing "scores" referring to *raw* scores—direct measurements of the attribute being assessed. A raw score is simply the numeric score on whatever measurement is being done. A raw score on the 6-year-old height investigation would be a number expressed in centimeters or inches. A raw score on the history midterm exam would simply be the score each student earned. A raw score on the Crossing Guard Aptitude Test would be the number of "yes" responses to the stimulus items; questions asking about presence or absence of children, grandchildren, the number of years living in the community where the school district is located. If we are only intending to use criterion-referenced scores, meaning that we have established a raw score cut-off, there may be no need to do any score transformation. We might do an analysis of all the data gathered during development of the Crossing Guard Aptitude Test and determine that individuals with a Crossing Guard Aptitude score of 50 or higher are 85% more likely to maintain employment, and so we set a raw score cut off at 50. We could then simply say that, based on our analyses, a Crossing Guard Aptitude Test raw score of 50 is necessary for employment.

On the other hand, we might be interested in getting a sense of a person's score in comparison to other peoples' scores to get a sense of relative standing. There are a multitude of occasions on which relative standing is very pertinent for making clinical recommendations to best assist a person. In those cases, the raw scores are transformed to standardized scores. Any standardized score is an expression of how the test taker's raw score performance compared to the raw score performance of other individuals who are roughly comparable to the test taker.

There are many different types of standardized scores. They include:

standard scores
percentiles
Z-scores
T-scores
stanines

The important piece to bear in mind, moving forward, is that all of these standardized scores are simply variations on the theme of relative standing. With this basic conceptual understanding, you can move forward confidently as you explore various assessment instruments. Having this conceptualization will enable you to interact competently with all aspects of assessment, ranging from helping parents understand the results of their children's testing at school or elsewhere, to interpreting scores you have recorded on a test taker, to choosing particular instruments to serve a purpose clinically in your work with clients.

Summary

This chapter has covered a broad range of information, beginning with the broad-brush conceptual issues such as construct validity, the whole way through specific analyses of sets of scores. Our hope is that this coverage has provided sufficient review to serve as a rich conceptual context for the subsequent chapters that will look at particular clinical categories of instruments.

Sound clinical instruments should always be accompanied by a technical manual that explains the constructs, the development of the instrument, and the reliability and validity coefficients that were attained in that development. A technical manual also typically offers explicit guidelines for accurate score interpretation on a given instrument. With the foundational information discussed in this chapter, and a technical manual, readers should be functionally literate in the realm of assessment as they perform their roles as mental health professionals.

Test Your Knowledge:

1. Measures of central tendency give us information about:
   a. The average age of the test takers in the standardization sample
   b. The most commonly occurring scores in a set of scores
   c. The likely political orientation of the test takers
   d. The skewness of the standardization sample

2. Measure of dispersion give us information about:
   a. How closely distributed the scores are around the mean
   b. The socioeconomic status of the test takers
   c. The soundness of the construct
   d. The geographic distribution of the sample

3. Construct validity refers to:
   a. How well constructed the test is
   b. The test developer's thought process as the test was created
   c. The evidential support for the ideas on which the test is based
   d. None of the above

4. If a test taker differs in some fundamental way from the individuals in the standardization sample, then:
   a. The test scores must be interpreted with significant caution as to what they mean
   b. The information yielded from the test will have diminished interpretive value
   c. There may be two levels of interpretation: one which is normative and quantitative, and one which is qualitative and functionally based
   d. All of the above

5. A good technical manual that accompanies a test should include:
   a. An operational definition of the construct on which the instrument is based
   b. Details about how the test was normed and standardized
   c. Directions for score interpretation
   d. All of the above

6. What is the relationship between the standard error of measurement and the reliability of a test?
   a. If the standard error of measurement is high, then the reliability is low
   b. If the standard error of measurement is high, then the reliability is also high
   c. If the standard error of measurement is low, then the reliability cannot be determined
   d. There is no relationship between standard error of measurement and reliability

7. In considering a frequency distribution, measures of central tendency include:
   a. Reliability indices
   b. Range and standard deviation
   c. Mean, median, mode
   d. Validity indices

8. In considering a frequency distribution, measures of dispersion include:
   a. Mean, median, mode
   b. Range and standard deviation
   c. Reliability indices
   d. Validity indices

9. The shape of the bell curve in a frequency distribution is determined by:
   a. The number of people in the sample
   b. The measures of both central tendency and dispersion
   c. The type of test being researched
   d. None of the above; bell curves are determined by the ages of the participants

10. Which of the following is true?
    a. A test can be valid without being reliable
    b. A test can be reliable without being valid
    c. Reliability and validity are inextricably related
    d. Reliability and validity are almost impossible to prove

Discussion Questions/Prompts:

1. What is your understanding of the difference between correlation and causation? What are some examples of times when reporting correlational data (such as in advertising) might be misleading and suggest cause and effect among variables when a causal relationship does not actually exist?
2. How might use of standardized information be a problem, as opposed to a support, in helping a client achieve his or her goals?
3. Imagine you are working with a person (either child or adult) who achieved a percentile rank equivalent of 38 on a measure of mathematical skill. Using lay language understandable to that individual, explain what that score means.
4. How comfortable are you in explaining psychometric principles to a client?
5. What areas of statistical analysis do you have the most concern with?

3 Ethical and Legal Issues in Psychological Assessment and Testing

Ellen C. Melton

Counselors often start out uncertain about the role that psychological assessment and testing will or should play in their practice. However, if asked, most counselors will endorse the need to understand basic concepts and issues of assessment and testing even if it is not a part of their counseling activities with clients. On the other hand, counseling assessment and testing is often an integral part of the counseling setting as in agency work in an inpatient or out-patient context; a therapeutic modality such as Cognitive Processing Therapy or Dialectical Behavior Therapy; diagnostic or referral purposes for specialized services in educational or behavioral contexts; or as a standalone activity such as an evaluation of depression, anxiety, or personality.

Regardless of the setting, the specific reason, or even the specific assessment, counselors must be aware of the ethical and legal considerations around psychological assessment and testing and their responsibilities within those standards, guidelines, and considerations. Ethical guidelines and assessment standards are typically provided by professional organizations that provide oversight for the administration and usage of psychological assessments and tests. Legal statutes and key court decisions have also defined how counselors may use and perform various assessment activities (Drummond, Sheperis, & Jones, 2016; Hays, 2013). In this chapter, some of the standards and guidelines for assessment and testing will be outlined, ethical considerations such as informed consent, confidentiality, and data management faced by clinicians will be presented, and finally, issues involving multicultural contexts and supervision in psychological testing and assessment will be discussed.

In laying a foundation for outlining the intersection between several sets of standards concerning the use of psychological assessment and testing procedures, it is useful to have a conceptualization of the importance and impact of the area of focus. According to the Standards for Educational and Psychological Testing, published by the American Educational Research Association (AERA), the American Psychological Association (APA), and the National Council on Measurement in Education (NCME) (2014), educational and psychological assessments and tests are among the most important contributions of the cognitive and behavioral sciences to our society, as they provide fundamental and significant information about individuals and groups.

Standards and Guidelines for Evaluating Tests and Test Usage

In this section, several professional organizations and their standards that relate specifically to assessment will be outlined and briefly described. The purpose of these standards is to provide criteria for the evaluation of assessments, tests, and testing practices; to provide a framework for interpreting scores; and to provide a frame of reference for assessing the validity of scores in relation to relevant issues and professional judgment. Counselors should make themselves familiar with each set of standards and/or guidelines for test usage, especially those associated with their specific licensure and the overarching standards that apply across applications of psychological assessment and testing (Drummond et al., 2016; Hays, 2013).

Among several important documents that affect clinical test usage are: the American Counseling Association *Code of Ethics* (ACA, 2014); the National Board for Certified Counselors *Code of Ethics* (NBCC, 2016); American Educational Research Association, American Psychological Association, and the National Council on Measurement in Education *Standards for Educational and Psychological Testing* (AERA, APA, & NCME, 2014); Association for Assessment and Research in Counseling *Responsibilities of Users of Standardized Tests* (AARC, 2003); American Counseling Association *Standards for Qualifications of Test Users* (ACA, 2014); and the Association for Assessment and Research in Counseling *Standards for Multicultural Assessment* (AARC, 2014).

ACA Code of Ethics

The American Counseling Association (ACA) *Code of Ethics* (2014) specifies principles of ethical conduct and standards of professional behavior for counselors and addresses key ethical issues. Section E of the 2014 code provides information on evaluation, assessment, and interpretation related to psychological assessment and testing. Section E of the code addresses general assessment, competence to use and interpret assessments and tests, informed consent, release of data, diagnosis using assessment tools, selection of assessment instruments, conditions and administration, multicultural issues, scoring, construction, and forensic evaluation (ACA, 2014).

NBCC Code of Ethics

The National Board for Certified Counselors (NBCC) *Code of Ethics* (2016) addresses issues of assessment and testing in 13 of the Directives in the code and includes issues of confidentiality and security, selection, usage, interpretation, diagnosis, and reporting results of psychological assessments and tests.

AERA, APA, and NCME Standards for Educational and Psychological Testing

The *Standards for Educational and Psychological Testing* (2014) is one of the more comprehensive documents on assessment standards and provides criteria for the evaluation and usage of psychological assessments and tests. Leaning heavily on the foundations of validity, reliability, and fairness in assessment and testing, the standards also go into test design and development, scoring, administration, rights and responsibilities, and testing applications in workplace, educational, program evaluation, and policy studies (NCME, 2014).

AARC Responsibilities of Users of Standardized Tests

The *Responsibilities of Users of Standardized Tests (RUST)* (2003) by the Association for Assessment and Research in Counseling (AARC) is organized around test user responsibilities in the following areas: qualifications of test users, technical knowledge, test selection, administration, scoring, interpretation, and communication of test results. It is designed to help counselors and other educators implement responsible testing practices.

ACA Standards for Qualifications of Test Users

The American Counseling Association *Standards for Qualifications of Test Users* (2014) proposes seven competencies as qualification to administer psychological assessments and tests:

practice and knowledge of testing; understanding of test construction and constructs; working knowledge of sampling, norming, and statistics involved in testing; ability to appropriately review and select tests and assessments; skill in administration, scoring, and interpretation; knowledge of the impact of diversity on testing; and a general understanding and consideration of appropriate test usage.

AARC Standards for Multicultural Assessment

The Association for Assessment and Research in Counseling's *Standards for Multicultural Assessment* (2014) include 38 multicultural assessment standards categorized into five major clusters: advocacy, selection of assessments, administration and scoring of assessment, interpretation and application of assessment results, and training in the use and uses of psychological assessments.

In addition, several specialty standards exist to guide testing practices in more specific counseling specialties. Among those are: *the Career Counselor Assessment and Evaluation Competencies* by the Association for Assessment and Research in Counseling (AARC) and National Career Development Association (NCDA) (2010); the *Marriage, Couple and Family Counseling Assessment Competencies* by the Association for Assessment in Counseling and Education (AACE) and International Association of Marriage and Family Counselors (IAMFC) (2010); the *Standards for Assessment in Mental Health Counseling* by the Association for Assessment and Research in Counseling (AARC) and the American Mental Health Counselors Association (AMHCA) (2010); the *Standards for Assessment in Substance Abuse Counseling* by the Association for Assessment and Research in Counseling (AARC) and the International Association of Addictions and Offender Counselors (IAAOC) (2010); and the *Competencies in Assessment and Evaluation for School Counselors* by the Association for Assessment and Research in Counseling (AARC) and the American School Counselor Association (ASCA) (1998).

While these codes, standards, and documents provide guidelines for professionals in the field, they do not, and cannot, provide answers to all ethical issues, considerations, and dilemmas. As professionals and clinicians, we are called on to reflect on what is in the best interest of each client and to follow best-practice guidelines in regard to test selection, administration, scoring, interpretation, and providing feedback with every assessment and with every client.

Qualification Considerations in Assessment and Testing

One can imagine a number of situations when ethical and legal considerations may be called into question when psychological tests and assessments are employed in counseling. Without question it could be argued that the most important ethical concern in assessment is the competence and qualification of the clinician in selecting, administering, scoring, and interpreting psychological tests and assessments. Different assessments across different testing domains require different levels of competency, sufficient knowledge, and a comprehensive understanding of the tests they select (Drummond et al., 2016; Hays, 2013). For this reason, several professional associations have outlined specific guidelines for the competencies of test users. The following is reproduced from the *Responsibilities of Users of Standardized Tests (RUST)* produced by the Association for Assessment in Research and Counseling (2003).

Qualifications of Test Users

Qualified test users demonstrate appropriate education, training, and experience in using tests for the purposes under consideration. They adhere to the highest degree of ethical codes, laws, and standards governing professional practice. Lack of essential qualifications or ethical and legal compliance can lead to errors and subsequent harm to clients. Each professional is responsible for making judgments in each testing situation and cannot leave that responsibility either to clients or others in authority. The individual test user must obtain appropriate education and training, or arrange for professional supervision and assistance when engaged in testing in order to provide valuable, ethical, and effective assessment services to the public. Qualifications of test users depend on at least four factors:

> *Purposes of Testing*: A clear purpose for testing should be established. Because the purposes of testing direct how the results are used, qualifications beyond general testing competencies may be needed to interpret and apply data.
>
> *Characteristics of Tests*: Understanding of the strengths and limitations of each instrument used is a requirement.
>
> *Settings and Conditions of Test Use*: Assessment of the quality and relevance of test user knowledge and skill to the situation is needed before deciding to test or participate in a testing program.
>
> *Roles of Test Selectors, Administrators, Scorers, and Interpreters*: The education, training, and experience of test users determine which tests they are qualified to administer and interpret.

Each test user must evaluate his or her qualifications and competence for selecting, administering, scoring, interpreting, reporting, or communicating test results. Test users must develop the skills and knowledge for each test he or she intends to use (AARC, 2003).

The American Counseling Association's (2014) *Standards for the Qualifications of Test Users* outlines these specific standards:

1. Skill in practice and knowledge of theory relevant to the testing context and type of counseling specialty.
2. A thorough understanding of testing theory, techniques of test construction, and test reliability and validity.
3. A working knowledge of sampling techniques, norms, and descriptive, correlational, and predictive statistics.
4. Ability to review, select, and administer tests appropriate for clients or students and the context of the counseling practice.
5. Skill in administration of tests and interpretation of test scores.
6. Knowledge of the impact of diversity on testing accuracy, including age, gender, ethnicity, race, disability, and linguistic differences.
7. Knowledge and skill in the professionally responsible use of assessment and evaluation practice.

Knowing the qualifications, however thoroughly, raises another more practical question: who determines if a counselor/clinician is qualified or competent to administer psychological tests and assessments? Hays (2013) indicates there are three sources that assist in identifying who is competent to employ tests and assessments: test publishers, professional associations, and individual state licensing statutes.

Drummond et al. (2016) and Naugle (2009) indicate that, for many years, the purchase of psychological tests and assessments was generally restricted to individuals who met certain educational and licensure qualifications. A graduated level system proposed by The Psychological Corporation was based on four levels (A, B, C, and Q) of competency for individuals, organizations, and agencies who purchased and used psychological assessments and tests. Interestingly, the level classification system, while officially dropped by the American Psychological Association (APA) over 40 years ago, continues to be supported by many of the standards of assessment and testing and enforced by many publishers, and the

Table 3.1 Assessment Qualifications of Professional Organizations

Qualifications	ACA	CACREP	NBCC	FACT	ATP	NCME
Coursework in appraisal, assessment, and testing	√	√	√	√	√	√
Master's, specialist, or doctorate in counseling or related field	√	√	√	√	√	√
Obtain passing score on the National Counselor Examination	√					
Qualifying experience under Supervision	√	√	√	√	√	√
Appropriate levels of training for specific tests	√	√	√	√	√	√
Need for assessment to assist with diagnosis, treatment planning, and intervention	√	√	√	√	√	√

Note: Reproduced in part from Naugle (2009); all information confirmed via the appropriate organization's website. ACA = American Counseling Association; CACREP = Council for Accreditation of Counseling and Related Educational Programs; NBCC = National Board for Certified Counselors; FACT = Fair Access Coalition on Testing; ATP = Association of Test Publishers; NCME = National Council on Measurement in Education

ability to purchase tests and assessments is often still dependent on background and experience, as denoted by the level originally required for purchase.

According to Hays (2013) counselors are also required to review their unique professional associations' ethical codes and other relevant documents to determine qualification and competence to administer tests and assessments. Fortunately, there is general agreement among those who determine competence that counselors who have graduated from a Council for the Accreditation of Counseling and Related Educational Program (CACREP) or CACREP-equivalent program will have met the basic qualifications to purchase and administer psychological tests and assessment. In addition, state licensure laws often parallel CACREP curricular standards and require passage of the National Counselor Examination (NCE) as well (Hays, 2013).

As part of their licensing and legal statutes, states attend to qualifications and competence of counselors as licensed and certified professionals. As such, states attend to testing and assessment use and recognize it as a potential and possibly necessary activity in the practice of counseling (Hays, 2013). The definition of assessment has been an instrumental factor in determining the scope of practice for counselors and Naugle (2009) noted that a majority of states specify *assessment* in the scope of counseling practice as a core area of curriculum. Further many states outline which assessment types can be administered by licensed counselors (Hays, 2013, Naugle, 2009).

Legal Considerations in Psychological Assessment and Testing

In addition to ethical codes, standards, and qualifications, state and national laws have also played a role in the regulation of psychological assessment and testing (Drummond et al., 2016, Hays, 2013).

Statutes and Regulations

Assessment is widely accepted as a regulated professional activity and has been defined in part by *statutes*, which are laws written by legislative bodies, *regulations*, which are created by government agencies, and *judicial decisions*, which are laws created by opinions from courts, often from litigation cases.

Among the more recent defining legislation are the following (Drummond et al., 2016; Hays, 2013):

Civil Rights Act, Title VII (1964, 1972, 1978, and 1991): assessments used in employment testing must not discriminate against individuals based on age, race, gender, pregnancy, religion, or national origin.

Family Educational Rights and Privacy Act (FERPA) (1974): student test records are to remain secure from unnecessary parties.

Americans with Disabilities Act (1990): tests used for employment or other selection purposes must accurately measure the individual's ability without being confounded by the disability itself; individuals with disabilities must receive test accommodations as needed.

Health Insurance Portability and Accountability Act (HIPAA) (1996): client records must remain secure and third parties are to obtain appropriate consent to access those records. Clients have the right to their health record.

No Child Left Behind Act (2001): states mandated to continually assess math and reading skills of students to ensure quality in schools; schools are held accountable for student test scores in these areas.

Individuals with Disabilities Education Improvement Act (2004): assessment requires informed consent of parents before testing children; schools must pay for testing and provide the least restrictive environment for learning.

Carl D. Perkins Vocational and Applied Technology Education Act (1984, 2006): individuals who are disadvantaged are entitled to receive vocational assessment and support; success will be determined through valid and reliable tests.

Judicial Decisions

Most of the judicial decisions involving and affecting psychological assessment and testing involve employment and educational tests. The following are among the noteworthy decisions (Drummond et al., 2016; Hays, 2013):

Larry P. v. Riles (1974): ruled that schools had used intelligence tests that were biased and disadvantaged African American students, placing them inappropriately in special education; counselors need proper documentation when placing children in special education.

Diana v. California State Board of Education (1970): schools are to provide tests to students both in their first language as well as English; counselors are to provide tests in an appropriate language for the client.

Sharif v. New York State Educational Development (1989): those working in New York schools, including school counselors, could not use Scholastic Aptitude Test (SAT) scores for making scholarship decisions.

Griff v. Duke Power Company (1971): a plaintiff must demonstrate job discrimination and an employer must demonstrate that hiring procedures are job-related and associated with job performance.

Bakke v. California (1978): colleges and universities cannot use a quota system for minority group admissions.

Key Ethical Issues and Dilemmas Involved in Psychological Assessment

In thinking of ethical issues involved in psychological assessment and testing, the first concern must always be client welfare. The welfare of the client must be the foremost consideration in the selection and use of tests and assessments (Drummond et al., 2016; Hays, 2013; Naugle,

2009). Issues of client confidentiality and privacy involved with testing and assessment are typically included and addressed in issues of informed consent, test security, diagnosis, and report writing, and will be discussed as inherent aspects of those topic areas.

Client Welfare

According to Drummond et al. (2016), while lack of confidentiality and invasion of privacy in testing and assessment are often viewed as more minor problems in the field of education, they are seen as much more serious problems in testing and assessment in counseling. It is of vital importance for professionals to have informed consent before testing an individual or releasing the results to a third party. With the possible exception of some court referrals, custody evaluations and determinations, or institutional testing programs, assessments and testing in counseling is employed to assist and/or benefit the counselor and client and not for other purposes. In this light, counselors overall have had fewer ethical problems in the use of tests than have various other professionals (Drummond et al., 2016; Hays, 2013).

Who Is the Client

According to Koocher and Rey-Casserly (2003) the counselor's simple act of setting up the appointment for testing and assessment may not bring about much thought regarding what specific duties or professional obligations are owed to which parties. If the client is simply the individual to be evaluated, assessed, or tested for their own benefit or insight, or for the counselor's assessment or diagnosis of the individual, and there are no layers of individuals or institutions expecting, or paying for, information or results, the client is not in question. In other circumstances, the individual being evaluated or tested may have had little choice in the matter or may wish to reserve the right to limit access to results of the evaluation. In still other instances, there may be direct conflicts between what one party is seeking and objectives of another party. The counselor is charged with considering the rights each layer of authority has in terms of factors such as the ability to compel cooperation, the right of access to test data and results, the right to dictate components of the assessment or evaluation, or the manner in which it is conducted (Koocher & Rey-Casserly, 2003). Assessments, testing, and evaluations conducted in the context of the educational system provide a good example of the complex layers of client status and information ownership that can be involved. Similar conflicts exist in competing interests within the legal system and the business world. In consideration of all of these reasons, it is critical that counselors clearly conceptualize, identify, and accurately represent their obligation to the client.

Informed Consent

The 2001 revision by the Ethics Code Task Force (ECTF) included a proposed standard referring specifically to obtaining informed consent for psychological assessment and testing. While the issue of informed consent is discussed extensively in the professional literature in areas of consent to treatment and consent for research participation, references to informed consent in the area of psychological assessment and testing have been quite limited. Certainly, counselors and other professionals involved in psychological assessment and testing would be wise to establish consistent informed consent routines in always obtaining written consent, informing and explaining procedures, and outlining, in detail, confidentiality and privacy issues. It is particularly wise to obtain written informed consent in situations that may have forensic implications, such as lawsuits and child custody litigation (Koocher & Rey-Casserly, 2003).

Professionals, such as counselors, qualified and engaged in psychological testing and assessment are expected to explain the nature and goals of the assessment or evaluation in language the client can readily understand, clarify any referral questions if necessary, outline and discuss what feedback the client will receive, and disclose who else will receive the information if applicable. Counselors must also be aware of the limitations of any assessment and tests they select and employ as well as any inherent potential for error either in scoring or interpretation. In keeping with ethical standards, counselors discuss any relevant limitations of the tests they would like to use with the client as a part of the initial discussion and informed consent procedures (Drummond et al., 2016; Hays, 2013).

To the extent possible, the clinician should be mindful of the goals of the client, clarify any misunderstandings about the assessments and their usage, and attend to any unrealistic expectations. For example, parents may seek a psychological evaluation or assessment with the expectation that the results will ensure that their child will be eligible for a gifted and talented program (Koocher & Rey-Casserly, 2003). Accident victims may anticipate that the evaluation or assessment will document or confirm their entitlement to damages, and job candidates may hope to become employed or qualify for advancement based on the outcome of the evaluation or assessment. While these expectations might certainly come to pass from the results, the counselor or clinician cannot reasonably comment on the outcome before valid data are obtained and in hand (Koocher & Rey-Casserly, 2003).

The key elements of informed consent are information, understanding, and voluntariness (Koocher & Rey-Casserly, 2003). In regard to information, does the client have all of the information that could reasonably influence their willingness to participate in the assessment process? This could include the purpose of the evaluation, who will have access to the results, and any financial responsibility the client will have to bear. Another consideration is whether the information is presented to the client in a manner or language they can understand, including use of appropriate language, vocabulary, and explanation of any terms that are confusing to the client.

In the realm of assessment, there are often circumstances or situations in which an element of coercion may be present. For example, the potential employee, admissions candidate, criminal defendant, or person seeking disability insurance coverage might prefer to avoid mandated testing and/or assessment. Clients such as those mentioned might agree to testing reluctantly because they feel they have no other choice. Conducting externally mandated evaluations such as those mentioned earlier in the chapter do not pose ethical problems as long as the nature of the evaluation, dispersion of the results, and obligations of the counselor or clinician are carefully and clearly defined and delineated at the outset. It is not necessary for the client who is to be evaluated to be pleased about the prospect of the evaluation, but they must understand and agree to the assessment and associated risks (Koocher & Rey-Cassler, 2003).

There exist also some additional issues of consent that can come into play when a counselor is called upon to evaluate a minor child, an individual with dementia, or other persons with reduced mental capacity as a result of a significant mental or physical disorder. These evaluations, when undertaken for the benefit of or service to the client, typically involve minimal risk. However, if the data or results might be used in legal proceedings, such as a competency or custody hearing, or in any way that might have significant or potentially adverse future consequences that the client is unable to competently understand or evaluate, a surrogate consent process should be used. A parent or legal guardian needs to be involved in granting permission for the evaluation, assessment, or testing, and must have the understanding of informed consent. Obtaining such permission assists in addressing and respecting the vulnerabilities and attendant obligations owed to individuals with reduced personal decision-making capacities (Koocher & Rey-Casserly, 2003).

Key Professional Issues in Assessment and Testing

In addressing the professional issues involved in psychological testing and assessment, there is a slight shift away from the ethical and legal aspects and more focus on the role of the clinician in light of their more traditional counseling role and their focus on process issues and the client relationship. Issues such as planning, test anxiety, and the possibility of coaching will be addressed.

Planning the Assessment

It should go without saying that an essential part of accepting the referral of a client for assessment, evaluation, or testing, or deciding to conduct assessment and testing with a new or existing client, will be planning the evaluation and any assessment or testing to be done. In this respect, the considerations in this process need to include the goals of the evaluation in the context of basic assessment science and the limitations of available techniques, strategies, or instruments. This is especially important when the referral originates with others or agencies who may be unaware of the limitations of testing or may have unrealistic expectations regarding what may be learned or gathered from test or assessment data (Koocher & Rey-Casserly, 2003). Counselors should generate and communicate a clear plan for the assessment or evaluation to the client as well as to any invested parties, addressing both expectations and limitations to those involved.

Counseling Process Issues

Counselors, especially those in private practice, typically use tests and assessments for problem-solving purposes to assist or benefit the client or to confirm or disconfirm a diagnosis. As such, at least in traditional counseling, testing and assessment results are almost always shared and discussed with clients. Often, such assessments are done as a means of assisting clients in making choices and/or in developing insight or self-awareness. In these instances, the client is seen as the primary user of any testing or assessment results, with the counselor acting more in the role of facilitator (Hays, 2013). Psychological tests and assessments can provide an opportunity to collect information that can be useful both in planning counseling interventions and to promote clients' understanding of themselves. Counselors can help clients explore and identify their abilities, personality characteristics, patterns of interests, and values for the purpose of making choices and changes that can improve their sense of well-being and/or their lifestyle (Hays, 2013).

When using psychological tests and assessments in more traditional counseling venues, the counselor must attempt to understand the client's frame of reference and goals. The more knowledgeable the counselor is about all aspects of testing and assessment, the better prepared the counselor is to assist the client in understanding the information that tests can provide. In interpreting test and assessment results then, the counselor must help clients understand the implications of the test results as well as their limitations, and also assist the client in integrating the test or assessment information into their self-perceptions and decision-making strategies (Hays, 2013).

Test Anxiety Issues

Another professional issue in psychological testing and assessment involves test anxiety, perhaps especially around those tests and assessments of ability. Small but significant negative relationships have been found between test anxiety and scores on tests of ability (Hays, 2013).

This relationship does not necessarily mean that high levels of test anxiety cause lower test scores but may reflect past performance in that those who have done poorly on these types of tests in the past may experience more anxiety.

If clients perceive the stakes are high for the assessment or evaluation, the act of testing or assessment itself can involve an excessive amount of worry or fear. In such cases, clients may have difficulty thinking clearly or organizing their thoughts or may experience mental blanking. It is imperative that clients are fully and adequately informed and apprised of the extent and nature of the assessment and/or testing that they will receive. In addition, interventions that counselors can use to assist individuals with this anxiety can include: emphasizing adequate preparation if applicable; cognitive-behavioral techniques such as challenging irrational beliefs and thought-stopping; desensitization techniques; and encouraging relaxation exercises. In general, testing procedures that are well organized and smoothly run, as well as that reassure and encourage, should help to reduce the anxiety that may be felt by highly anxious test takers (Hays, 2013).

Administration, Scoring, and Interpreting Results

Selection of Instrument

Certainly, identifying and selecting the most appropriate assessment or testing instrument or strategy for each client and for each situation is a critical decision (Drummond et al., 2016; Hays, 2013; AARC, 2003). In this light, there is general agreement that the selection of assessment methods and specific tests involves careful consideration and evaluation of available instruments. With literally thousands of formal and informal instruments available to assess an almost equal multitude of abilities, traits, attitudes, and more, counselors need to know how to access and locate information about available testing and assessment instruments. One such source for information about commercial psychological tests and assessments remains the *Mental Measurements Yearbook*, now in its 20th edition (MMY, 2017). Other sources of information about psychological tests and assessments are professional organizations, Internet resources including publisher websites, and research literature.

Drummond et al. (2016) indicate the choice of instrument or strategy can depend on several factors that include: type of information needed, needs of the client, resource constraints, available time frame, quality of assessment instrument, and qualifications of the counselor. Hays (2013) indicates that from a therapeutic point of view, clients should collaborate in deciding what questions they wish to answer by use of tests or other assessment procedures. Hays (2013) also indicates that if clients are convinced of the test or assessment's usefulness, clients may be more motivated to not only do their best but may also be more likely to accept the results with less defensiveness.

Administration and Proctoring

How psychological assessments and tests are administered varies as a process dependent on the audience, purpose, and format (Hays, 2013). Indeed, there are numerous ways that tests and assessment can be administered to a client, each having distinct advantages and disadvantages. Drummond et al. (2016) outline the following modes of administering assessment and testing instruments: self-administered, individually administered, group administered, computer administered, video administered, audio administered, American Sign Language, and nonverbal administration. Regardless of the mode or format in which the assessment or test is administered, the counselor or clinician is responsible for being aware of and following all administration procedures including activities that take place before, during, and after administration.

Hays indicates that inexperienced test users often do not fully appreciate the importance of the test administrator's role (2013). The first major responsibility of the test user as a counselor, or clinician, is to know all about the instrument. Counselors should review the manual, forms, answer sheets, and other materials and become familiar with the content of the instrument, the type of items, and the directions for administering the test or assessment before the client comes to take the assessment or test (Drummond et al., 2016).

Koocher and Rey-Casserly (2003) indicate that a conducive climate is critical to the collection of useful and valid test and assessment data. In this respect, counselors should strive to create appropriate rapport with clients by helping them to feel physically comfortable and emotionally at ease, as appropriate to the context. The counselor should have prepared a suitable testing environment in advance, strive to appreciate the attitudes of the client, address any issues raised regarding the tests and assessments, and check in on client anxiety.

Technology in Testing

The increasing automation of psychological testing and assessment can make administration of tests and assessments, and certainly scoring, more efficient. Technology may also result in more extensive and complex testing in a shorter amount of time. Many test publishers have embraced Internet testing over traditional paper-and-pencil tests for reasons of efficiency not only in administering but also in updating. Internet tests and assessments can provide multimedia, better graphics, and relevant resources and are thought to allow for the assessment of higher order abilities and types of skills not easily measured by paper-and-pencil tests (Hays, 2013). Naturally, the use of technology in testing and assessment brings its own challenges and problems: security, privacy, computer viruses, hacking, cheating, and copyright issues. Navigating these challenges is left to the counselor as to when and where the tests and assessments are taken or given. When the counselor or clinician is not present at the time the test or assessment is taken, these challenges will be out of the counselor's control (Hays, 2013).

Along with the other technology issues in Internet testing, there is also a continuing need for the ethical and professional use of tests and assessments that are supported by reliability and validity. The growth of career resources on the Internet has in turn resulted in, and been driven by, a curiosity and fascination that has resulted in many short career interest quizzes, brief personality measures, and other such quizzes and tests that have no evidence of norms, reliability, or validity. The counselor is charged with making it clear that these unproven instruments are no substitute for true standardized assessment instruments (Hays, 2013).

Interpretation of Tests and Assessments

In counseling, interpretation of tests and assessment includes much more than simply scoring an assessment tool or testing instrument. Interpretation includes sharing initial findings and incorporating interpretation of test and assessment data into the general counseling process. As Hays (2013) indicates, the more intentional counselors are about bringing testing and assessment interpretation into their work with individuals, the more therapeutic the assessment process can be. The manner in which assessment and testing tools can aid in self-awareness, insight, and decision-making can save time and money for clients. In addition, and more important to the therapeutic relationship, communication of test and assessment results can almost always yield a richer dialogue and better treatment planning. In this light, when making inferences about a test taker's past, present, and potential future behaviors and other characteristics from test scores, the counselor should also consider other available data that support or challenge the inferences or interpretations being made and communicated.

Another potential role of interpretation might include the responsibility of interpreting results of psychological tests and assessments to parents, teachers, and other professionals. Responsible interpretation of assessment and test results requires counselors to have knowledge and understanding of the test results themselves in order to be able to communicate those results in a manner that can be understood by those the counselor may be working with, whether the actual client or an interested or invested party (Drummond et al., 2016).

Also according to Drummond et al. (2016), when interpreting scores, counselors should understand and consider the properties—psychometric (such as validity and reliability), as well as normative (individual) and ipsative (intraindividual) properties—of the tests and assessments that were administered. Counselors should be well informed about the various types of scores, such as percentiles, standard scores, and age and grade equivalents in interpreting and communicating as well. Counselors should also consider major differences between the normative group and the actual test taker and the impact of any modification(s) of administration procedures on the results. And finally, computer-based assessment instruments often provide canned computer-generated reports or narratives. These reports may contain complex and detailed statements or paragraphs that should not be viewed or communicated as standalone interpretations without other contextual elements such as the client's personal history, life events, current stressors, and motivation (Drummond et al., 2016). Ultimately, regardless of how scores and interpretations are obtained, it is the counselor or clinician who is both responsible and accountable for the accuracy of any and all interpretations.

Report Preparation and Data Management

Preparation of a report that interprets and communicates the results of psychological testing and assessment is a critical part of the assessment process. Conveying tests and assessment results with language that the test taker, parents, teachers, or other interested and invested parties can understand is one of the key elements in helping others understand the meaning and usefulness of the test results (Drummond et al., 2016). To keep written reports clear and understandable, the language should be specific and concrete rather than abstract and ambiguous. Drummond et al. (2016) advises the following: avoid jargon and abbreviations; refer to yourself in the third person (e.g., "the examiner found" rather than "I found"); use concise sentences; avoid needless words and phrases; avoid unnecessary redundancies; write background information in past tense and assessment results in present tense; pay attention to professional form and style of report.

While there is no single, optimal report format suitable for every setting and assessment, there are some sections of a typical psychological assessment report for a client: title (e.g., Mental Health Evaluation, Psychological Evaluation); identifying information; reason for referral; background information; behavioral observations; assessment instruments and procedures; assessment results and interpretation; summary; and recommendations (Drummond et al., 2016). The exact format of an assessment report depends on the audience, referral question(s), assessment instruments or tests, and strategies used in the administration of the assessment. As a rule, only include the results of any tests and assessments that are relevant to the overall purpose of the evaluation.

The release of data and who should and needs to have access to the data involved in a psychological assessment is yet another necessary focus of the counselor or clinician. A large part of the intent of ethical standards for psychological testing and assessment is to minimize harm and misuse of data. Under longstanding accepted ethical practices, psychologists may release test data to another clinician, qualified professional, or interested party after being authorized to do so by the client or by another valid release or court order (Koocher & Rey-Casserly, 2003). In this respect, counselors are advised to restrain from releasing test or assessment data to individuals who are not qualified or entitled to such information, except as required by law or court order to an attorney or court based on a client's valid release of information, or to the client as an appropriate part of therapy or intervention.

Counselors may worry about exactly how far their responsibility goes in upholding such standards. It is one thing to express reservations about releasing data, but it is another issue to be in violation of a court order or contend with the legal system when the counselor may be worried about possible harm from the data. When in doubt, the counselor is always advised to seek and retain legal counsel to navigate issues of ethical and legal responsibility. As Koocher and Rey-Casserly (2003) indicate, counselors and other clinicians should always seek and maintain appropriate confidentiality measures and competence assurances; such professionals cannot use the ethics code as a shield to resist release of testing and assessment information.

Multicultural Assessment and Testing

As the population continues to diversify, counselors are naturally expected to recognize special considerations and challenges in assessing diverse populations. According to Hays (2013), when assessing an individual from another culture the general rule seems to be that the less the counselor knows of the individual's culture, the more errors the counselor is likely to make based on their lack of understanding. While it is important to be knowledgeable about the culture of the individual being assessed, it is also equally important not to "overculturalize," attributing every behavior and variable to culture. Although minimizing cultural bias in assessment is a goal, attempting to remove all cultural differences from an assessment may result in compromising the validity of the behavior it was designed to assess (Hays, 2013). To further complicate the issue, assessment practices, assessment tools, instruments, and tests are often far from being fair for all individuals and for all groups. As Hays (2013) states: fairness in assessment becomes something that counselors and clinicians strive toward but yet never fully achieve.

Fairness in psychological testing and assessment refers to efforts to create equitable experiences for test takers, free from bias. Hays (2013) defines bias as differences in scores or findings, either artificially high or low, that lead to differential ways in which the data are used for groups and subgroups. Bias can have significant consequences for clients that can lead to misdiagnosis or other interpretation or evaluation errors that may affect what counseling interventions or placements clients receive (Hays, 2013). The *Standards for Educational and Psychological Testing* (AERA, APA, & NCME, 2014) define fairness in four ways: the absence of bias; there is equitable treatment of all test takers; those with equal standing on a particular test construct should score equally no matter the group membership; and test takers have had an equal opportunity to learn. The *Standards* further categorize bias in two ways: bias associated with test content, as inappropriate selection of test items or general content coverage; and bias associated with response processes referring to situations when items elicit responses not intended by the test such as a response set.

Hays (2013) indicates there are many cultural factors that may influence the assessment process and thus introduce bias into assessment and testing as well as into the counseling process and outcomes. Hays lists a few of those factors as: the culture of the counselor and counseling process, counselor discrimination, mental disorder rates, test and assessment sophistication, client motivation and, obviously, language.

Clients of diverse backgrounds, and counselors of different backgrounds, may have various levels of understanding and acceptance of counseling in general, and "counselor" and "therapist" can have different meanings across racial and ethnic groups (Hays, 2013). In thinking about the issue of assessment bias, the counselor must understand and distinguish between test results and innate aptitude. Racism, sexism, and other forms of discrimination such as heterosexism and classism occur in assessment when counselors use cultural group membership as the explanation for assessment or testing findings (Hays, 2013). In this respect, counselor discrimination also affects clinical decision-making in assessing the degree and severity of a client's symptoms, the client's level of functioning, and the client's prognosis. Research by Good, James, Good, and Becker (2003) found that when counselors were unaware of the client's racial, ethnic, and gender identity, they tended to provide less severe diagnoses as when they were aware of that information.

Relatedly, the disproportionate rates of mental disorders across cultural groups, particularly racial and ethnic minorities, are understood to play a role in bias as well. In 2005, Paniagua presented some weaknesses in how prevalence and incidence data have historically been collected that produced a picture that seemed to indicate that mental disorders in general are higher for racial and ethnic minorities. Recent research has shown that when different and more culturally appropriate, and more sophisticated assessment and testing tools are used, those differences are minimized.

A basic assumption of psychological testing and assessment is that the test taker is willing to provide obvious information and to give a performance, or authentic answers, to someone they may not know well, or may not know at all. Motivation across cultures to perform may not be equal and may certainly be reflected in the assessment and test results. And lastly, language can also serve as a significant barrier and result in unintentional bias. Limited proficiency in the language of the test, issues with translation or test adaptation may also impact the fairness of the assessment process and produce bias that may impact the evaluation and subsequently any interpretation or recommendations (Hays, 2013).

According to Hays (2013), gender differences in assessment and interpretation may also be attributed to gender bias in some manner. The counselor must note that instruments tend to reflect only male and female comparisons. Information regarding how assessment findings relate to transgender or intersex populations is, at least to date, very limited. Further, because sexual orientation overlaps gender in some ways and because items typically represent traditional views of gender characteristics, they also end up depicting heterosexual characteristics and counselors must use caution in interpreting and applying the results of any assessments that use gender loadings and data.

Counselors must also recognize the influence of variables such as race, ethnicity, and socioeconomic variables in psychological testing and assessment. According to Hays (2013), a frequent argument is that tests and measures of cognitive aptitude are constructed by and for White middle-class individuals and are therefore biased against lower socioeconomic individuals and others who are not members of the majority culture. This cultural bias could potentially be found in items suburban children might exhibit more familiarity with than urban or rural children. Another instance might be children brought up in a home where a dialect, nonstandard American English, or broken English is used being less able to comprehend the language used on assessment and testing instruments. In understanding and competently interpreting test and assessment data with clients of diverse backgrounds, Hays (2013) indicates from previous research that social class is correlated with race and ethnicity and, when socioeconomic class is controlled, many cultural differences disappear.

The *Standards for Multicultural Assessment* (AACE, 2012) charge counselors with understanding the influence of culture, background, and individual characteristics when using testing and assessment as well as reporting results and designing interventions from test and assessment data. These standards also charge counselors to recognize how the effects of stigma, oppression, and discrimination impact the interpretation and application of assessment results for culturally diverse clients. The wise counselor researches and collaborates to eliminate biases, prejudices, and discriminatory contexts in conducting evaluations, making interpretations, providing feedback, and implementing interventions.

Also worth noting and discussing are issues that may be involved with assessing and testing individuals with disability. Types of disability include deafness, blindness, developmental delays, intellectual disability, psychiatric illness, traumatic brain injury, and many others. The specific disability must be taken into account in the selection and provision of any evaluation, testing, and assessment, and appropriate assessment accommodations must be provided. In using tests and assessments with clients with disabilities, using instruments with items related to general health and physical symptoms may appear to produce "deviant" scores by individuals who are physically ill or physically disabled, and therefore may be difficult to interpret or easily misinterpreted (Hays, 2013). In cases such as this, some instruments exist for use with disabled populations and could potentially yield not only more normative scores in consideration of the disability, but also yield more useful and helpful data and information.

The same considerations can be carried over into thinking about assessment with older adults. According to Hays (2013), the need to assess both the mental health and cognitive functioning of older adults has led to the development of instruments specifically designed to assess older clients. When assessing older adults, counselors should be sensitive to and aware of possible fatigue and the possible influence of medical issues and/or medications. After initial testing, the assessment data can function as a baseline against which to potentially compare future changes in the mental health or cognitive functioning of the individual.

The Association for Assessment in Counseling and Education's (AACE) *Standards for Multicultural Assessment* (2012) indicates that the 4th revision of the standards addresses more specifically the role of social advocacy in assessment. The document also speaks to the importance of effectively selecting, administering, and interpreting assessments, tests, and diagnostic techniques. The intent of the revision is to enhance counselors' knowledge of as well as the public's awareness and support for culturally appropriate assessment and testing. In regard to the Standards, they make the following statements before addressing each content area:

Advocacy: culturally competent professional counselors recognize the importance of social justice advocacy; they integrate understanding of age, gender, ability, race, ethnic group, national origin, religion, sexual orientation, linguistic background, and other personal characteristics in order to provide appropriate assessment and diagnostic techniques.

Selection of Assessments: Content and Purpose, Norming, Reliability, and Validity: culturally competent professional counselors select assessments and diagnostic techniques that are appropriate and effective for diverse client populations.

Administration and Scoring of Assessments: culturally competent professional counselors recognize challenges inherent in assessment of persons and seek to provide administration and scoring of assessment to clients respecting age, gender, ability, race, ethnic group, national origin, religion, sexual orientation, linguistic background, and other personal characteristics.

Interpretation and Application of Assessment Results: culturally competent professional counselors acknowledge the importance of social justice advocacy in interpretation and communication of assessment results with diverse populations.

Training in the Uses of Assessments: culturally competent professional counselors seek training and supervised experience to ensure they provide appropriate assessment and diagnostic techniques for diverse client populations.

Supervision and Consultation in Assessment and Testing

In stark contrast to the vast and robust literature on best practices in psychotherapy and counseling, ethics among all mental health practitioners, and the actual process of testing and assessment, the topic of supervision in psychological testing and assessment has been relatively neglected across the fields in which they are most frequently used—psychology and counseling. In fact, Watkins published a call to action regarding what he termed "a serious deficiency" in the supervision of testing and assessment in 1991. Iwanicki and Peterson (2017) indicate there has been little notable progress regarding this issue in the empirical literature despite that call to action many years ago. In fact, they report that a psycINFO search in March 2016 with the subject headings "psychotherapy and supervision" and "psychological assessment and supervision" yielded little literature or research actually focused on the supervision of psychological testing and assessment outside of formal educational programs and/or internships. A number of recent searches by this author, using the same search terms, replicated those findings in numerous psycINFO searches in May and June 2017. These searches yielded very limited literature and/or research on the actual supervision of testing and assessment. Of those that were found, many will be cited in this section.

Dumont and Willis (2003) assert that given the important decisions that are often made from psychological test and assessment results, competence in administration, scoring, and interpretation of assessment instruments and tools is of paramount importance. They go on to state that experienced, as well as inexperienced, test administrators and users often do not fully grasp the importance of standardized administration procedures and protocols and are often not fully aware of the potential for errors in administration and scoring. In effect, these errors may result in substantial, meaningful differences between scores on the recording form and the scores the individual may have truly earned or have been able to earn if the test administration and/or scoring had been without error (Kaufman, 1994). For Dumont and Willis, this adds up to a "serious concern" in the type and amount of supervision in assessment that mental health professionals have been given, or sought, over the course of their careers.

While there are a number of models of clinical supervision, a psycINFO database search in June 2017 yielded only one model of supervision specifically designed to provide a framework to guide the supervision and professional development of novice test users. The model was proposed in 1997 by Finkelstein and Tuckman and was presented with yet another call to "spur further work in this unfairly neglected area." They went on to outline their model, which included the following areas of focus: learning the basics of test administration and scoring; generating primary inferences; clustering related hypotheses; from outline to written word; internalizing diagnostic norms; autonomy with consultation; striking off on one's own; and passing the torch.

If there is a dearth of information regarding supervision of mental health clinicians and counselors, there is an even greater lacuna in the literature regarding consultation in psychological assessment and testing. Evans and Finn (2016 state that mental health clinicians frequently recognize the need for ongoing consultation and peer support for their work with clients regarding psychotherapy and counseling but not with psychological testing and assessment. They offer that psychotherapy consultation groups exist in abundance but consultation groups for psychological assessment are not to be found. Evans and Finn (2015) assert in no uncertain terms that the complexities inherent in practicing psychological testing and assessment are such that regular consultation is greatly needed—whether it is focused on test scoring, test interpretation, report writing, or communicating with the client, family member(s), or other concerned or invested parties about the results of the tests or assessment. Evans and Finn (2015) have developed a model of collaborative assessment consultation that focuses on advanced case presentation and group collaboration sessions. In their thinking, regular consultation helps maintain and increase professional competence, acts to stimulate professional growth, and results in assessment practice being less daunting for practitioners and more sustainable over time. More importantly, however, the practices of supervision and consultation ensure the client is receiving the best, most competent, most ethical, most reliable, and valid assessment possible.

Test Your Knowledge:

1. Among the ethical and legal considerations in psychological testing and assessment, which is not true?
   a. It is the counselor's responsibility to be aware of the legal and ethical issues involved in testing and assessment
   b. There are very few clear guidelines or standards regarding testing and assessment
   c. There are several sets of standards and guidelines from state to national levels regarding testing and assessment
   d. Ethical guidelines and standards are typically provided by professional organizations that oversee the administration and usage of tests and assessments

2. In the Standards for the Qualifications of Test Users outlined by the American Counseling Association, which is not a standard for test users?
   a. A thorough understanding of testing theory, techniques of test construction, and test reliability and validity
   b. Skill in administration of tests and interpretation of test scores
   c. Knowledge of the impact of diversity on testing accuracy, including age, gender, ethnicity, race, disability, and linguistic differences
   d. A desire to help a client to achieve a specific goal by using a test or assessment

3. Which of the following is always the first concern in psychological testing and assessment?
   a. Client attitude
   b. A suitable testing area
   c. Client welfare
   d. Method of payment

4. Which of the following is not true concerning identification of the client in testing and assessment?
   a. Conflicts can exist in competing interests for the information provided by a psychological assessment
   b. The counselor is charged with considering the rights of each layer of authority in terms of access to data and results
   c. Whoever is paying the bill has exclusive rights to the test results
   d. Counselors are charged with conceptualizing, identifying, and representing the client

5. Informed consent includes all but which one of the following?
   a. Information
   b. Understanding
   c. Voluntariness
   d. Exclusive rights to the data

6. The responsibility for proper use of a psychological test or assessment falls on the
   _____.
   a. Publisher
   b. Counselor who uses the test
   c. Client
   d. Test developer

7. Which of the following is not a key professional issue in psychological assessment and testing?
   a. Planning the assessment
   b. Counseling process issues
   c. Test anxiety issues
   d. All of the above are key professional issues

8. Interpretation of psychological tests and assessments include much more than simply scoring the test. Which of the following is not an important consideration in administering, scoring, and interpreting results?
   a. Intentionality and responsibility of what is reported
   b. Communication of what is reported
   c. Cultural considerations in what is reported and how
   d. Let the data speak for itself

9. There are many cultural factors that may influence the assessment process and introduce bias into assessment and testing. Some of the cultural factors mentioned were:
   a. Culture of the client and culture of the counselor
   b. Culture of the individual ordering the assessment
   c. Mental disorder rates and the influence of culture on those rates
   d. Client motivation and language barriers

10. Which of the following is not true about supervision and consultation in the realm of psychological testing and assessment?
    a. If you have received training in your counseling program, you have been well prepared to administer tests and assessments and do not need to worry about supervision or consultation
    b. There is an obvious lack of empirically based literature and research regarding supervision and consultation of testing and assessment
    c. While psychotherapy and counseling supervision groups can be found, it is often difficult to find supervision or consultation of psychological testing and assessment
    d. In view of some of the important decisions that often rest on psychological testing and assessment, counselors who engage in those activities would be wise to seek supervision and consultation

4 Mental Status Examinations and Intake Assessments

Robin Leichtman and Kathryn C. MacCluskie

This chapter is designed to help counselors feel more comfortable achieving two seemingly disparate goals in an intake interview: gathering objective diagnostic information and beginning the relationship development process. Each agency that provides human services will likely have a preferred procedure for doing intakes. We will talk about gathering initial information and about how to respond empathically while still getting the information you need in the first session, one of the most important sessions of all. An initial session typically involves gathering foundational information about a person. Intake appointments may include an intake interview, a mental status exam, screening inventories, suicide risk assessment, clinical diagnosis and identification of treatment goals. In addition to the assessments, pertinent information is shared with the potential client such as informed consent, the importance of confidentiality, client's rights and explaining how therapy works. Throughout the chapter, ideas on how to create an interview environment that is welcoming, comfortable and safe will also be provided.

A typical scenario involves an individual calling a mental health service provider and making an appointment. When the individual arrives at their scheduled appointment time, as part of the intake process, individuals are asked to complete several forms including demographic details, insurance information, physical health screening/medical history, emergency contact information and photocopies of pertinent identification (e.g., driver's license and insurance card). Potential clients are provided with a written copy of their rights, responsibilities and privacy policy including grievance procedures and a copy of the agency policies. Agency guidelines may include cancelation and missed appointments policies, fees for services and arrangement for payment and an explanation of services being offered.

The initial paperwork (e.g., financial information) may be administered by support staff depending on the type of office you work in (e.g., private practice, community mental health agency, hospital setting). If someone else is managing this paperwork on your behalf, recognize that the client has been completing paperwork for a good length of time and may be starting to feel anxious about meeting with you. Impressions are formed within the first few moments of meeting someone and you want to instill a sense of warmth, safety and assurance. How can you convey that message in the first moments of meeting an individual and throughout the clinical interview? For instance, as part of my introduction, I say things such as: "I appreciate that you took the time and energy to meet with me today" or "I am glad you are here." During the initial moments and throughout the interview, counselors are encouraged to maintain an intention to create a psychological climate of safety in which clients will not feel threatened and to encourage an open dialogue to assist the individual to drop any pretense or defenses.

Mental Status Examinations

The specific term "mental status examination" refers specifically to assessing an individual's level of consciousness and awareness of his or her surroundings. Mental status exams, in contrast to "intake assessments," are more likely done in medical settings. Examples of when someone might need a mental status exam would be a person who recently suffered a stroke or who sustained some other type of head injury. The Mini-Mental State Exam (MMSE, Folstein, Folstein, & McHugh, 1975) is a commonly used tool for assessing level of consciousness. The categories of cognitive processing assessed by the MMSE are orientation to person, place and time; attention; calculation; recall; registration; repetition; and understanding complex demands. There is a very high correlation between a reduced score on the MMSE and likelihood of organic impairment (i.e., changes in brain tissue or function as the result of a physical ailment). In general, when "mental status" is included as a component of an intake interview, it is referring to some subset of these categories.

Intake Interviews

The main purpose of the initial assessment is to gather information. The Intake or Mental Health Assessment essentially attempts to capture the current functioning of an individual as well as his or her physical, mental and spiritual developmental history. It includes the presenting problem and as much information as a counselor can acquire to best address current concerns. Most agencies have a standard format and train new clinicians in completing paperwork to meet compliance with state regulatory boards. Some states have recommended forms; for example, in the State of Ohio, the Alcohol, Drug, and Mental Health Services Board of Cuyahoga County provides links for the components of an intake and mental status exam: http://adamhscc.org/en-US/member-agency.aspx.

During the intake, there are a variety of procedural protocols that must be completed. By law, counselors are responsible to inform potential clients of agency policies, informed consent and confidentiality limitations (e.g., we are mandated reporters to prevent harm to self and others as well as report alleged or suspected abuse). Once informed consent and limits of confidentiality are explained and consent forms signed, the intake interview begins.

Relational Considerations

While there are numerous content areas pertaining to discovery, the process of gathering data is somewhat dependent upon the counselor's skill in establishing rapport and developing the therapeutic relationship. With an increased sense of safety and trust, individuals feel more comfortable sharing more content information. Content information is very important both from an objective angle and also from the angle of empathy and contextual understanding of the behaviors, thoughts, and feelings the client is disclosing. Therefore, perhaps in an intake assessment more than any other dimension of evaluation, relationship development is at least as important as gathering valid data from which to make clinical decisions. "An effective initial interview is a balance between gathering information and building a therapeutic relationship" (Whiston, 2017, p. 141). The quality of that relationship will sustain the work and predict therapeutic outcomes. The initial session sets up the ground to allow for this work to develop. "Of those factors directly related to treatment outcomes, one of the largest contributors to outcome is the therapeutic relationship" (Hubble, Duncan, Miller & Wampold, 2010, p. 37).

Students who are in their internships and learning how to do intake assessments often struggle with finding an appropriate balance between gathering objective information and establishing therapeutic rapport. As we become more skilled in this work, it becomes easier to be carefully observing verbal and nonverbal behavior of a client while simultaneously responding empathically. This is a form of divided attention and multi-tasking. As Malcolm Gladwell (2008) demonstrated in his seminal memoir, *Outliers*, a minimum of 10,000 hours of "deliberate practice" is necessary to develop one's skill set in any profession. Becoming skilled in the general principles of clinical interviewing, especially the initial interview, requires practice at active listening, empathic responding, meeting and overcoming the potential client's resistances and, overall, finding a comfortable meeting ground to collect the data and gain an understanding and awareness of the individual's process.

In order to work from a common foundation of conceptualizing therapeutic relationships, we will spend some time summarizing approaches for optimal relationship development. Note that use of "optimal" means creating interpersonal and extrapersonal contexts with the highest possible likelihood of another person feeling comfortable. We recognize that none of us can "make" another person feel comfortable, that control lies within the client. From Person-Centered Therapy, the characteristics to develop a healthy, healing therapeutic condition include "an ability to understand the client's meanings and feelings; a sensitivity to the client's attitudes; a warm interest without any emotional over-involvement" (Rogers, 1961, p. 44); overall, an expression of unconditional positive regard for the purpose of facilitating growth and development. The strength of the interview is indicated by the degree of understanding the interviewer conveys to the client.

Joyce and Sills (2010) recommend three questions to determine the strength of a working alliance:

1. Does the client have confidence in you as the therapist and trust that you are genuinely being helpful?
2. Are you both on the same page? It is important for the therapist to understand the presenting concern that brought the individual to seek counseling. Is there clarity and agreement regarding treatment goals?
3. Is there a commitment to treatment even when challenges arise?

An array of interviewing techniques may be used to gather information while building an alliance. One way to organize the interview is to follow these steps (Ivey & Ivey, 2007; Whiston, 2017):

Stage 1: Building rapport and developing a therapeutic alliance
   "Hello. I appreciate that you took the time and energy to come in today."

Stage 2: Gathering information and defining issues
   "What brings you in today?" "What is your concern?" "To what extent is this problem impacting your relationships with family and friends or your work?" "On a scale of 1–10, where 1 is not at all and 10 is a great deal, how would you rate the severity of the problem?" "Tell me more about the symptoms you are experiencing and be as specific as possible."

Stage 3: Determining outcomes
   "If you were to write a treatment goal, what would it be?"

Stage 4: Identify methods used in the past to solve the problem
   "What have you tried to solve this problem?" "Have you discussed these concerns with anyone in the past?" "How have you been successful in the past when dealing with this issue?"

Stage 5: Gather history
   Is there a medical history? Are there significant developmental events that are impacting current functioning (social/developmental history)? Is there a family history? Are there perceived internal and external barriers due to race/ethnicity, socioeconomic status and/or sexual orientation (cultural influences)?

Information Gathered in the Initial Interview

- Referral source
- Identifying information (name, address, best number to reach, age, gender, marital status, school or occupation information, insurance information)
- Presenting problem
- Past counseling experiences or psychiatric history
- Present level of functioning in work/school, relationships (family and peers) and social/leisure activities and the degree to which the presenting concern impacts the individual's ability to function in each of these areas
- Social development and any significant history that may influence present concerns
- Family history and current status including marital status, living arrangements, others living in the home, any children, history or current trauma (physical, verbal, sexual, domestic violence or exploitation), influences of family of origin and/or current family members impacting ability to function and/or influencing current presenting problem, family history of alcohol/substance use and mental illness
- Medical history and current status including date of last health physical, sleep, diet and exercise patterns, medications prescribed, alcohol and/or substance use
- Education and job history
- Religious and cultural influences
- Legal history
- Military history

Interviewing Tips

The content of an interview refers to the specific data provided by the client (e.g., client discloses struggling with math). Process refers to the communication implied though not plainly expressed (e.g., loss of confidence in her ability as evidenced by statements like "I'm stupid" or "I can't do it."). To establish rapport, the therapist needs to communicate a sense of understanding. The following offers suggestions for demonstrating understanding, empathy and respect. This is not an exhaustive list. I have highlighted four areas of interviewing skills that promote building a therapeutic alliance while obtaining information. Basic listening skills including attending behaviors; using open and closed questions; and encouraging, paraphrasing and summarizing, demonstrating to the client that you want to hear their story and concerns. Observation skills will help you respond empathically and respectfully as well as guide you in diagnosing and treatment planning.

Attending Behaviors

Appropriate visuals (eye contact), vocal qualities, verbal tracking skills and body language are examples of attending behaviors. Attending behaviors encourage dialogue and assist the client in sharing their thoughts and feelings. They communicate to the client that you are interested and "see" the individual, and they are expressed both verbally and nonverbally. Active, authentic listening builds trust and rapport as it enables the client to continue to talk and explore. These messages impact the effectiveness of the clinical interview.

Buber (1970) explained that there are two ways to be in contact: I and It or I and Thou. From this approach (Buber, 1970), connections made from an I-It perspective treat the other as an object, pushing "it" around to suit one's needs and judging "it" based on stereotypes and assumptions. I–It is the experience of purpose of having to meet a goal without recognizing the needs of the other or attending to the relationship. For instance, we can use the example of having the goal to complete an intake. In an I–It relationship, the client is treated as an object, someone to "fix." An I–Thou stance offers a relational approach, seeing and acknowledging the other by way of honoring the inherent humanity of the relationship.

> You can develop a person to person dialogue with clients by adopting an "I–Thou" attitude towards them. This involves turning your being to their being, addressing them with real respect, being genuinely interested, accepting and confirming of them as they are now and not as a means to an end.
>
> (Mackewn, 1997, p. 82)

This, by itself, is immensely therapeutic.

Self-understanding and self-awareness are key components in monitoring your patterns of attending to another individual. Develop an awareness of your individual style. As a treatment provider, I need to be aware of my behaviors and the impact my behaviors have during the interview. Moreover, I need to have an awareness of my contact style and how I regulate contact during the interview.

> Awareness is the way in which we understand ourselves and what we need and also the way in which we organize our field and make meaning of our experience. It is our capacity to be in touch with our own existence, to know how we are feeling, sensing, thinking, reacting, or making meaning from moment to moment . . . it enables us to perceive and make sense of what is going on inside and outside ourselves and allows us the possibility of ascertaining what we can do to make ourselves, others or the environment better.
>
> (Mackewn, 1997, p. 113)

Open and Closed Questions

In interviewing, open-ended questions are often used to encourage the individual to elaborate on a subject and to avoid leading or unduly influencing the client. "What brought you to counseling?" is an example of an open-ended question and requires the individual to construct a response. A closed question, in general, elicits a yes or no response. For instance, I might say, "Per the Intake report, I see you came to counseling because you feel depressed." Client response: "Yes, that is correct." This can be followed by an open-ended question such as, "Tell me more about your depression"; however, the client may be less likely to open up about other issues. In interviewing, counselors are encouraged to consider what questions enable the client to engage in the interviewing process. Questions can encourage or discourage the client in being forthcoming with information.

Typically, open-ended questions begin with *what, how, why* or *could* (Ivey & Ivey, 2007, p. 94). Examples: *What is your earliest memory of feeling this way? How do you make meaning of the situation? Why do you imagine others respond to you in a negative way? Could you remember a time when you felt differently?*

Close-ended questions often begin with *is, are* or *do* (Ivey & Ivey, 2007, p. 94). Examples: *Is this a new symptom? Are you on any medications? Do you have a support system in place other than therapy?*

Something else to consider is using vocabulary the client will understand; in other words, keep in mind the client's educational and social background. It is also important to note that assessing children requires patience and knowledge of basic developmental stages. Children may think they are being brought to counseling because they are in trouble. Creating a safe, engaging environment through the use of therapeutic art or play will assist in building trust between you and the child. Additionally, children tend to be more concrete in their thinking. Keeping the questions simple and incorporating other ways to gather information (e.g., "Tell me about your picture") will establish rapport and encourage the child to participate. Adolescents, in general, present with a capacity for abstract reasoning skills and may appear to understand the interview process. However, avoid making assumptions based on adult norms. Consider the individual's emotional development and ability to regulate their emotions, and show respect.

Encouraging, Paraphrasing and Summarizing

Avoid technical jargon and encourage the interview process by using encouragers, paraphrasing and summarizing. These techniques let the client know you are actively listening and assist in establishing an alliance.

Encouragers are verbal prompts or nonverbal gestures that encourage individuals to continue, such as saying "uh-huh" or nodding your head in understanding. The repetition of key words or restating something (e.g., "I heard you use the word 'fear' or 'scared' several times") will encourage an individual to say more about that feeling. Appropriate display of emotions, such as smiling, demonstrates interpersonal warmth and encourages the possibility for positive outcomes, as well as helps clients feel comfortable and safe.

Paraphrasing helps to clarify the individual's disclosure(s). Paraphrasing is restating what you heard the client say in your own words. For instance, client reports that she plays softball and runs track at school. Therapist paraphrases by saying, "Sounds like you enjoy sports. How does your participation as an athlete impact your mood?"

Summarizing is used to process and/or clarify information. Summarizing helps to organize the data. After summarizing the events and issues surrounding the presenting problem, I might ask, "What else is there to add to the story?" or, "Have we missed anything that is important to consider in treatment?" Summarizing provides an opportunity for the client to add more details. Perhaps, more importantly, the client leaves feeling understood.

Client Observation Skills

In the next section, I will introduce the mental status exam, which lists specific behaviors to observe. Three basic observation skills to assist in understanding the dynamic between therapist and client include nonverbal behavior, verbal behavior, and discrepancies and conflict (Ivey & Ivey, 2007).

Pay close attention to nonverbal messages (e.g., eye contact, facial expressions, hand gestures, activity level, posture) and be curious as to what the individual may be communicating without interpreting or making assumptions. I have heard it said that 85% or more of communication is nonverbal. Whether this is an accurate percentage or not, it is to your benefit and therapeutic outcomes to be aware of what is not being said. For instance, if a client appears fidgety, do not assume they have ADHD; they might just be nervous or had too much coffee that day. I might say something like, "I am noticing a lot of movement in your chair. I move around in a similar way when I am uncomfortable." Usually, the individual will respond in a manner that explains what the movement means for them. In this way, several messages are conveyed: 1) I am not being judgmental; 2) I am increasing the client's awareness and understanding of their own way of being and how they present to others; 3) I am building ground for a therapeutic relationship; 4) I am engaging the individual in the therapeutic process.

Verbal statements offer insight into the individual's thought patterns, cognitive development and ability; the level of ownership of their own thoughts, feelings and behaviors (e.g., do they use "I"-statements or tend to blame others); and demonstration of insight. The communication exchange is imperative to understanding and responding to the individual's needs. Earlier I discussed the I-Thou stance (Buber, 1970); another important consideration as a therapist is to manage your patterns of selective attention. Selective attention refers to stimuli one chooses to pay attention to while ignoring other information. Depending on your theoretical orientation, you may be processing information to fit a particular theory. For instance, behavioral therapists are listening for symptoms and concrete data that are measurable and observable; existential therapists are listening for meaning-making; and Adlerian therapists are listening for social context. Your personal style and theory will impact how clients respond in the interview and talk about their concerns (Ivey & Ivey, 2007).

Listening for key words may provide a clue in noticing what is important to a client. Further, observing client topic changes may be evidence of difficulty tracking a conversation or distracting from a difficult topic. I might help the individual by commenting, "A few moments ago you mentioned _____." The client may respond in a number of ways (e.g., "I got distracted" or "I lost my train of thought" or "I decided midway I didn't want to talk about that" or "I noticed I was getting emotional and needed to deflect"), which represents data and will help to assess the client's thought processes. In addition to listening for key words/phrases, notice the client's conversational style. Where is it on the continuum between concrete/situational and abstract? Clients closer to the concrete style provide specifics and tend to use lots of examples and stories. Abstract thinkers tend to self-reflect and analyze their thoughts and behaviors.

To demonstrate, here is a transcript of a concrete/situational dialogue in which a parent describes her 7-year-old daughter:

> *When [client] gets anxious, she shuts down, doesn't want to talk and starts crying. It happened once this week and couple of times last week. Last week, she was so anxious, I had to keep her home from school. In the past, it happens after a long school break and sometimes after the weekend. It usually happens at the beginning of the school year.*

A transcript from a 30-year-old female exemplifying abstract thinking:

> *My mind is always going. What's the next goal? I appreciate what is good about the now and at the same time, I stay disconnected from the moment.*

While I share these examples to explain concrete versus abstract thinking, I also provide these transcripts as illustrations of age-appropriate mental processes and concerns. Attending to an individual's thought processes will guide the decision of best treatment practices to meet the needs of the client. Individuals who present with difficulty in abstract thinking or who are exclusively concrete thinkers exhibit struggles to learn, empathize and relate to other people. In general, behavioral approaches will be more suited for these individuals. Further, an inability to think abstractly may be indicative of developmental and/or neurological concerns (e.g., autism spectrum). On the other hand, people who are abstract thinkers may use intellectualizing as a means of reducing emotional intensity.

Observing discrepancies, mixed messages, conflicts or incongruities during the interview is another important task (Ivey & Ivey, 2007). The following examples are provided to help illuminate the many ways discrepancies may present:

Discrepancy in verbal statement: *He's a great kid, but he doesn't listen to me.*

Discrepancy in nonverbal communication: *I can talk about that (eyes tearing, face flushed, hands wringing, eyes averted).*

Discrepancy between what is said and nonverbal observation: *Of course, I love my family (spoken loudly almost shouting, feels/sounds angry, eyes averted, hands fisted, tense body; or, that same statement spoken with no vocal inflection or shift in facial expression).*

Discrepancy between people: *I will go crazy if I have to live with my mother (and mother doesn't understand the problem).*

Discrepancy between client and situation: *I did everything I could and they still failed me (from the student who never did their homework, skipped classes, several reported suspensions).*

Discrepancy between client and prospects: *When I grow up, I'm going to be in the NBA (never practices basketball).*

During the intake process, it is important to note these discrepancies as the therapeutic goals may include ways to assist the client in working through the conflict. However, if it is not in the client's interest to work on these goals, meet the client where "they are available for meeting, accepting, and exploring" (Mackewn, 1997, p. 34) their individual aims and reasons for coming to therapy. In this first meeting it is important to establish rapport and assist the client in articulating their treatment goals: "listen to their stories, summarize what you have heard and say what you understand to be their longing or need, checking whether or not the client feels you have 'got' what he or she is saying" (Mackewn, 1997, p. 34–35).

Mental Status Examination

A mental status exam considers the variables that may be impacting an individual's functioning. The Mental Status Examination (MSE) may be done in a checklist format or a written paragraph or two that describes:

- Attitude/Appearance/Behavior:

  - Is the individual forthcoming with information? Do they appear friendly, cooperative, engaged, indifferent, confused, suspicious, worried, angry, hostile, etc.?
  - Is the individual's appearance appropriate to age, weather, setting, and situation? Does the individual appear to have acceptable grooming and hygiene? Is there any evidence of health problems? Is there any evidence of alcohol or substance use? Is the individual's height and weight proportionate? Are there any distinguishing features (e.g., tattoos, piercings, scarring, bruising, birthmarks, etc.)?
  - Does the individual make eye contact? Notice if eye contact is nonexistent, indirect, fixed, fleeting, glaring, or darting.

- Affect/Mood/Psychomotor Activity:

  - Is the individual's presentation congruent or incongruent with the individual's narrative? For instance, are they smiling/laughing as they share how sad and depressed they have been feeling.
  - What does the individual's facial expression indicate regarding their mood? Does the individual appear happy, sad, perplexed, preoccupied, bored, dazed, tense, etc.?
  - How would you describe the individual's posture (stooped, relaxed, stiff, shaky, slouched, etc.)? How would you describe their gait (slow, hesitant, shuffling, normal, ataxic, uncoordinated, brisk, etc.)? Are there any bizarre mannerisms? Does the

individual present with abnormal movement such as tics; twitches; grimaces; ritualistic behavior; rocking; pacing; nail biting; skin, scalp, or hair picking, or other body-focused repetitive behaviors? Does the individual appear to exhibit other symptoms associated with obsessive-compulsive behaviors?

- Orientation/Memory/Cognition:
  - Do they appear oriented to person, place, time, and space/situation?
  - Does the individual appear and/or report to have sufficient attention and concentration or are they easily distracted, exhibit a short attention span, or preoccupied?
  - Memory can be assessed by asking about recent meals or general knowledge (e.g., news or sports events). Long-term memory can be assessed by way of creating a personal timeline of events that can be confirmed by a family member or significant other.
  - Is there an intellectual impairment/mental retardation? Are they able to think abstractly or is their thinking more concrete?

- Thought Process/Content:
  - Describe the individual's thought processes (coherent, incoherent, disorganized, blocked, circumstantiality, tangentiality, magical thinking, vague, flight of ideas/rapid thoughts, etc.).
  - Is the thought content consistent with reality? Notice if there are any obsessions (unwanted, recurring thoughts), delusions (e.g., grandiose or persecutory thinking), or hallucinations (e.g., visual or auditory).

- Speech:
  - Are any of the following disorders apparent?
  - Blocking: a sudden interruption of thought or speech
  - Mutism: refusal to speak
  - Echolalia: unsolicited repetition of words spoken by another person
  - Neologisms: use of new words or made-up words
  - Flight of ideas: rapidly shifting the topic of conversation, making it difficult to follow
  - Perseveration: uncontrollable persistence or repetition of a thought or action despite the absence or cessation of a stimulus
  - Word salad: disorganized speech in which random words or phrases used together lack coherence or comprehension (e.g., dogs sleep coffee rings glasses)
  - Pressure of speech: rapid speech (e.g., motor mouth) difficult to interrupt; also known as "cluttered speech"
  - Tangential speech: conversation drifts and never gets to the point
  - Circumstantiality: nonlinear speech in which an individual has difficulty getting to the point; conversation drifts but eventually does get to the point

- Insight/Judgment:
  - Does the individual have the ability to recognize their own issues/problems?

- Suicidal/Homicidal Ideation

The MSE is based on clinical observation and statements made throughout the intake interview. The clinician may ask additional questions if there was concern; for instance, if the client described feeling depressed throughout the interview, a suicide/homicide assessment would be appropriate and necessary. The next section highlights checklists and rating scales often used when there are specific concerns.

Checklists and Rating Scales

Clinical interviews are the most commonly used assessments in gathering information; however, self-report, objective instruments should be considered to substantiate or challenge clinical observations and analysis. Clients may not have been able to disclose pertinent information during the interview for various reasons (e.g., shame or embarrassment). Information from a checklist may assist in identifying issues that did not present during the interview. Additionally, rating scales offer an indication of the extent of the problem and a baseline from which we can measure treatment outcomes.

The Symptom Checklist 90-Revised (Derogatis, 1994) and the *Brief Symptoms Inventory* (Derogatis, 1983) are favored instruments used in mental health settings in which the client endorses symptoms using a 5-point Likert scale in which a score of "0" indicates no presentation and "4" indicates extreme sensing. The instrument is normed for individuals 13 years and older and is written at a 6th grade reading level. Each provides measures on nine scales: somatization, obsessive-compulsive, interpersonal sensitivity, depression, anxiety, hostility, phobic anxiety, paranoid ideation and psychoticism. Global indices are provided to measure overall psychological distress level, intensity of symptoms, and total number of self-reported symptoms.

Outcome Questionnaire 45.2 (Lambert, Morton, et al., 2004) is a 45-item self-report instrument used to screen symptom distress (depression and anxiety), interpersonal relations, social roles (school/work and home), alcohol and/or substance use and suicidal/homicidal ideation. It is designed for use as an outcome measure; in other words, the assessment would be administered periodically throughout treatment to record progress.

Other Screening Instruments

Of all the disorders listed in the DSM, perhaps the category of greatest concern in a first meeting would be depression because a) it is a very common category of disorders, and b) it has a high degree of concomitance with suicidality. The *Beck Depression Inventory-II* (BDI-II) is comprised of 21 items aligned with the *Diagnostic and Statistical Manual of Mental Disorders-Fourth Edition* (DSM-IV) criteria for depression. The assessment of depression includes both the type and severity. In cases of depression, a suicide assessment should also be administered. Readers are referred to Chapter 11 of this book, where suicide assessment is covered in more detail. Suicide assessment checklists have been developed by Aaron Beck including the *Beck Scale for Suicide Ideation* (Beck & Steer, 1991) and *Beck Hopelessness Scale* (Beck & Steer, 1993). William Reynolds (1988) developed the *Suicidal Ideation Questionnaire* (for grades 10 through 12), *SIQ-JR* (for grades 7 through 9) and the *Adult Suicidal Ideation Questionnaire* (Reynolds, 1988). Rogers et al. (1994) developed the *Suicide Assessment Checklist* (SAC) comprised of 12 items assessing suicide plan, suicide history, psychiatric history, drug use and demographics, as well as nine items based on the therapist's ratings of suicide risk factors including hopelessness, worthlessness, social isolation, depression, impulsivity, hostility, intent to die, environmental stress and future time perspective.

Substance Abuse Subtle Screening Inventory 3 (SASSI-3; Miller, 1997) has a 93% rate of accuracy in identifying individuals with substance-related disorders as reported by the SASSI Institute. The SASSI-A2 (Miller, 2001) is designed for adolescents. Chapter 7 of this text discusses substance use screening and is important to mention here to determine if alcohol or substance use is a problem. Therapists will also need to assess whether or not they can provide the appropriate services for a client.

There are several interpersonal violence (IPV) assessments used in public and mental health settings that screen for abuse, domestic violence, and victimization scales. "The effects of IPV for both survivors and perpetrators are long-lasting, and violent behaviors and notions of what constitutes a relationship have been found to pervade across relationships and generations" (Hays, 2013, p. 286). Similarly, child abuse (physical, sexual, psychological, or neglect) has immediate and long-term effects. Internalizing symptoms (such as low self-esteem, anger, hypervigilance, fear, depression or withdrawal) and externalizing symptoms (such as aggression toward siblings and peers, self-injurious behaviors, negative perceptions and/or preoccupation with sexuality inconsistent with the individual's age) are red flags. Individuals may be uncomfortable sharing details of IPV and/or abuse during a clinical interview. Often there will be accompanying symptoms of trauma. For these reasons, people are sometimes more comfortable sharing this type of information in a more impersonal context such as a paper-and-pencil questionnaire.

Genograms

Genograms are most often used in family counseling, as they serve as a tool for charting family patterns. A standardized format was developed in the early 1980s; however, several modifications have been made since that time. McGoldrick, Gerson and Petry (2008) suggest "the genogram is constructed from information gathered during the first meeting with a client/patient and revised as new information becomes available." In general, the genogram depicts three generations of family members highlighting critical events. Using this picture, both therapist and client can view family relationships in both a current and historical perspective.

Projectives

Projective techniques ask the client to respond to ambiguous stimuli. Individuals are believed to "project" their personality by way of their responses based on the theory of "projective hypothesis." The *Rorschach Ink Blot Test* and *Rotter Incomplete Sentences Blanks, Second Edition* are good examples of projective assessments. However, they would be impractical to use in an intake. Drawing techniques are more easily accessible and further help to build rapport. House-Tree-Person or kinetic drawings are often used to gain insight into the client's worldview and experience.

House-Tree-Person (H-T-P) is a personality assessment used with persons aged 3 and older. The individual is asked to draw three separate pictures—one of a house, one of a tree and one of a person. There is also a *Draw-A-Person* projective assessment in which the individual draws three pictures—one of a man, one of a woman and one of self. *Kinetic Family Drawing* (KFD) asks the individual to draw their entire family including themselves doing something together. The child or adult's drawings and discussion regarding their drawings provide a measure of self-perceptions and attitudes.

A drawing technique I often use provides a window into a client's personality traits and also the degree of insight they have about self. I will ask the client their preference between colored pencils or markers. I hand them an 8–1/2 x 11 sheet of paper and ask them to fold the paper in half and then I ask them to fold it in half again so when they open the paper, they have four squares. In the top square, I ask them to draw a picture of an animal that would best represent who they are; in the next square, I ask them to draw a picture of a type of transportation (car, train, skateboard, bus, etc.) that describes how they move in the world; in the next square, draw a piece of furniture that best describes you; and in the last square, draw a drink or food that best describes you. An example is shown in Figure 4.1.

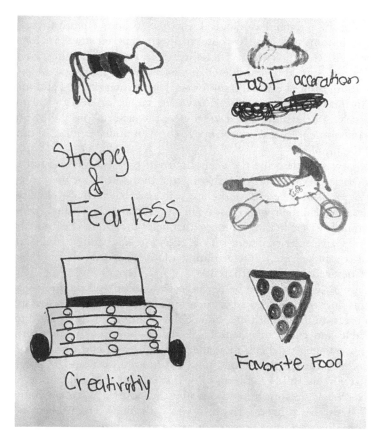

Figure 4.1 Drawing as Assessment Data

In the drawing the client described himself as a tiger (strong and fearless) and, like a motorcycle, he accelerates fast. He described himself as creative, which he depicted by drawing a TV on top of a dresser. His favorite food is pizza.

Another favorite drawing technique I use is the name and four corners. In the center of the paper, I ask the individual to write their name and decorate their name in a way that describes who they are. In the top left corner, I ask them to draw a picture (use shapes or words if they are uncomfortable drawing) of something they do when they are alone. In the top right corner, I ask them to draw something that they do when they are with someone else or a group of people. In the bottom left corner, something that makes them angry/frustrated and in the bottom right corner, something they fear.

In the first drawing exercise, a good measure of one's self-perceptions is revealed. In the second exercise, I gain an understanding of how the individual relates to others and their strengths and limitations.

Diagnosis and Treatment Goals

All of the information gathered from the intake should provide you with useful information in making a clinical diagnosis and treatment goal(s). Counselors need to become familiar with the DSM-5 and diagnostic criteria determining a mental illness. While a full discussion of the DSM-5 is beyond the scope of this chapter, it is important to mention because diagnostic impressions and treatment formulation are a part of the intake process. Psycho-pathology can often be reframed as a logical response to one's circumstances and developmental history. Symptoms may arise as contextually appropriate strategies for meeting one's needs in a pathogenic family system. Therefore, in treatment planning, environment and developmental history should be considered as well as the diagnosis.

Hays (2013) distinguishes between symptom-oriented interviewing and insight-oriented interviewing. An intake incorporates both as we are gathering data to learn of the client's behaviors, necessary to determine if behaviors meet the criteria for a DSM-5 diagnosis, and the individual's phenomenological experience to form an understanding of the meaning and implications of the problem.

A diagnosis is a way to describe the client's current presentation and not meant to be a life-long sentence; neither is therapy for that matter. Individuals, for the most part, come to therapy to solve a problem. The goal of therapy is to assist clients in developing an awareness of their strengths as well as their weaknesses. Therapists further individuals' personal and professional development by facilitating a process that helps individuals become the best version of self they can be given their current set of "tools" (e.g., cognitive ability, developmental stage, emotional vocabulary, etc.). "Determining a DSM diagnosis should be looked on as a process, not a static event" (Hays, 2013, p. 138).

Similarly, treatment goals need to be periodically assessed and progress monitored. Outcome assessments and rating scales were mentioned earlier and offer therapists a baseline from which to measure treatment outcomes. There is an increased demand to hold professionals accountable and collecting quantitative data is one way of monitoring outcomes. Therapists are encouraged to check in at the beginning and end of a session to track the client's experience. At the beginning of a session, I inquire, "Is there anything from the last time we met that you are still holding on to or that you want to talk about?" At the end of the session, I ask, "What are your impressions after this hour?" "What are you making of this process so far?" "How has it been for you to talk with me?" "Has it been useful?" "This is important as it can give you some sense of impact and effectiveness of one session and what adjustments you may need to make" (Joyce & Sills, 2010, p. 232).

Concluding an Intake Session

At the close of this first meeting, it is important to allow time for individuals to ask questions and to clarify boundaries and conditions of treatment (e.g., next scheduled appointment day/time, gentle reminder of cancelation policies and fees, ways to contact you). I usually end with a statement like, "I appreciate your commitment and openness to the therapeutic setting. I am looking forward to working with you."

Summary

Throughout the chapter there has been an ongoing emphasis on the relational aspects of an intake interview. Relationships are enhanced when a person feels heard and understood, and so use of active listening skills in response to client disclosure can be conducive to development of rapport. There may be no other aspect of assessment in which relationship development is more important than during intake assessments. We have provided readers with some simple active listening strategies to implement during an intake process. This chapter is written based on the assumption of a client being seen in a general mental health setting, not a specialized treatment facility. In some cases in which there is a particular type of disorder for which a client is being assessed, the nature of the intake information may very well shift toward a much more detailed assessment of particular precipitants and/or symptoms.

Test Your Knowledge:

1. Which of the following categories of information are not recommended as a component of an intake:
   a. Level of education
   b. Type of car the client drives
   c. Medical conditions
   d. Legal history

2. Clients may be more willing to answer honestly to a paper-and-pencil questionnaire than during a one-on-one interview because:
   a. They might have a hearing problem
   b. They might be stressed about their finances
   c. They might feel less embarrassed
   d. This is a trick question—clients always tell their counselors the truth

3. Which of the following categories of information is not covered by the Mini-Mental State Exam?
   a. Tolerance of frustration
   b. Attention
   c. Orientation to person, place, time
   d. Understanding complex instructions

4. Which of the following statements about intakes and treatment plans is true?
   a. Treatment plans are inessential to the counseling process
   b. Treatment plans should not be identified until the counselor has had many sessions and opportunity to establish rapport
   c. Treatment plans should be dynamic and changing organically as the client grows
   d. Treatment plans should be based solely on the counselor's diagnosis of the problem since he or she is the expert

5. It is inadvisable to explain limits of confidentiality in a first counseling session because it reduces the likelihood that the client will be honest.
   T or F

6. Screening instruments can help a counselor gauge the "typicality" of particular symptoms.
   T or F

7. It is most important to prioritize getting background information and intake information over establishing a relationship in a first session with a new client.
   T or F

8. Structured screening instruments are always preferable to projective instruments for gathering information in an intake interview.
   T or F

9. Mental Status Examinations should only be administered by psychiatrists.
   T or F

10. Questions about history of being abused should be avoided at all costs in a first session as it might scare the client away from disclosing private personal information.
   T or F

Discussion Questions/Prompts:

1. Rehearse aloud or role play with a colleague meeting a client for the first time. Be aware of your nonverbal messages; in other words, notice your posture, your facial expressions, the tone of your voice. Consider ways that you promote a safe environment (e.g., offer a tour of the facility before going directly to your office).
2. What are common components of an intake interview?
3. Describe the major categories of the MSE.
4. In what ways are checklists or rating scales helpful?
5. What intake and/or MSE assessment questions make you most uncomfortable?

5 Career Assessments and Personality Inventories

Bill McHenry

Introduction

From early in the development of the counseling profession, career advisement, career counseling and career assessments have been a central focus (Gysbers, Heppner, & Johnston, 2009). Counselors are called upon to serve clients in various capacities related to career decision-making (Zunker, 2015). Tools for such efforts have been sharpened over the years, allowing for a more robust and detailed assessment of a client's likes, dislikes, skills, abilities and temperament. While career development and career counseling instruments can be highly useful in the process of helping an individual make informed decisions about what major to take, what area of jobs (cluster) they might fit well in, and/or how to attain greater job satisfaction, the instrument itself (and the associated results) should be reinforced and processed with the client to ascertain fit and agreement. Failure to do so can actually damage the counseling relationship and have the client lose faith in the counseling process.

For example, when I (Bill) was in high school, I recall taking a career assessment and then receiving results back that basically said I matched well with three occupations. Sharing results with my friends, we laughed at the strange job titles some of us received. I suspect some you reading this had a similar experience. Now, that's not to say that the results were inaccurate. In actuality, I recall mine were pretty close to what I have become as a professional. The missing piece was that there was no follow-up and simply left kids (teenagers) to figure out what the results meant to them. As counselors, we can and should do better.

When I became a school counselor I decided that I would have all of the 9th grade students in my school take an online career assessment inventory. I also decided that I would spend at least 30 minutes with each student reviewing their results and helping them make meaning from them. Assuredly, not all schools have the luxury we had to dedicate so much time to this effort. For me, there becomes an ethical question regarding the use of assessments without taking the time to work with the recipient of the results. I believe that having clients take assessments without processing the data is akin to teachers giving students a test and then not grading them.

Career Assessments

There are a significant number of career assessments and career decision-making inventories on the market. Some are available online, some are paper-pencil; some assessments are self-report, others have ability testing built into the tool; some assessments allow for instant (self-scored) results while others require the instrument be sent off to be scored and returned at a later date. Regardless of the mechanics (e.g., online) of the assessment, career assessments should return results that forward the client's awareness of self and his or her place in the world of work.

Different assessments in the career area have been developed for specific career-related issues. For example, instruments have been developed to measure *career beliefs* (the Career Beliefs Inventory—CBI), *self-efficacy in career decision-making* (Career Decision-Making Self-Efficacy Scale—CDMSE), while some instruments are designed for age-specific assessment results such as the *Adult Career Concerns Inventory* (ACCI) and the *Cognitive Vocational Maturity Test* (CVMT), which was designed to assess career awareness and possibilities in students grade 6 and beyond. Most counselors who work a lot with career issues find two or three instruments that serve their population well. The following case uses a prolific instrument, *Holland's Self-Directed Search* (SDS).

Holland's Self-Directed Search is considered widely as a strong instrument for use in career decision-making and career counseling. It is based on John Holland's theory that individuals choose to work in settings and environments in occupations that meet their personal needs across six different categories. These categories are identified as being:

- Realistic (R)
  - These individuals usually prefer to work with things rather than people. They usually have mechanical and athletic abilities and lean toward jobs that are outdoors, active and involve tools and/or machines.

- Investigative (I)
  - These individuals like to work alone and use skills in the areas of math and science to better understand the world around them. They prefer to solve problems rather than persuade those around them.

- Artistic (A)
  - These individuals like to create new works, have a strong imagination and typically have good artistic and creativity skills.

- Social (S)
  - These individuals like to work with and help other people. They are interested in relationships and prefer to talk with people over using technical or mechanical skills.

- Enterprising (E)
  - These individuals prefer to persuade others, enjoy leadership roles and are interested in money and politics. They like to influence the world around them.

- Conventional (C)
  - These individuals prefer to have organized and orderly routines in their world. They do not enjoy ambiguity or disorder. They prefer to work indoors (Holland & Messer, 2013).

It should be noted that these are simply very brief descriptions of each of the categories. Counselors using the SDS need to acquire a much greater knowledge of each of the six defined categories prior to use of the instrument with clients.

Personality Instruments

There exist a litany of tests and assessments available to detect a client's personality. Among them, the more popular instruments include the Myers–Briggs Personality Type Indicator

(MBTI) and the 16 Personality Factor Questionnaire (16PF). The 16PF was developed using factor analysis to whittle down from thousands of adjectives to just 16 primary traits. From these traits, an individual's personality can be better understood across dimensions such as trust, control, assertiveness, etc. Built by Cattell and others, the 16PF categorizes individuals by personality type (Drummond, Sheperis, & Jones, 2016).

The MBTI, ironically, has 16 personality types into which clients are classified. This instrument is built upon the work of Carl Jung and considers personality flexible and changing throughout the lifespan. The designers of the instrument suggest that the classification of an individual into a "type" is a way of recognizing their *preferences* along eight primary constructs: *extroversion, introversion, sensing, intuition, thinking, feeling, judging and perceiving* (CPP, 2017).

The eight recognized preferences in the MBTI coding system are as follows:

- Extraversion (E)

  - People who tend to focus on the outer world of people and things. They gain energy from being around and among other people.

- Introversion (I)

  - People who seem to focus more on the inner world including ideas and impressions. They gain energy from being alone to reflect.

- Sensing (S)

  - People who are focused on the present and pay a lot of attention to information they acquire from their senses.

- Intuition (N)

  - People who appear to attend more to the future and to possibilities. These individuals pay attention to patterns in the world.

- Thinking (T)

  - People who use a logic-based model to make decisions about the world. These individuals focus on cause and effect.

- Feeling (F)

  - People who base their reactions, thoughts and beliefs on subjective evaluation of the events around them.

- Judging (J)

  - People who prefer a well-planned and highly organized life.

- Perceiving (P)

  - People who are flexible and spontaneous and like to remain open about life (Myers, 1998).

It should be noted that the above (very brief) descriptions are simply that—brief descriptions. Readers interested in using the MBTI need to acquire a deep and full understanding of these eight preferences. Additionally, although each of the four sets (E-I, S-N, T-F, J-P) can be considered as being binary in nature, rather, they are a continuum on which each client has tentative preferences.

Table 5.1 Key Aspects of the MBTI and Holland's SDS

Type of Instrument	Strengths	Weaknesses	Ideal Populations	Typical Referral Questions
Holland's Self-Directed Search (SDS)	★Well researched ★Stable results over time ★Used with various populations ★Self-directed ★Ties to other career tools (e.g., O★NET) ★Fast administration	★Self-report ★Potential scoring errors ★Possible lack of differentiation in scores	★Literate ★Psychologically balanced ★Motivated ★12 years or older	★Career indecision ★Career counseling ★Career planning
Myers-Briggs Personality Type Indicator (MBTI)	★Well grounded in theory ★Fast administration ★Results can make great intuitive sense to the client	★Limited test-retest reliability ★Can be misunderstood as being "the" exact personality ★Depends on client honesty	★Literate ★12 years or older ★Motivated	★Career issues ★Relationship issues ★Work issues

While these are but two common current personality tools, numerous other examples exist in the world of therapy. Examples include the Eysenck Personality Inventory (EPI), which is used with high school-aged students and older and describes the client's personality across two dimensions (introversion–extroversion and neuroticism-stability). The NEO Personality Inventory (NEO-PI-3) measures personality across five constructs: neuroticism, extraversion, openness, agreeability and conscientiousness. The subscales for this instrument include domains such as anger, assertiveness, vulnerability, warmth and trust (Costa & McCrae, 2010).

The case presented in this chapter uses the MBTI as part of the assessment process.

Specialized Training

The SDS does not require any special training or advanced coursework for counselors to administer and help the client interpret the results. Counselors should review the *professional User's Guide* and become familiar with the information contained within. Further, it is recommended that counselors take and successfully pass with a score of 100% the "Counselor Self-Test" located at the end of the manual.

Although the MBTI does not require specialized training for counselors to administer and help the client make meaning from the results, there are several levels of training associated with the MBTI that can be completed by counselors wanting to better understand the instrument, its results, and how to interpret client scores.

Ethical Considerations Specific to Holland's SDS and the MBTI

There are several American Counseling Association (ACA) ethical guidelines that inform the use of these instruments by professional counselors. While self-scored instruments, as is the case for both the SDS and MBTI, can appear benign and simple to both the counselor and client, counselors should be well versed not only in the administration of the instruments, but also the analysis of data with the client. For example, standard C.2.a. describes the importance of counselors to practice within their particular scope of competence.

C.2.a. Boundaries of Competence

Counselors practice only within the boundaries of their competence, based on their education, training, supervised experience, state and national professional credentials and appropriate professional experience. Whereas multicultural counseling competency is required across all counseling specialties, counselors gain knowledge, personal awareness, sensitivity, dispositions and skills pertinent to being a culturally competent counselor in working with a diverse client population.

While a counselor may meet the published test manufacturer's skill and educational level for use of the instruments, the ACA holds counselors to a higher standard. Basically, meeting the minimum requirements by a test maker does not in itself allow a counselor to use the instruments. In reality, a professional counselor should have practiced with the instrument, read all of the necessary guidebooks and literature and have consulted with/been supervised by another counselor on the use of the instruments. If these requirements are met, then the counselor has most likely met the criteria for practicing within his or her scope of competence with the MBTI and the SDS.

In the case presented in this chapter, the counselor has been trained, supervised and well educated on the administration and interpretation of results of both the SDS and MBTI.

E.6.a. Appropriateness of Instruments

Counselors carefully consider the validity, reliability, psychometric limitations and appropriateness of instruments when selecting assessments and, when possible, use multiple forms of assessment, data, and/or instruments in forming conclusions, diagnoses or recommendations.

When considering the use of ANY assessment tool, counselors should consider the value of the particular instrument they have in mind. Questions a counselor should ask include whether the instrument is appropriate for the case scenario and client issue(s), if any limitations exist in the instrument that may cause the results to be less useful than other measures, and what other data/information/assessments can be incorporated to enhance the therapeutic process.

In the case presented in this chapter, the MBTI and SDS are both good candidates for offering useful data and information to the client in regard to her issue. Additionally, the use of multiple measures, including other data beyond the instruments allows for a more fully integrated meaningful feedback session.

E.9.a. Reporting

When counselors report assessment results, they consider the client's personal and cultural background, the level of the client's understanding of the results and the impact of the results on the client. In reporting assessment results, counselors indicate reservations that exist regarding validity or reliability due to circumstances of the assessment or inappropriateness of the norms for the person tested.

When reporting assessment results, it is incumbent upon the counselor to help find ways to make the results meaningful to the client. In some cases, such meaning may be a clear affirmative response by the client that the results fit, while in others, meaning from the results may be that the client and counselor determine the results are not accurate (perhaps based on testing environment, unique internal conditions within the client when testing—such as being angry, sad, feeling bad about herself, etc.).

In the case presented in this chapter, the counselor uses an approach that is respectful of the client's self-awareness and to what degree the client makes immediate connections with the results. Further, the counselor works to ascertain meaning attributed by the client to parts of the results that do not immediately ring true.

Overview of the Case

Suzie arrives for counseling based on some career indecision. She is a bright, articulate, Caucasian age 32. She has been enrolled in the local counseling program for three semesters and is still having some lingering indecision.

At the core of her presenting career issue is that she has competing interests and feels unable to move forward assertively with her career for fear of "ignoring" a big part of self. The two major aspects of self that she has identified as being at odds with one another are her artistic expression and her strong interest in helping others. She does not see either as a hobby or a fad, but rather as part of her core being.

Interestingly, Suzie is a bit reluctant to share her concerns and indecision with her peers and professors for fear that they may see it as non-commitment or even ask her to leave the program. She knows that she wants to be a counselor but does not know how to best fit all of her pieces of self into her profession.

Initial Session

During the initial session with Suzie, the counselor explores what has brought her to seek counseling and what options she has considered in resolving her felt career indecision. Through active reflective listening and empathy, the counselor helps Suzie clarify her concerns and goal for counseling: *to meaningfully connect her pieces of self into her career direction*. If this goal is attained, Suzie will feel relief from the stress and anxiety of her career indecision, be more apt to fully embrace her life direction and feel more honorable to herself.

During the initial session, the counselor and client agree that a good direction for them to move forward with is through the use of formal assessments. The two decide that Holland's SDS and the MBTI are the best candidates to help Suzie ascertain further insight, direction and clarity with her career issue.

During the initial session, Suzie shared the following:

Suzie: I have competing interests. I would love to be a painter, but I cannot make any money doing that. I would love to figure out a way to be a therapist and still be an artist on the side, show work and sell my work.

Counselor: So, you've got a competition here. A part of you is passionate about making art and the other is passionate about counseling.

Suzie: Yes! I thought about art therapy too.

It is very important to understand career counseling cases as not only helping clients who have no idea what they want to do, but also those clients who have a lot of possibilities. In the latter, helping them refine their career goals is especially helpful. Through the use of assessment data and good counseling, clients can find meaning and make career decisions more effectively and with more conviction.

Session 2

The second session begins with Suzie taking both the SDS and MBTI. Because both instruments can be scored immediately after administration and because of her cognitive level/functioning, Suzie is asked to score the instruments herself.

The counselor takes the time to describe both instruments, discuss the limitations of both and express that the results are tentative at best. Suzie successfully completes and scores the instruments and the following results emerge.

Counselor: Let's look at your results and see what's consistent, inconsistent with you. See what meaning we can make from it.

Note here that the counselor gets out a blank piece of paper and several colored pens. The process of considering the results can be best accomplished through artistic representation (as the client has already espoused a strong lean toward artistic presentation). The counselor and Suzie begin by placing the paper between them and having the instruments beside them. They also have the results code information available for reference. Observing from the outside, it would appear that they are working together to solve a mystery with the clues on the table in front of them.

Counselor: Suzie, does the ASI code for the SDS seem to fit with you?
Suzie: Yes. Well, after reading the possible letters, I think it's the right fit. Some days I think I am ASI, others probably SAI. But, yes, it seems to fit.
Counselor: Let's look at the MBTI next. After reading over the code and the associated description, does that seem to fit as well?
Suzie: Yes. It fits better than any of the other descriptions.
Counselor: Ok—Which words or phrase leap out at you as most significant?
Suzie: Seek to understand people, loyal and curious. And "flexible." Oh, and idea too.
Counselor: Tell me about understanding people. How does that fit into your world and how you know yourself?
Suzie: I guess I'm really curious about people and that's what led me to the profession. I love to hear their stories and try to imagine what it's like to be them.
Counselor: Do you see a connection between your MBTI and Holland code?
Suzie: Hmm . . . I'm not sure.
Counselor: Well, the first thing you mentioned from the MBTI is that you are curious about people.
Suzie: Oh yeah, I see the social part of me.
Counselor: Yes, but also the "I." Investigative and curious seem close as well, don't they, Suzie.
Suzie: (nearly yells) Oh yeah!
Counselor: Understanding people, what does that connect with on your SDS code?
Suzie: Well, the social part for sure.
Counselor: Tell me more about being flexible.
Suzie: I'm spontaneous and if plans change I just go with the flow, it doesn't stress me out.
Counselor: So is that an artistic rhythm? An organic approach to living?
Suzie: Yes! For sure.
Counselor: Ok, tell me about loyalty.
Suzie: I'm just a really consistent friend. I just am consistent with people. I don't cut off relationships.
Counselor: Ok, so your "I" and "C" were one point away from one another. Am I correct that you are consistent in following the rules of relationships with others? Almost have a conventional approach to relationships.
Suzie: Absolutely. But you know, I got a high score on that one because I did a lot of administration jobs. I know how to do that stuff but I hate it as work.

Counselor:	So part of your personality, loyalty, is connected, consistency in the relationship. But in work you want the artistic part to approach but not the conventional as much. Does that make sense?
Suzie:	Yeah, yeah, that's really helpful.
Counselor:	What's jumping out at you as we are drawing all over this paper?
Suzie:	Well, it's making a lot more sense to the profession I am pursuing. It makes me feel more confident in moving forward as a counselor because it seems like, um, these things are more about being a therapist than an artist. I am less unsure I guess about not being an artist. Or letting that part of me not be the focal part.
Counselor:	I hear you talking through your "I" and "C" lens. That it's binary, either/or.
Suzie:	Yeah.
Counselor:	If you went through your "A" lens, how would you define your ability to counsel and do art?
Suzie:	Yeah, maybe art therapy, or incorporating some of those qualities into the therapeutic approach.
Counselor:	Ok, you've thought about that.
Suzie:	Yes, I have.
Counselor:	You still had indecision.
Suzie:	Yeah, I just felt like I had to choose because art therapy just isn't that common. It seems like there's not a market for it.
Counselor:	So you investigated it?
Suzie:	Yes.
Counselor:	Your investigation made you foreclose on the idea.
Suzie:	But that was just me coming to my own decision. Not really being open.
Counselor:	Can we look at the validity of your research?
Suzie:	Yeah. If I could do art therapy, that would make me really happy.
Counselor:	When you said that, your eyes lit up.
Suzie:	[Laughing . . .]
Counselor:	It would satisfy you?
Suzie:	Yes, the introverted part of me, doing art, being investigative and getting to help them would be my perfect career.
Counselor:	Ok—what would prevent you from doing that?
Suzie:	Getting special training. I would need special training.
Counselor:	Can you use your I and C to help you get the answers you need to move forward?

Review of the Case

In this case and transcript, we can see the value of assessment results as they tie directly to the client and her concerns. Throughout the process, the counselor and client used the results to make meaning of self-direction and opportunities for future growth. Interestingly, the client had already been considering the possibility of becoming an art therapist, but had foreclosed on that possibility prior to really investigating it. The counselor used the assessment results to highlight skills the client might use to further consider this option.

In this session, the following actions, professional approaches and counseling skills were demonstrated; the counselor did the following:

1. Described clearly the instruments and possible limitations of the results.
2. Worked with the client on making meaning from the results.
3. Demonstrated a tentative approach to reading and accepting the results as facts.

4. Helped the client recognize connections across the results of both instruments as well as her way of being in the world.
5. Assumed a position of "not knowing" the right direction for the client.
6. Used the actual results such as the data from the MBTI and the Holland Codes (e.g., Artistic, Investigative, etc.) as a means to disseminate the results themselves AND as tools to better understand the client.
7. Used the results as a strength on which the client can call to further investigate her career.

Intentions of the Case Example

I wanted to write this chapter in this way because as counseling students, you yourself may have a similar career question (or may know someone in your counseling program who has a similar career question). Though Suzie had a good sense of what she wanted to do, it was through the skillful use of results that she was able to have the story of her next career move come to life. This is so important for you to understand as assessment and tests results are not THE story, but rather are aides in the development of the client's narrative and personal story.

Additionally, I wanted to use this case to highlight the fact that tests and assessments do not have to be used only for those clients in serious life distress. Assuredly, Suzie had some discomfort, and she had been ruminating on this question for some time. But she did not need immediate psychological intervention at a deep level. Rather, she needed to go through a formal process that allowed her to better understand herself and her options.

Summary

Career interest inventories, assessments, tests of personality, etc., can be used with clients ranging from minor career indecision discomfort to cases of severe career crisis. Although such results can be delivered in ways that make them appear factually accurate and definitive, it is wise to approach results with an eye toward making meaning and helping the client realize them as connecting or not to their individual life story.

Test Your Knowledge:

1. The MBTI code is:
   a. Considered stable over time
   b. Never the same from one administration to the other
   c. Tentative, as the code may actually differ from administration to administration
   d. Changing all the time

2. The SDS code is:
   a. Considered stable over time
   b. Never the same from one administration to the other
   c. Tentative, as the code may actually differ from administration to administration
   d. Changing all the time

3. Both the SDS and MBTI are suggested to be used with clients who are:
   a. Literate
   b. 12 and older
   c. Motivated
   d. All of the above

4. The use of multiple instruments is:
   a.   Preferred over one instrument
   b.   Considered the same as using one good instrument
   c.   The research is not clear on which is a better approach
   d.   Only suggested when there is serious psychological impairment

5. Self-scored instruments allow for:
   a.   Immediate results in the session
   b.   More accurate results
   c.   More buy-in by the client
   d.   All of the above are correct

6. In the case, the role of the counselor was to:
   a.   Make sure the client was comfortable with the results as they were obviously reliable and valid
   b.   Help the client make meaning of the results in relation to the presenting issue
   c.   Analyze the results and look for discrepancies that could be the problem with the client
   d.   All of the above are correct

7. The client needed:
   a.   Direction from the counselor
   b.   A definitive answer/direction
   c.   A better awareness of self
   d.   More information through data and discussion with the counselor to help her fit things together better in her life

8. Inherent in the case provided was a woman who had:
   a.   Career indecision
   b.   A need for more information
   c.   Support in finding her path
   d.   All of the above are correct

9. The counselor deciding to use an artistic process of delivering and discussing the results with the client was anchored in actual assessment results.
   T or F?

10. The fact that the counselor used instruments that are self-scored and based on self-observations by the client make the results less definitive than a more formal assessment tool.
    T or F?

Discussion Questions/Prompts:

1.   What has your experience been with assessments that provide you data that suggest your personality type?
2.   What limitations can you imagine exist in regard to self-report, self-scored instruments?
3.   How might you have provided the feedback to the client regarding her results?
4.   How do you see the intertwined connection between career decision-making and identity development playing out in this case?
5.   If you had no experience or knowledge of the MBTI or SDS, would you administer these instruments? Why or why not?

6 Assessment Techniques in Substance Use Disorders in Counseling

Enobong J. Inyang

Introduction

This chapter examines assessment instruments and techniques that can assist the clinician in the personalized assessment and the development of individualized treatment plan for adults presenting with substance use disorders (SUDs). A thorough and comprehensive assessment is an integral and important first step in effective treatment of SUDs (Allen, 2003; Connors & Volk, 2003; Donovan, 2013). Samuel Shem (1978) in a novel entitled *The House of God* provides an earlier perspective on the role of assessment in the counseling process that can inform age-old counselors and other healthcare professionals in the process of SUD assessment and treatment: "If you don't take a temperature, you cannot find a fever" (p. 420). This dictum underscores the inevitability of assessment as the first line of action in the prevention and treatment of SUDs. Greenfield and Hennessy (2008) also indicated that a "successful treatment of substance use disorders depends on a careful, accurate assessment and diagnosis" (p. 55). Foundational to the discussion in this chapter are the *Addiction Counseling Competencies: The Knowledge, Skills, and Attitudes of Professional Practice*, in the Technical Assistance Publication Series 21 (TAP 21) created by the Center for Substance Abuse Treatment (CSAT, 2006) and the American Psychiatric Association (2013), 5th edition of the *Diagnostic Statistical Manual of Mental Disorders* (DSM-5) SUDs classification.

The *competencies model* is an evidence-based, best-practice approach to assessment and treatment of SUDs intended to replace the 12 Core Functions of addiction counseling that was based on pseudoscience (Phelps, 2013). It focuses on three dimensions of competency—knowledge, skill and attitudes (KSA), which will be examined in detail later in the chapter.

The DSM-5 SUDs classification includes 10 specific substances with associated severity specifiers ranging from mild, moderate and severe. Although there are several screening and assessment instruments at the disposal of the counselor, only the SASSI-4 and Addiction Severity Index 6 (ASI-6) are covered because of their psychometrics properties, extensive use, and personal familiarity with them as screening and assessment instruments, respectively.

Background to Substance Use Disorders Assessment

To understand the role of screening and a comprehensive, thorough assessment in the treatment of SUDs, it is important for the professional to become familiar with the complexity and dynamics inherent in the onset and maintenance of SUD behaviors and addiction. It is also important to examine the cost of SUD to society. Those considerations provide the background for a comprehensive and thorough assessment as integral to effective treatment of SUDs in this chapter. SUDs (which include alcohol use disorders [AUDs] and nicotine use disorders [NUDs], use of illegal drugs such as cocaine, narcotics, hallucinogens, marijuana and prescription drugs) is the most prevalent mental health disorder society faces today with high human and material cost (Doweiko, 2015, Kilts, 2004). According to Doweiko (2015, p. 2), some of the direct and indirect costs of SUDs in the United States are:

- Approximately 25% of patients seen by the primary care physician have an SUD
- Excessive alcohol use was a factor in 50% of all deaths from acute traumatic injuries
- Approximately 1 million hospital emergency room visits are the result of illicit drug abuse
- Approximately 40% of all hospital admissions can somehow be tied either directly or indirectly to alcohol use/abuse
- Hospitalized persons with an SUD are more likely to require rehospitalization within 30 days of discharge than nonusers
- Approximately 25% of those individuals on Medicaid have an SUD. As this group ages, their medical costs increase at a higher rate than for age-matched individuals without an SUD

Other researchers have pointed to how SUD comorbid with psychiatric and mental health problems with high healthcare cost (Karch, Dahlberg, & Patel, 2010; Scott & Marcotte, 2010; Parrott & Giancola, 2006; Winerman, 2013). Scott and Marcotte indicated that between 40% and 60% of individuals who committed suicide were intoxicated at the time of their deaths. Parrott and Giancola indicated that the use of illicit drugs increases the woman's chance of being murdered by as much as 28-fold, even if the woman was not using drugs herself at the time of her death. Comorbidity of SUDs with other mental health issues further underscores the complexity of SUDs and the need for a thorough and comprehensive assessment using valid and reliable instruments. Although at some point healthcare professionals were unaware of the possibility of dual-diagnosis or clients presenting with both SUD and psychiatric conditions (Seppala, 2004), dual-diagnosis clients are actually "the norm rather than the exception" (Doweiko, 2015, p. 339). According to Doweiko (2015), most of the SUD clients seen in treatment programs will have symptoms of other mental illnesses at the time they initiate treatment.

SUDs and the related costs is not only the United States' problem. Globally, about half of the world's population has used drugs once with alcohol being the most commonly used drug and marijuana the most commonly abused illicit substance (Leamon, Wright, & Myrick, 2008). The American Society on Addiction Medicine (ASAM, 2001) indicated that addiction is a primary, chronic, neurobiological disease with genetic, psychological, cultural, and environmental factors influencing its development and manifestation. Due to multiple factors that underpin the onset and maintenance of SUDs, assessment becomes a complex and challenging process. The neurobiological, genetic, psychological, cultural and environmental components that may be unique to an individual must be assessed if treatment is to be successful.

The assessor must possess the requisite knowledge, skills, and attitudes (KSA) in SUDs assessment (instrument selection, administration, and interpretation) and mental health disorders. It is against this background that the imperative for careful, thorough, evidence-based clinical assessment based on the *competencies model* or TAP 21 is examined in this chapter. Even so, an examination of techniques in the assessment of different components related to SUDs is extensive and beyond the scope of a single chapter.

Theoretical Background of Substance Use Disorders Assessment in Counseling

From the discussion thus far, SUDs assessment is a complex and challenging process with life-long implications for clients, their families, employment opportunities, and society at large. For example, it will be a grievous disservice to say that an individual with a single "dirty" urine toxicology test for marijuana and other illicit drugs is addicted and in need of treatment. Such a screening result is just an alert to the counselor for a complete SUD assessment to determine the extent of the problem, if any (Doweiko, 2015). As another expert indicted, the process of assessment is "more than a one-time paperwork procedure conducted at the onset of treatment to simply gather minimal facts and secure a diagnosis" (Juhnke, 2002, p. vii). It is rather a three-stage process; the intake/interview, screening and assessment (Mignon, 2015). Mignon stated that the purpose of the assessment process is: 1) identifying the individuals who are in need of professional assistance; 2) provide justification for admitting an individual to a particular level of care; 3) identify the individual strengths and weakness or protective and risk factors; and 4) establish treatment goals and relapse prevention.

The rest of this chapter focuses on the process of assessing adults with SUD based on the *Addiction Counseling Competencies: The Knowledge, Skills, and Attitudes of Professional Practice*, Technical Assistance Publication Series 21, TAP 21 (2006) and the SUD criteria of the American Psychiatric Association's (2013) 5th edition of the *Diagnostic Statistical Manual* (DSM-5). Our guiding premise is that accurate client assessment is fundamental to treatment effectiveness. Effective treatment outcome is measured by a reduction or abstinence from substance use (Mignon, 2015; National Institute of Drug Abuse (NIDA), 2012a & b).

The DSM-5 Changes and Assessment of SUDs

Pivotal to a comprehensive and thorough assessment is that the assessor must be familiar with the changes in the DSM-5, understand how the changes affect SUD criteria and be able to integrate the changes into the assessment process (Mignon, 2015). A detailed discussion of each of the criteria is beyond the scope of this chapter. The reader is encouraged to refer to the DSM-5 for full discussion in the section entitled Substance-Related and Addictive Disorders. The changes do have implications in terms of specialized knowledge, skills and attitude (KSA) for assessment and treatment of SUDs. For example, there is no other DSM-5 disorder class that requires a specific license or certification with states and/or national certification bodies, except for SUDs treatment. Henriksen, Nelson, and Watts (2010) are critical of such specific licensure and/or certification for SUD professionals; arguing that the practice implies that only a small proportion of the counseling professional can work with SUD problems. Bobby (2013) indicated that specialized licensure and certification for SUD counseling is an approach that can promote accountability in the era of managed care and this writer agrees.

The new DSM-5 Substance-Related and Addictive Disorders classification consists of 10 separate classes of drugs:

- Alcohol-related disorders
- Caffeine-related disorders
- Cannabis-related disorders
- Hallucinogen-related disorders
- Inhalant-related disorders
- Opioid-related disorders
- Sedative- or hypnotic-related disorders
- Stimulant-related disorders
- Tobacco-related disorders
- Other or unknown substance disorders

In the DSM-5, each of the disorders listed is classified as use, intoxication, withdrawal, other induced disorder and unspecified related disorder with severity specifiers on a continuum from mild to moderate to severe. For example, alcohol problems are classified as Alcohol-Related Disorders in the DSM-5 and include alcohol use, alcohol intoxication, alcohol withdrawal, other alcohol-induced disorders and unspecified alcohol-related disorder. The DSM-5 diagnostic criteria for alcohol-related disorders are: "A problematic pattern of alcohol use leading to clinically significant impairment or distress, as manifested by at least one of [the 11 criteria], occurring within a 12-month period" (DSM-5, p. 490). The severity of the disorder can be mild (305.00, F10.01), moderate (303.90; F10.20), or severe (303.90, F10.20). The diagnostic criteria and severity apply to each of the 10 DSM-5 substance-related disorders. The screening and assessment process helps the assessor to determine the presence and severity of any of the DSM-5 SUDs that a particular individual seeking treatment fits into.

Screening and Assessment Techniques in SUDs in Counseling

Discussion of screening and assessment techniques in this chapter is based on the TAP 21, *competencies model*, introduced earlier. TAP 21 *competencies model* was created to provide the required competencies for a comprehensive assessment of SUDs, within Practice *Dimension* 1 (PD 1). The section of TAP 21 entitled clinical evaluation consists of two distinct elements, screening and assessment. Both comprise competencies 24 through 36 of the 123 competencies of the *competencies model*. Each competency comes with the expected knowledge, skills, and attitudes (KSA) that the assessor must demonstrate, as described in the following sections.

Clinical Evaluation

Clinical evaluation is "the systematic approach to screening and assessment of individuals thought to have a substance use disorder, being considered for admission to addiction-related services, or presenting in a crisis situation" (TAP 21, p. 39).

Screening

There are numerous definitions of screening, from narrow focus to very broad coverage. For example, Connors and Volk (2003) define the term or concept as, "skillful use of empirically based procedures for identifying individuals with alcohol-related [substance-related] problems or consequences or those who are at risk for such difficulties" (p. 21). In the *competencies model*, the term is defined as, "the process by which the counselor, the client, and available significant others review the current situation, symptoms, and other available information to determine the most appropriate initial course of action, given the client's needs and characteristics and the available resources within the community" (TAP 21, p. 39). The *competencies model* requires the assessor to demonstrate competencies in three areas: knowledge, skills, and attitude consistent with each of the related competencies at the screening phase.

Competency 24: Establishing rapport, including management of crisis situations and determination of need for additional assistance.

Knowledge

- Importance and purpose of rapport building
- Rapport-building methods and issues
- The range of human emotions and feelings

- What constitutes a crisis
- Steps in crisis prevention and management
- Situations and conditions for which additional professional assistance may be necessary
- Available sources of assistance

Skills

- Demonstrate effective verbal and non-verbal communication in establishing rapport
- Accurately identifying the client's beliefs and frame of reference
- Reflecting the client's feelings and message
- Recognizing and defusing volatile or dangerous situations
- Demonstrating empathy, respect, and genuineness

Attitudes

- Recognition of personal biases, values and beliefs and their effect on communication and treatment process
- Willingness to establish rapport

Competency 25: Gathering data systematically from the client and other available collateral sources, using screening instruments and other methods that are sensitive to age, developmental level, culture, and gender. At a minimum, data should include current and historic substance use; health, mental health, and substance-related treatment histories; mental and functional statuses; and current social, environmental, and/or economic constraints.

- Knowledge of:

  - Validated screening instruments for substance use and mental health status, including their purposes, application, and limitations
  - Concepts of reliability and validity as they apply to screening instruments
  - How to interpret the result of screening
  - How to gather and use information from collateral sources
  - How age, developmental level, culture, and gender affect communication
  - Client mental status—presenting features and relationship to substance use disorders and psychiatric conditions
  - How to apply confidentiality rules and regulations

- Skills

  - Administering and scoring screening instruments
  - Screening for physical and mental health status
  - Facilitating information sharing and data collection from a variety of sources
  - Communicating effectively in emotionally charged situations
  - Writing accurately, concisely, and legibly

- Attitudes

  - Appreciation of the value of data gathering

- **Competency 26:** Screen for psychoactive substances toxicity, intoxication, and withdrawal symptoms, aggression or danger to others, potential for self-inflicted harm or suicide, and co-occurring mental disorders.

- Knowledge of:
    - Symptoms of intoxication, withdrawal, toxicity for all psychoactive substances, alone and in interaction with one another
    - Physical, pharmacological, and psychological implications of psychoactive substances
    - Effects of chronic psychoactive substance use or intoxication on cognitive abilities
    - Available resources for help with drug reactions, withdrawal, and violent behavior
    - When to refer for toxicity screening or additional professional help
    - Basic concepts of toxicity screening options, limitations, and legal implications
    - Toxicology reporting language and meaning of toxicology reports
    - Relationship between psychoactive substance use and violence
    - Basic diagnostic criteria for suicide risk, danger to others, withdrawal syndromes, and major psychiatric conditions
    - Mental and physical conditions that mimic drug intoxication, toxicity, and withdrawal
    - Legal requirements concerning suicide and violence potential and mandatory reporting for abuse and neglect
- Skills
    - Eliciting pertinent information from the client and relevant others
    - Intervening appropriately with client who may be intoxicated
    - Assessing suicide and/or violence potential using approved risk-assessment tool
    - Assessing risks of abuse and neglect of children and others
    - Preventing and managing crisis in collaboration with health, mental health, and public safety
- Attitudes
    - Willingness to be respectful toward the client in his or her presenting state
    - Appreciation of the importance of empathy in the face of feelings of anger, hopelessness, or suicidal or violent thoughts and feelings
    - Appreciation of the importance of legal and administrative obligations
- **Competency 27:** Assist the client in identifying the effect of substance use on his or her current life problems and the effects on continued harmful use or abuse
    - Knowledge of:
        - The progression and characteristics of substance use disorders
        - The effects of psychoactive substances on behavior, thinking, feelings, health status, and relationships
        - Denial and other defense mechanisms in client resistance
    - Skills
        - Establish a therapeutic relationship
        - Demonstrating effective communication and interviewing skills
        - Determining and confirming with the client the effects of substance use on life problems
        - Assessing client readiness to address substance use issues
        - Interpreting the client's perception of his or her experiences

- Attitudes

  - Respect for the client's perception of his or her experiences

- **Competency 28**: Determine the client's readiness for treatment and change, as well as the needs of others involved in the current situation.

  - Knowledge of:

    - Current validated instruments for assessing readiness to change
    - Treatment options
    - Stages of readiness
    - Stage-of-change models
    - The role of family and significant others in supporting or hindering change

  - Skills

    - Assessing client readiness for treatment
    - Assessing extrinsic and intrinsic motivators
    - Assessing the needs of family members, including children for appropriate levels of care and providing support and recommending follow-up services

  - Attitudes

    - Acceptance of nonreadiness as a stage of change
    - Appreciation that motivation is not a prerequisite for treatment
    - Recognition of the importance of the client's self-assessment

- **Competency 29:** Review the treatment options that are appropriate for the client's needs, characteristics, goals, and financial resources.

  - Knowledge

    - Treatment options and their philosophies and characteristics
    - Relationship among client needs, available treatment options, and other community resources

  - Skills

    - Eliciting and determining relevant client characteristics, needs, and goals
    - Making appropriate recommendations for treatment and use of other available community resources
    - Collaborating with client to determine the best course of action

  - Attitudes

    - Recognition of one's own treatment biases
    - Appreciation of various treatment approaches
    - Willingness to link client with a variety of helping resources

- **Competency 30:** Applying accepted criteria for diagnosis of substance use disorders in making treatment recommendations.

  - Knowledge

    - The continuum of care and available range of treatment modalities
    - Current *Diagnostic and Statistical Manual of Mental Disorders* (DSM) or other acceptable criteria for substance use disorders, including strengths and limitations of such criteria

- Use of commonly accepted criteria for client placement into levels of care
- Multiaxis diagnostic criteria

- Skills

  - Using current FDSM or other accepted diagnostic standards
  - Using appropriate placement criteria
  - Obtaining information necessary to develop a diagnostic impression

- Attitudes

  - Recognition of personal and professional limitations of practice, based on knowledge and training
  - Willingness to base treatment recommendations on client's best interest and preferences

- **Competency 31:** Construct with the client and appropriate others an initial action plan based on client needs, client preferences, and resources available.

  - Knowledge of:

    - Appropriate content and format of initial action plan
    - The client's needs and preferences
    - Available resources for admission or referral

  - Skills

    - Developing an action plan in collaboration with the client and appropriate others
    - Documenting the action plan
    - Contracting with the client concerning the initial action plan

  - Attitudes

    - Willingness to work collaboratively with the client and others

- **Competency 32:** Based on the initial action plan, take specific steps to initiate an admission or referral and ensure follow-through.

  - Knowledge

    - Admission and referral protocols
    - Resources for referral
    - Ethical standards regarding referrals
    - Appropriate documentation
    - How to apply confidentiality rules and regulations
    - Client's rights to privacy

  - Skills

    - Communicating clearly and appropriately
    - Networking and advocating client admissions to appropriate treatment resources
    - Facilitating client follow-through
    - Documenting accurately and appropriately

  - Attitudes

    - Willingness to renegotiate

Overall, a primary objective of screening is to identify individuals with an SUD problem. A secondary objective of screening for the individual is to initiate a more comprehensive and thorough individualized assessment that can guide the development of a treatment plan and interventions. As Connors and Volk (2003) indicated, screening benefits society by minimizing both the human and economic cost of SUDs through early detection and interventions.

There are essentially two categories of screening tools or instruments for SUDs; those that can be given orally during the intake and the longer, written questionnaires that are completed by the individual seeking treatment. Regardless of which format, screening instruments help to answer two essential questions: Is there a substance use disorder problem? What is the immediacy of the problem? (Doweiko, 2015). Ability to select appropriate screening means that the screener demonstrates specific knowledge, skills, and attitudes (KSA) consistent with the *competencies model* discussed earlier. For example, the screener must have knowledge of validated screening tools, including their purpose, application, and limitations; have a concept of reliability and validity of the screening instruments; and demonstrate the skills to administer, score, and communicate the results effectively to the individual. The screener must also demonstrate the attitude of the value of data gathering as part of the screening process.

Assessment

SUD assessment should answer the question: how severe is the nature and what is the extent of the substance use disorder problem? The answer to this question should help determine treatment, referral, inpatient or outpatient placement, and whether detoxification and medication is necessary. The *competencies model* distinguishes assessment from screening as "an ongoing process through which the counselor collaborates with the client and others to gather and interpret information necessary for planning treatment and evaluating the client progress" (TAP 21, p. 46). It comprises four essential competencies and related KSAs:

- **Competency 33:** Select and use a comprehensive assessment process [instruments] that is sensitive to age, gender, racial, and ethnic culture, and disabilities that include but are not limited to:

  - History of alcohol use
  - Physical health, mental health, and addiction treatment histories
  - Family issues
  - Work history and career issues
  - History of criminality
  - Psychological, emotional, and worldview concerns
  - Current status of physical health, mental health, and substance use
  - Spiritual concerns of the client
  - Educational and basic life skills
  - Socioeconomic characteristics, lifestyle, and current legal status
  - Use of community resources
  - Treatment readiness
  - Level of cognitive and behavioral functioning.
  - Knowledge of:

    - Basic concepts of test validity and reliability
    - Current validated assessment instruments and protocols
    - Appropriate use of limitations of standardized instruments
    - The range of life areas to be assessed in a comprehensive assessment

- How age, developmental level, cognitive and behavioral functioning, racial and ethnic culture, gender, and disabilities can influence the validity and appropriateness of assessment instruments and interview protocols

- Skills

  - Selecting and administering appropriate assessment instruments and protocols within the counselor's scope of practice
  - Introducing and explaining the purpose of assessment
  - Addressing client perceptions and providing appropriate explanations of issues being discussed
  - Conducting comprehensive assessment interviews and collecting information from collateral sources

- Attitudes

  - Respect for the limits of assessment instruments and one's ability to interpret them
  - Willingness to refer for additional specialized assessment

- **Competency 34**: Analyze and interpret the data to determine treatment recommendations.

  - Knowledge of:

    - Appropriate scoring methodology for assessment instruments
    - How to analyze and interpret assessment results
    - The range of available treatment options

  - Skills

    - Scoring assessment tolls
    - Interpreting data relevant to the client
    - Using results to identify client needs and appropriate treatment options
    - Communicating recommendations to the client and appropriate service providers

  - Attitudes

    - Respect for the value of assessment in determining appropriate treatment plans

- **Competency 35:** Seek appropriate supervision and consultation [in the assessment process].

  - Knowledge of:

    - The counselor's role, responsibilities, and scope of practice
    - Limits of the counselor's training and education
    - The supervisor's role and how supervision can contribute to quality assurance and improvement of clinical skills
    - Available consultation services and roles of consultants
    - The multidisciplinary assessment approach

  - Skills

    - Recognizing the need for review by or assistance from supervisor
    - Recognizing when consultation is appropriate
    - Providing appropriate documentation
    - Communicating oral and written information clearly

- Incorporating information from supervision and consultation into assessment findings
- Attitudes

  - Commitment to professionalism
  - Acceptance of one's own personal and professional limitations
  - Willingness to continue learning and improving the clinical skills

- **Competency 36:** Document assessment findings [results] and treatment recommendations.

  - Knowledge

    - Agency-specific protocols and procedures
    - Appropriate terminology
    - Legal implications of actions and documentation
    - How to apply confidentiality rules and regulations and clients' rights to privacy

  - Skills

    - Providing clear, concise, and legible documentation
    - Incorporating information from various sources
    - Preparing and clearly presenting, in oral and written form, assessment finding to the client and other professionals within the bounds of confidentiality rules and regulations

  - Attitudes

    - Recognition of the value of accurate documentation

It is imperative that the assessor demonstrates the competencies listed above and their related KSAs as he or she proceeds in the assessment process. The *competencies model* is based on research as part of the ongoing evolution of treatment of SUDs (Phelps, 2013).

Screening and Assessment Techniques in Counseling

Choice of Instruments

Choice of instruments for both screening and assessment is an important component of the *competencies model* because it affects treatment outcomes. The *model* provides guidelines about the required knowledge, skills, and attitudes on choice of instruments. For example, the assessor must have knowledge of validated screening and assessment instruments; the skills to administer, score, and interpret instruments; and appreciation for the value of the data in the screening and assessment process. Choice of instrument should satisfy two basic psychometric standards: validity and reliability (Tarter, 2011; Donovan, 2013, Lewis, 2014). In addition, Lewis indicated that selection of assessment instrument is predicated on consideration of certain components pertinent to the onset and continuance of substance use behaviors. Typical areas to consider are to verify if the instrument has scales that cover history of substance use, current substance use (frequency, amount, administration), prior substance abuse treatment history, current functioning, psychological and psychiatric issues, recreational issues, job-related problems, medical issues, legal issues, family history of substance abuse, religious or spiritual beliefs, cultural issues, and sexual disorders (Lewis, 2014; Craig, 2004).

Table 6.1 provides a list of suggested instruments for screening and assessment. They are suggested because of their established psychometric properties, wide use, and familiarity of

Table 6.1 Selected Screening and Assessment Instruments for Adults SUDs

Type of Instrument and Source Screening Tools	Description	Administration and Scoring	Strengths	Weaknesses
CAGE-AID Questionnaire (Ewing, 1984; www.partnersagainstpain.com/printouts/A7012DA4.pdf)	Binary yes/no to four questions. Screening for alcohol and drug abuse	Oral or self-administration in less than 1 minute. Scored instantaneously by the tester. Two or more yes answers signals the need for further assessment	Brevity. Easy to score. Interpretation not required. No training required for administration and interpretation	Insensitive to women. Subjectivity. Only identifies late-stage alcohol/drug problems
Alcohol Use Disorders Identification Test (AUDIT; Barbor, de la Fuente, Saunders, & Grant, 1992) Whqlibdoc.who.int/hq/2001/who_msd_msb_01.6a.pdf Thomas F. Babor Alcohol Research Center, University of Connecticut, Farmington, CT	10 items, three subscales developed by the World Health Organization to identify persons with harmful alcohol use. Screen for risk rather than the presence of diagnosable SUD	Training required for administration. Pencil-and-paper self-administered or interview within two minutes. Hand-scored	Brevity. Detailed user's manual and videotaped training manual explain administration, scoring, and interpretation. Test and manual are free. Appropriate for a number of populations including college students, criminals, armed forces personnel, and psychiatric patients	Does not screen for drugs
Substance Abuse Subtle Screening Inventory-3 and -A2 (SASSI-3 and -A2; www.sassi.com/, 800-726-0526)	93 items, 10 scales. Paper-and-pencil formats, PC versions, seven online. Administered by professional trained staff. Robust validity/reliability	Requires 15 to 20 minutes administration time and 10 minutes to score by hand. Electronic scoring available	Graphed scores by scales. Provides profile scores. Has both face validity. Can detect denial, random responding, and defensiveness. Is available in Spanish. Has versions for adolescents, clients with disabilities, and deaf or hard of hearing	Requires training. Is costly

Assessment Instruments	Description	Administration and Scoring	Strengths	Weaknesses
Addiction Severity Index-6 (ASI-6; www.tresearch.org/ASI.htm or www.evinceassessment.com/)	Most widely used assessment tool Comprehensive, semi-structured interview with 140 items covering seven domains Score is produced for each of the domains	About one hour to administer by a trained technician or clinician Scoring is done by computer	Assess seven relevant SUD domains: alcohol use, drug use, psychiatric status, employment status, medical status, legal status, family/social relationships Easy to follow manual and available in online, in Spanish and adolescent version	Extensive training for scoring and interpretation of results Expensive
Composite International Diagnostic Interview (CIDI core; Version 2.1 314-286-2267, mccrarysl@epi.wustl.edu)	Covers alcohol, tobacco, and nine categories of other illicit drugs Determines if alcohol use disorder was ever present, or within the last year, last six months and last two weeks Available in hard and computerized formats Has 20 major questions and 59 sub-questions and three subscales on dependency, abuse, and withdrawal	Pencil-and-paper self-administration, interview by a trained assessor, and computer self-administered versions About 15 minutes to administer Scoring/interpretation is about 20 minutes	Translated into many African, Asian, and European languages Include questions on time of first use	Requires extensive training for administration and interpretation
Drug Use Screening Inventory (revised) (DUSI-R; Ralph Tarter University of Pittsburgh, School of Pharmacy Pittsburgh, PA, 15261)	DUSI-R contains 159 items with 11 subscales that assess severity of SUD in 10 domains and contains a lie scale and substance preference and specific substance with the greatest problem	Can be self-administered in pencil-and-paper and computer formats or by interviewer Self-administered version requires 5th grade reading level Manual administration	Identifies current use, areas in need of prevention, and use for follow-up assessment. High reliability and validity.	Expensive: paper version costs $3 each and computer administration and scoring runs about $495.00

.

the write with them. The assessor is at liberty to choose among a wide variety of available instruments. In so doing it is advisable to be mindful of the reliability and validity of the instrument and training as required.

Techniques in Conducting SUD Screening and Assessment in Counseling

Screening

Screening is the first step in clinical evaluation in SUD treatment. The purpose is to determine if there is substance use problem that warrants further assessment and treatment. There are a number of screening tools at the disposal of the counselor. For the purpose of this chapter, the CAGE and the SASSI-3 are selected. The CAGE is a very brief, nonconfrontational tool that is helpful in establishing rapport during the initial contact with an individual seeking help. It is a mnemonic from the following four questions that the individual can answer yes or no to:

> Have you ever felt you should **c**ut down on your drinking?
> Have people **a**nnoyed you by criticizing your drinking?
> Have you ever felt bad or **g**uilty about your drinking?
> Have you ever had a drink first thing in the morning to steady your nerves or to get rid of a hangover (**e**ye opener)?

The CAGE can be used with both adults and adolescents over 16 years old. Scoring is instantaneous. Two or more yes answers to the four questions is indicative of the need for a referral for full assessment. The validity and reliability of the CAGE are well established (Mayfield, McLeod, & Hall, 1974; Ewing, 1984; Fiellin, Reid, & O'Connor, 2000).

Although the CAGE has been widely used and its psychometrics established, it is a self-report tool that cannot detect deception. Craig (2004) indicated that, as a group, substance abusers are known to lie, manipulate, and deny the true nature of their use disorders; hence the need for an instrument that is more robust in the screening process. The SASSI-3, now in its 4th edition, provides the opportunity to get a better picture of the substance use issue and possibility of deception. The adult version can detect individuals who may have a high probability of alcohol and other drug problems with 93% accuracy (Allen, 2003). A number of validation studies have confirmed the SASSI-3 to have high reliability and validity (Piazza, Martin & Dildine, 2000). The case illustration section will put the screening process in context.

Assessment

If the result of screening suggests the presence of substance use issues, the individual is given a full assessment to determine the extent of the problem. As stated earlier, the assessor must demonstrate the required assessment competencies based on the *competencies model* and be able to choose the appropriate assessment instrument. Sometimes the ability of the counselor to choose an instrument is limited because the agency where she or he works has a manualized treatment process that includes a specific assessment instrument. For the purpose of this chapter, the ASI, now in its 6th edition, is recommended because it covers some of the pertinent components that Morgan (2017) has suggested for SUD assessment.

Confidentiality

Before presentation of a case illustration of SUD screening and assessment process, it is important to discuss confidentiality of client records based on federal laws and regulations and the *competencies model*. Confidentiality of SUD records is protected by federal laws and regulations to the extent that treatment program staff or clinicians may not even admit to anybody outside the treatment setting that a client is even receiving services (Craig, 2004). The only allowances for such disclosure of confidential information are when the client has given consent in writing, the disclosure is allowed by a court order, or the disclosure is for medical emergency or necessity (U.S. Department of Health & Human Services, 1987).

Competency 65 of the *competencies model* also requires the assessor to be competent in applying federal, state, and local confidentiality rules and regulations as they apply to SUD appropriately. The related knowledge is the ability of the assessor to ethically apply confidentiality rules and regulations to the documentation and sharing of client information, including in emergency situations such as medical/suicide prevention/mandatory reports of child/elder abuse or neglect situations. The required skills include skill to explain and apply confidentiality rules and regulations, obtain informed consent, and communicate with family and others the boundaries of existing federal rules and regulations. Two related attitudes that apply to the assessor's attitudes in the *competencies model* are 1) recognition of the importance of the confidentiality rules and regulations, and 2) respect for the SUD client's right to privacy.

Case Illustration

Putting it All Together

This section puts both the screening and assessment process in context using a fictitious SUD client based on elements that are often encountered among clients in clinical settings. Any resemblance to an actual client is coincidental. The reader should note that no single case scenario can encompass all the elements discussed, nor are the elements exhaustive. It should also be understood that there is no single assessment instrument that captures the breadth of all the necessary components essential for understanding the extent or severity of the client's substance use problem. However, a thorough and comprehensive assessment ought to address numerous domains of the client's life or lifestyle and how the nuances of that lifestyle directly or indirectly relate to substance use. Hence, our case illustration examines specific components identified by Lewis (2014) essential for assessment purposes and predicated on establishing rapport as the generic skill for engaging clients in any phase of SUD counseling. Recall that the first competency in clinical evaluation of the *competencies model* is establish rapport, which includes management of a crisis situation and determination of the need for additional professional assistance (TAP 21, 2006). Indeed, Juhnke (2002) indicated that establishing rapport humanizes the assessment encounter.

Referral Source

Knowing the referral source or reason for referral is important for accountability and expectations, even when the client is self-referred. The assessor should establish the reason the client seeks help now. For our case illustration, Bob is presented. Bob is a 56-year-old Caucasian male who is mandated by court to undergo and successfully complete substance abuse treatment following arrest for driving under the influence (DUI). Although Bob's court intake paperwork may help to establish the presence of SUDs, his results on the CAGE questionnaire (with a score of 3 out of 4) amplifies the immediate need for professional treatment.

CAGE Screening Results

Bob was asked the four CAGE questions and he responded yes to three of the four questions, indicating that he needed additional screening and assessment. The SASSI-3 was administered.

Have you ever felt you should **c**ut down on your drinking?   (Yes)
Have people **a**nnoyed you by criticizing your drinking?   (Yes)
Have you ever felt bad or **g**uilty about your drinking?   (Yes)
Have you ever had a drink first thing in the morning to steady your nerves or to get rid of a hangover (**e**ye opener)?   (No)

Bob's SASSI-3 Screening Results

Bob's SASSI screening yielded the results shown in Table 6.2, suggesting the need for further assessment. It corroborates the CAGE results.

Bob's SASSI-3 results indicate that a comprehensive assessment is necessary to fully understand the extent of his SUD problem and other related issues that may be implicated. The most important indicators of Bob's problem are the CAGE score of 3 out of 4, his elevated FVOD of 10, FAV of 11, and OAT of 8. Individuals with Bob's pattern of scores would usually acknowledge behavioral problems that may be implicated in substance use, but are less likely to make the connection between acknowledgement of high-risk behavioral problems and the impact on their substance use and overall lifestyle. His SYM score of 8 correlates with individuals who are likely to be exposed to environment, people, and things dominated by substance use.

Table 6.2 Bob's SASSI-3 Results

FAV	FVOD	SYM	OAT	SAT	DEF	SAM	COR	FAM
11	10	8	8	6	6	6	12	11

FVA&FVOD = Face validity; SYM = Symptoms; OAT = Obvious attributes; SAT = Subtle attribute; DEF = Defensiveness; SAM = Supplemental Addiction Measures; COR = correctional; FAM = Family versus control

Bob's Screening Results Overview

Name: Bob   **Date of Test:** 04/25/2017
Age: 56   **Sex:** Male
Marital Status: Single
DUI Arrest: 01/01/2017
Prior Treatments: 3   **Highest Grade Completed:** 12
Employment: Yes (self-employed)
Weekly Net Income: $850   **Family Members in Household:** 0

Random Responding: Results indicate NO evidence of random responding (High FAV & FVOD)
Alcohol or Other Drug Problem: High probability of severe SUD (High SYM)
Acting Out: High risk of acting out problem (Moderate SAT, COR)
Defensiveness: Indication of a problem (Elevated DEF score)
Indication of Emotional Past: Yes (elevated SAT)
Prescription Drug Abuse: High risk of a problem

Based on Bob's screening results, a comprehensive assessment is warranted. Researchers have identified certain areas that are important to assess to determine the extent of the SUD problem and some of the underlying factors that may contribute to onset, maintenance, treatment failure, and relapse prevention (Lewis, 2014; Craig, 2004; Morgen, 2017). Our choice of assessment instrument is the Addiction Severity Index-6 (ASI-6), adult version, because it covers most of the domains identified in research by Lewis, Craig, and Morgen and pertinent for diagnosis, treatment planning, and interventions. Bob's ASI-6 narrative report is presented as the following:

ADDICTION SEVERITY INDEX -6 (ASI-) NARRATIVE REPORT
BOB, M
111 ABAK ROAD
NOWHERE, TX 77777

DOB: 07/24/1962
SS #: 222–44–5555
Date of Interview: 04/29/2017
Type of Interview: Assessment
Assessor Name: Tom Alright

Site ID# 089
Beginning Time: 9:00 am
End Time: 10:00 am
Assessor ID#: 242

General Information Section

This section is a summary of Bob's self-report about his lifetime and current medical, employment, substance use, legal, family/social, and psychological issues. Each section includes the assessor's rating of how severe the issue is and a recommendation for treatment.

Bob is a 56-year-old, Caucasian male. He reported that he is a Christian but does not have a denomination preference and the spirituality is very important to his life. However, he admitted that he has not been to any church in many years but reads books on spirituality from time to time and reported that spirituality has been helpful in "staying clean" for years. He lives alone in a house that he owns across the street from his mother's house and adjacent to his father's house. Bob states earning about $850 weekly as a real estate appraiser and sometimes buys, fixes, and flips houses. Bob reports being in prison a couple of times for alcohol- and drug-related offenses. He was arrested for driving under the influence about 2:00 am in January 2017 after a night of "partying" with a girl who provided cocaine following a memorial for his mother who died in early December 2016. He spent about a week in jail. Bob reported that he had been clean for 10 years prior to this incident and has not used any illicit drug since then. This last statement was contrary to his intake report conducted five days prior in which he admitted that he had used substances the day before intake.

Alcohol and Drug Section

Lifetime and Recent Alcohol Use: Bob reported that he drank all the time throughout his life until about 10 years ago when he joined AA. He reported that he does not like the taste of alcohol anymore and had not had any drink or spent any money on alcohol in the past 30 days. He reported that when he was drinking he spent more than $100 monthly.

Lifetime and Recent Drug Use: Bob reported a lifetime history of regular cocaine use dating back to high school. He reports "off and on" experimentation with opiates and tranquilizers and other drugs that one can think of. He reports a long history of cannabis use dating back to high school. He reported never using inhalants. He stated that he never overdosed on drugs and had never been detoxed. In the past 30 days, Bob reported not using any drugs whatsoever, except prescribed medication for anxiety. In the past 30 days, Bob reported not spending any money on illicit drugs.

Alcohol and Drug Treatment History: Bob has been in intensive treatment about three times for alcohol and drugs while in prison. He reported attending AA and staying clean for about 10 years until it ended four months ago. He has been participating in alcohol and drug group sessions once a week for about one month now. The group is a 12-Step-based group but provided by a non-recovering group leader in a mental health agency.

Client Perception of Severity of Alcohol and Drug Problems and Desire for Treatment: My clinical impression is that Bob understood all the interview questions but deliberately misrepresented the seriousness of his alcohol and drug problems. It seems unlikely that Bob is forthcoming with information about his current alcohol and drug use. Bob appears to engage in impression management and is downplaying the severity of his SUD problem. Based on his past and current drug-related legal problems, Bob's drug problem appears very substantial and needs to be addressed in outpatient treatment. Such treatment should initially focus on establishing rapport to help break Bob's denial. However, Bob appears motivated to obtain treatment for his SUD.

Family/Social Section

Marital and Living Situation for the Past Three Years: Bob is currently living alone, having been divorced for more than 15 years, but is currently seeing different women. Bob reported that he still sees one of the women who gave him cocaine the night he was arrested for DUI. He has two grown daughters who live in another city but with whom he stays in touch.

Recovery Environment and Social Contacts: Bob reports that he has two close friends who he has known since high school who are still regular alcohol and drug users, but who respect his recovery efforts. He reports that one of the two friends is the woman who gave him cocaine the night of his mother's memorial service. No one resides with him now and he spends his time in "isolation" reading and going to the lake to enjoy quiet time.

Lifetime Relationship Problems: In the past 30 days Bob reports no relationship problems with his friends other than annoying texts from his lady friend. He reported that in the past 30 days he has enjoyed a trusting relationship with his father and step-mother for whom he is house sitting currently. He reported that he feels very excited that his father has the trust in him to house sit after he trashed the house and stole his alcohol and partied in the house the last time when he was asked to house sit about a year ago. Bob reports that regaining his father's trust was very important and meant a lot to him. He reports that he is not in any serious relationship currently. He reported that he had a very close relationship with his mother when she was alive.

Client Perception of Severity of Family and Social Problem and Desire for Treatment

Bob reports no family problems in the past 30 days. He gets along with his two daughters, father, and step-mother. He reports no need for treatment for family problems. He reported no problems with others and can get along with anybody and likes to keep to himself, except occasionally when he joins his friend for dinner, even though they drink and use drugs. He believes that he cannot abandon them now because "they need what I've got."

Psychiatric Section

Serious Emotional and Psychological Problem—Lifetime: Bob reports a history of serious anxiety problems for which has been prescribed different antianxiety medications. He does not receive financial benefits for psychological disability.

Recent Serious Emotional and Psychological Problems: Bob has had serious problems with anxiety and depression in the past 30 days as a result of his mother's death, his DUI, and his legal problems. Bob related that he has not had treatment for bereavement and does not believe that he needs grief work. He reported that he did not want to talk about his mother during the interview, teared up when he was referring to his mother, and indicated that they were very close.

Client Perception of Severity of Emotional and Psychological Problems and Desires for Treatment: Bob reported experiencing emotional problems related to his legal problem and mother's death most of the past 30 days. He reports that staying busy at work helps take his mind off his mother and the legal problem. He reports taking psychoactive medication for his anxiety and depressive issues. He reports that therapy for grief is important and will help him to ensure that he does not go back to using to self-medicate.

Assessor Impressions and Recommendations: The impression of the assessor is that Bob understood all the questions and was not in denial about his psychological problems. Bob appears to have moderate emotional issues that need psychotherapy. Bob can benefit from grief work.

Legal Section

History of Charges and Arrest: Bob is participating in SUD evaluation as a result of a referral from the court for both individual and group treatment because of his DUI arrest. He reports a long history of involvement in the criminal justice system and incarceration because of drugs, the most recent being four months prior to this assessment. He is on deferred adjudication pending successful completion of substance abuse treatment.

Client Perception of Severity of Legal Problems and Desire for Treatment: Bob is very bothered by his current legal problem and believes that completing counseling successfully is important to "keep them off my back." He is on deferred adjudication.

Assessor Impressions and Recommendation—Legal: The impression of the assessor is that Bob understood all the questions. He was not in denial about his legal problems and did not attempt to minimize them. He appears to understand that completing substance abuse counseling will help his legal problems. He reports that he has legal representation for his legal issues. There is no additional comment on Bob's legal issues at this time.

Medical Section

Medical History: Bob reported no serious medical history.

Client Perception of Severity of Medical Problems and Desire for Treatment: Bob did not report any known medical history.

Assessor Impressions and Recommendations: Bob understood all the questions that pertain to his medical situation. He appeared to answer them truthfully. He does not appear to need any medical treatment at this time.

Employment Section

Employment History: Bob is self-employed as a contractor/consultant appraising houses for different companies. He reports that he sometimes buys and "flips" houses when he believes he can make a profit.

Current Financial Resources: Bob states that he worked five days a week in the last 30 days making an average of $850 weekly. He indicates that sometimes he does not have business for a week or two depending of the time of year. He denied receiving any unemployment compensation or welfare benefits from the government and has not made any money illegally. He does not have any dependents and is not paying alimony. He does not have credit card or other debts.

Education and Training and Resources: Bob has a high school diploma and credentials in real estate appraisal. He appears to have the required skills for the type of work or business that he is engaged in. He reports that he has a valid, unrestricted driver's license and has the truck he inherited from his mother for work and leisure purposes.

Client Perception of Severity of Employment Problems and Desire for Treatment: Bob reports no employment problems. He is not troubled in any way about employment if he can avoid drug-related legal issues. Bob does not need help with securing employment.

Additional Employment Comments: Bob reports that he is satisfied with his employment situation. He is skilled in what he does and has no employment-related concerns other than if he cannot flip his property quick enough.

Overall Assessor Comments: The information in this ASI narrative report is based on Bob's responses to each component of the assessment instrument. It is intended as a demonstration to complete a comprehensive assessment using a valid instrument that can be used to guide diagnosis, treatment planning, and interventions in SUD treatment.

Assessment Feedback and Recommendations

Lewis (2014) underscores feedback as the most critical aspect in the assessment process. The feedback should be informative and accurate. The assessor style matters to ensure that the client does not put up defense and resistance. Lewis provides the "elicit-provide-elicit" (p. 65) formula for providing assessment feedback. The assessor should first elicit from the client what the client wants to know about the problem. The assessor then provides information based on the assessment results only. Lastly, the assessor elicits from the client his or her thoughts about the feedback received. Bob's ASI assessment results provide the counselor with specific areas that need attention in his treatment that should be elicited from Bob. The assessor's clinical impressions are integrated as recommendations to the counselor for treatment. In Bob's case, his denial is one area to pay attention to with the understanding that denial is a common problem among individuals initiating SUD treatment. It highlights the importance of rapport in the assessment process. Bob appears to recognize the detrimental effect of continuing to engage in a high-risk lifestyle. He continues to engage in high-risk situations (people, places, and things) that expose him to substances. Bob needs to replace high-risk people, places, and things with positive people, places, and things as protective factors. Given Bob's history of drug use and legal involvement, he needs help to successfully complete treatment. The assessor then elicits from Bob what he thinks about the impressions shared.

Ethical Issues in Assessment

The assessor should recognize the magnitude of confidentiality with SUD clients. Unlike other areas of counseling practices, confidentiality of SUD client records is governed by federal laws and regulations. Ethical assessment also requires that informed consent must be provided the client prior to beginning assessment. The National Association for Alcoholism and Drug Abuse Counselors (NAADAC) is an organization dedicated to inform substance abuse counselors about ethical practices with SUD clients (Brook & McHenry, 2009). The reader is encouraged to access the NAADAC code of ethics for additional guidelines.

Multicultural Considerations

Cultural consideration should guide the assessment process as it does treatment itself.

Whereas most of the SUD counselors are White and the majority of the clients seeking treatment for SUDs are non-White, multicultural competence becomes an important competence. The assessor should inquire about the client's cultural background to understand the role of culture in recovery (Craig, 2004). The assessor is encouraged to examine his or her worldviews, values, and attitudes about non-White clients and seek competency in multicultural assessment. For help in cultural competency with SUD clients, a useful source is TIP 59 by Substance Abuse and Mental Health Services Administration (SAMHSA, 2014).

Test Your Knowledge:

1. Which of the following is (are) elements of clinical evaluation according to the *competencies model* discussed in this chapter?
   a. Assessment
   b. Interview
   c. Screening
   d. Both A and B

2. What does KSA in the *competencies model* denote?
   a. Knowledge, system, attitudes
   b. Knowledge, skills, appraisal
   c. Knowledge, skills, attitudes
   d. Knowledge, skills, actions

3. Elicit-provide-elicit is a recommended strategy for providing assessment feedback to clients discussed in this chapter.
   T or F?

4. Which of the following is NOT a screening instrument identified in the chapter?
   a. Addiction Severity Index (ASI)
   b. SASSI
   c. CAGE
   d. All of the above

5. The CAGE is useful in determining the client _____.
   a. Substance use severity
   b. Probability of having substance use disorder
   c. Placement in treatment
   d. All of the above

6. The CAGE can be used with:
   a. Adolescents over 16
   b. Adults
   c. Children
   d. Both A and B

7. When comparing the CAGE and SASSI, in regard to detecting the honesty of the client, the instruments produce results that are:
   a. The same
   b. The CAGE is better
   c. The SASSI is better
   d. We do not really know

8. Bob has a strong social network.
   T or F?

9. Bob's assessment results seemed consistent, but he seemed to be minimizing his response to treatment. Therefore, the counselor can infer that the assessment results (instruments used) are more reliable and therefore he is not in denial.
   T or F?

10. Bob's grief and loss issues have nothing to do with the case.
    T or F?

Discussion Questions/Prompts:

1. Discuss the importance of evaluating Bob from multiple data points.
2. Describe and discuss the strengths and weaknesses of both the CAGE and SASSI.
3. Discuss how the mental health and social issues in Bob's case connect to his assessment results.
4. When considering this case, what aspects of Bob's story make this case the most challenging?
5. What ethical considerations do you see in this case?

7 Utilizing Assessment in Counseling with Children

Teri Ann Sartor

As counselors of children and adolescents, we understand the different skill sets necessary for working with this unique population. Just as distinctive as the skill set, the assessment measures are specialized as well. Despite the primary purpose of counseling the child client, counselors must realize conducting assessments in therapy with children may also require them to assess their parents or guardians as well. In some cases, caregivers may bring a child to counseling as a result of them "testing positive" for a mental health diagnosis at the primary care physician's office. As mental health professionals, we know that there is not a "test" that indicates a diagnosis; however, there are assessments that can support diagnosis. As a result of this miscommunication or misinformation to the caregivers, it is important for counselors to provide education on the purposes of further assessment and the treatment process.

The purpose of this chapter is to discuss relevant assessment material pertaining to counseling children. The chapter will review the basic protocols counselors must follow in the assessment process of counseling children, the ethical consideration in assessing children, two common assessment instruments (Child Behavior Checklist and the Parent Stress Index) and how they can be used in conjunction, and will present a fictional case example to further the understanding of the uses of assessment in the counseling process.

Ethical Implications in Providing Counseling Assessment for Children

American Counseling Association's *Code of Ethics* (ACA, 2014) and its division of the Association for Assessment in Research in Counseling (AARC, 2017) provide guidance to counselors who participate in counseling assessment. Additionally, the state's rules and regulations in which a counselor practices should also be referred to when assessing children in counseling. Counselors who work with children should remember the process of assessment involves gathering information about the client for a wide range of reasons including client decision-making and treatment planning through both qualitative and quantitative means (ACA, 2014). The readers should refer to Section E: Evaluation, Assessment, and Interpretation of the *Code of Ethics* (ACA, 2014) and the AARC's website (http://aarc-counseling.org/resources) for resources specifically related to assessment.

When children are assessed for the purposes of counseling, additional considerations come into play as a result of a child's inability to consent, effectively communicate concerns, and other various developmental challenges. First and foremost, the child's parents have the right to informed consent in regard to testing and assessment protocols (ACA, 2014). The clinician should adequately explain the purpose of the testing and results of the assessment to the parents, guardian, or caregiver of the child. Helping parents or caregivers understand the purpose of the assessment can assist in the counselor gaining the needed information to appropriately and adequately provide treatment to the child and ensure the child's welfare. Additionally, the counselor should acknowledge and inform the caregiver(s) both verbally and in writing that assessments do not determine the diagnosis of the child; rather, it helps the clinician obtain additional data to support the diagnosis given to the child (Drummond, Sheperis, & Jones, 2016). Because children rely on adults for their basic needs the counselor should also assess the parents' motivations behind seeking assessment and counseling as a way to further protect the child. While as counselors, we hope parents want what is in the best interest of the child, we must remember this may not always be the case—thus, advocacy for the child may also be necessary on some occasions. Also, a counselor's view of what is in the child's best interest might be misaligned with the caregivers' view of what constitutes the child's best interest. Thus, as a counselor, client welfare (in this case, the primary client is the child) should always be the top priority (ACA, 2014).

Training Prior to the Assessment Process

Before a counselor even considers assessing a child (or any person), they should ensure they have received the proper supervised training in assessment procedures (ACA, 2014). This training should extend beyond the basic assessment course required of a master-level counselor. More specifically, counselors should be aware of any additional training that is sometimes required to administer, score, and interpret specific testing instruments related to counseling children. Simply put, by reading one article or because a specific testing instrument is readily available, it does not necessarily mean the counselor has the ability to administer it or that it's the "best" choice.

Beginning the Assessment Process

Prior to beginning counseling with a child it is important for the counselor to gather background and treatment information pertaining to the child, the family, and of course informed consent for treatment of the child. When parents or guardians of the child are divorced or separated, it is imperative for the counselor to have copies of and follow the legal guidelines as set out by a divorce decree or separation agreement (Sartor, McHenry, & McHenry, 2017). A counselor's failure to do so could not only have a negative impact on the treatment process due to unforeseen conflict in parental relationships, child-parent relationships, child-counselor relationships, or parent-counselor relationships, but it could also open the counselor up to malpractice concerns related to consent.

After the informed consent process is ethically completed, the clinical interview can be conducted with the parent(s) or guardian(s); it may not be developmentally appropriate for the child to be present in the clinical interview. Geldard, Geldard, and Yin Foo (2013) commented prior to beginning work with a child that they generally find it helpful to consult with parents without the child being present. Thus, when the child is not present, parents can freely talk about their concerns without feeling inhibited by the child.

The clinical interview should consist of collecting the child's background information including the reason for referral. Basic background information such as the child's history (psychosocial, family, medical, psychiatric, legal, out-of-home placements, etc.) will be pertinent throughout the assessment, conceptualization, and treatment process. However, in conducting assessment, the reason for referral will dictate the types of testing instruments utilized along with the treatment provided, treatment goals set, and the objectives that will need to be met (Drummond et al., 2016). Thus, the first goal of assessment is finding the reason of referral.

Timing of Assessments and Choosing Instruments

When choosing an assessment instrument or test, the counselor should be aware of the child's abilities to "sit" for the test and the time it takes to administer. Because some children may struggle with specific time allotments or the concentration skills necessary, pencil–paper tests may not be appropriate. In cases involving young or delayed children, they may experience difficulties in communication, either written or verbal, and thus the clinicians should consider using assessment tools with parent and teacher rating forms (Drummond et al., 2016). Much like clinicians do in counseling, it is important we are doing what best fits the needs of the child with consideration of their developmental level. Additionally, when working with children, it is important for the counselor to remember parental stresses often affect those of the child and vice versa (Lawson, 2007; Soltis, Davidson, Moreland, Felton, & Dumas, 2015). Thus, it may be important to discuss and assess the parental stress levels and parenting skills through the process of consultation. Ultimately, counselors working with children must remember that, in the hours when the counselor is not present, the parent is the child's "counselor."

In choosing testing instruments many options are available for various reasons of referral and treatment needs of the client. It is extremely important that counselors ensure the instrument(s) are reliable and there is evidence of validity relevant to the purpose for the assessment (Drummond et al., 2016). Counselors must always remember that just because a testing instrument is readily available, it does not mean it is appropriate. While it is not possible to provide a list of every single possible testing instrument, counselors should be thoughtful in choosing the assessment and conduct research prior to making a choice. This research should include the purpose and usage of the testing instruments, population type, cultural and ethical implications, reliability, validity, scoring, and interpretation procedures, etc.

In considering options, counselors should refer to *Tests in Print* or the *Mental Measurements Yearbook* for basic information and purposes for testing instruments. Other test options may also be available by reviewing *Test Critiques, Tests,* counseling organization websites, and test publishers' websites such as Achenbach, Western Psychological Services, Sigma, Pearson Assessments, etc. Caution should be warranted when utilizing only the publishers' website, as not all valuable information may be provided (Drummond et al., 2016). While various possible avenues provide direction in choosing assessments, counselors should remember no list is exhaustive but can provide a good starting point for clinicians who embark on the continuous process of assessing children throughout the counseling process.

Assessing a Child with Concerned Parents

In this section, a case study will be discussed along with the assessment and procedures related to making recommendations for treatment. The case is of a fictional character who was created solely for the purpose of illustrating and describing the assessment processes with children. Because an assessment generally consists of more than one assessment or test, two testing instruments will be discussed in detail in relation to how they can be utilized with the particular case of the child involved. As the case is described, readers are encouraged to pay attention to the details and occurrences, as one minor detail can change the assessment process or decision-making process for the counselor. Now, let's review the case and determine which assessment(s) should be used for Charlie!

Meet Charlie

Mark and Tiffany are interested in seeking counseling for their 6-year-old child, Charlie. During the initial contact, Tiffany communicated they are worried about Charlie as a result of his recent behaviors. The behaviors include behavioral difficulties at home and at school, nightmares, "accidents" during the day and night, and "moodiness." As the licensed counselor, John set up an initial interview session to meet with both Mark and Tiffany to cover the necessary information to adequately assess how to best provide treatment to Charlie.

Prior to the initial interview meeting, John requested Tiffany and Mark jointly fill out and return the "Child Background Information Sheet" and "Family Information Sheet," and review the informed consent information posted on his website. John informed Tiffany and Mark about the importance of receiving these documents prior to clinical interview and that they be emailed back to him as soon as they are completed, but that they must be received prior to the day before the scheduled interview. After the information sheets were received and reviewed, but prior to the initial interview, John noticed Tiffany and Mark had two separate addresses. To ensure his ethical obligations were met in accordance with his state's counseling board rules and administrative codes, he contacted Tiffany and asked her and Mark to provide him with a copy of divorce decree or separation agreement to his office for review. At this time he instructed her that services cannot be provided without reviewing the document for specifics regarding custodial parenting rights. John then asked that both parents arrive 30 minutes prior to the session to complete the necessary assessment forms (to be discussed later).

The initial interview meeting was scheduled during Charlie's "school day" and both Tiffany and Mark were present with the separation agreement in hand. John reviewed (and made a copy of) the separation agreement, which noted that both parents have consenting rights and must mutually agree on medical and mental health treatments. After Mark and Tiffany individually completed the assessments, John reviewed (and signed) the informed consent process and purpose of assessment with them. At this time, Mark and Tiffany were also invited to ask questions and discuss any concerns. Mark indicated that his main concern is the behavioral difficulties Charlie is having at school because it is a reflection of their parenting ability. Tiffany chimed in and commented her main concern is how "the divorce" is affecting Charlie because most of his struggles began around the same time. Charlie's parents acknowledged they have only recently decided to get a divorce but maintain a good relationship otherwise. They both communicated with John that they want to ensure this transition goes smoothly for Charlie and hope to remain friends and good co-parents.

Family Background History

Charlie is the only child of his parents, Mark and Tiffany. His mother is currently employed as a middle school teacher. His father is employed as an electrical engineer and is in a supervisor role at the company. Charlie's parents have separated within the past two to three months and are moving toward divorce proceedings. Mark and Tiffany reported that marital problems have been occurring over the past year and a half but they have "tried to keep it contained for Charlie's sake." His parents indicate this is a mutual decision and they feel they are better friends than spouses.

When not at kindergarten or daycare, Charlie currently spends most of his time under his mother's care. Charlie lives with his mother in the home that used to be shared with his father. Charlie's father currently lives in an apartment in the neighboring city. Charlie visits his father's apartment approximately two times per week, including alternating weekends. They reported that they are not aware of any type of mental illness on either side of the family.

Charlie's Background History

Charlie's parents reported Charlie as being a typical kindergartener along with a well-rounded, healthy, and happy child up until his 6th birthday. They noted this was around the time his father moved out of the house. Tiffany reported this was when she first started noticing difficulties. Mark indicated he began noticing difficulties around this time as well and commented, "It was like he was a different child" when he visited his apartment for the first time. Parents reported that problem behaviors at home and at school may seem minor but they are concerned because it is "out of character for Charlie."

Charlie's Medical History

Mark and Tiffany reported no major medical history. They indicated tubes were put in his ears around 2.5 years of age and he had his tonsils removed around age 3. They commented he received no other medical treatment outside of regular check-ups. They reported that up until this point he has not received any treatment for behavioral difficulties but decided to seek counseling after consulting with his primary care physician.

Considerations for Assessment and Choosing the Instruments

In assessing and treating Charlie, there are several considerations concerning this situation. At the forefront is the reason for referral. Charlie's parents indicated their ultimate concern is to ensure a smooth transition as they proceed with a divorce. While some counselors may want to immediately go into "couple's counselor mode," it is important to remember the primary client is Charlie, and thus concerning treatment, only parent consultation and training may occur for Mark and Tiffany.

A divorce, separation, or any change in the family may affect the individual stress levels of separate units in the family; thus it is important to examine how these changes can affect the levels of stress the caretakers experience and the child's interaction with them. Soltis et al. (2015) suggested parental stress levels not only influence how the child is perceived but can also influence the child's academic performance. Thus, as discussed earlier, a parent's stresses tend to influence the overall stress level of the child throughout various aspects of their life including the child's functioning and ability to cope with stressful situations (Cappa, Begle, Conger, Dumas, & Conger, 2011). Furthermore, Schoppe-Sullivan, Schermerhorn, and Cummings (2007) provided evidence that marital conflict may also impact a child's ability to adjust indirectly through parenting strategies. Additionally, Tavassolie, Dudding Madigan, Thorvardarson, and Winsler (2016) noted the importance of understanding the relationship between parents' perceptions of their personal and partner parenting style as it relates to marital conflict and child behavioral problems.

In addition to Charlie's behavioral problems, which may be related to stress from his parents' separation, we must also consider his stage of development. Because Charlie is considered to be in Piaget's pre-operational stage of development, additional implications exist in terms of cognitive and verbal abilities.

At 6 years of age, Charlie is most likely to be egocentric and struggle with verbal and written expression; thus a parent or teacher form is more appropriate than a pencil-paper test. As a result of him being egocentric, he may also believe he is the cause of the "crisis" or the separation of his parents. This is a "noteworthy" consideration because it relates to the primary concern of the parents. Additionally, as a result of the lack of verbal expression and vocabulary, it is likely Charlie cannot verbally express his emotions; thus they may be displayed through his behaviors at home and in school. Van der Veen-Mulders, Hauta, Timmerman, van den Hoffdakker, and Hoekstra (2017) commented that parents are the most important informants for a child's behavioral difficulties due to the amount of time they spend at home. Thus, getting the parents' and possibly his teachers' perspectives and experiences regarding his behavioral difficulties may provide valuable information about what

Table 7.1 Assessments Used in Counseling Children and Adolescents

Instrument	Child Age Range	Strength	Weakness	Usage
Child Behavior Checklist	6–18 years	DSM-5-oriented scales Extensive empirical data and backing	Limited social competency scales	Assesses behaviors, problems, and adaptive functioning
Parent Stress Index	1 month to 12 years	Considers the interaction between the child's characteristics and the parents' level of stress	Limited assessment of stressors outside the child-parent relationship	Assesses the parents' stress levels and risks related to parenting concerns

Charlie's symptoms are specifically and how they may contribute to diagnosis and further inform treatment.

For the purpose of Charlie's assessment, the Achenbach System of Empirically Based Assessment's (ASEBA; Achenbach, 2009) Child Behavior Checklist/6–18 and the Parent Stress Index-4 (Abidin, 2012) were chosen. These assessments are appropriate in accordance to the reason for referral, child's developmental level, and the intended use.

Prior to choosing the assessments, John referred to the *Mental Measurements Yearbook* and *Test Critiques* to get an idea of what would be most appropriate for Charlie. In conducting his research, he thought about using the Strength and Difficulties Questionnaire (SDQ) because it is comparable to the CBCL (Carballo, Serrano-Drozdowskyj et al., 2014) and it's free, along with the Behavioral Assessment System for Children, 3rd edition (BASC-3; Reynolds & Kamphaus, 2015) due to it being more linked to the *Diagnostic and Statistical Manual*'s behavioral definitions. Ultimately, he decided to utilize the CBCL because of the specificity, scales utilized, and the general reason of referral for assessment.

The PSI-4 (Abidin, 2012) was also chosen to assess Mark's and Tiffany's stress levels and how those relate to their parenting of Charlie and associated stressors. The BASC-3, Parenting Relationship Scale (PRS) (Reynolds & Kamphaus, 2015), was also considered but because of the concern regarding Mark's and Tiffany's divorce (and the stresses associated), the PSI-4 was chosen due to the specificity of evaluation of stress and how it influences the relationship between the child and parent(s). Additionally, because parenting stress was found to negatively associate with child coping competencies (Soltis et al., 2015) and differences in parenting styles can influence a child's behavioral problems (Tavassolie et al., 2016), John wanted to assess how these stresses may impact Charlie and his abilities to cope with stressful situations. Highlights of the CBCL and PSI-4 can be viewed in Table 7.1.

The Child Behavior Checklist

The Achenbach System of Empirically Based Assessment (ASEBA) is a widely used report for parents, teachers, and youth (for older children) for both child and adolescent behaviors, problems, and adaptive functioning (Achenbach & Rescorla, 2001; Achenbach, 2009; Achenbach & Rescorla, 2001, 2007, 2015; Read, Settipani et al., 2015; Tavassolie et al., 2016). It has been effectively and extensively utilized as both a clinical and research test for psychiatric, neurological, and other types of medical conditions (Piper, Gray, Raber, & Birkett, 2014). ASEBA has several different types of forms that allow for gaining multiple perspectives of a child's behavior across various settings. Forms include the rating form by parents (CBCL), teachers (TRF), youth (YRF), Structured Clinical Interview for Children and Adolescents (SCICA), and direct observation form (DOF), which can be used by other observers and for training clinicians. The forms are quick to administer and score, have a strong research base, and can be used periodically as a way to justify and document services needed as a result of the difficulties the child is experiencing (Achenbach & Rescorla, 2001). These forms are ideal across settings such as private practice, group homes, community counseling clinics, residential treatment, acute care hospitals, and educational settings. It is suggested that the forms be filled out prior to the clinical interview as the results can provide beginning points of discussion to further clarify treatment needs and goals. More specifically, this type of information provides standardized documentation detailing the needs for intervention and a baseline for which the changes can be assessed in the child. For the purpose of this chapter the focus will primarily be on the CBCL form, more specifically the CBCL/6–18 version.

The reassessment of children is recommended for six or 12 months between administrations and can be helpful in determining changes in the problem behavior, the particular course, and treatment of presenting problems in children (Achenbach & Rescorla, 2001). The CBCL is widely used as a continuous assessment to evaluate progress toward goals in treatment in addition to clinical observations, interviews, and progress in sessions (through self or other [parent] report).

CBCL Scales

Because the CBCL/6–18 is intended to measure an accurate picture of parents' perceptions related to their child's emotional and behavioral difficulties, several scales and subscales are included within the instrument (Achenbach, 2009). Competence scales are comprised of the child's activities, social life, and academic performance; the total competency score combines all scores. The competency profile helps identify the child's strengths and areas for growth (Doll, Furlong, & Wood, 1998). The eight syndrome scales are comprised of three separate categories: internalizing, externalizing, and total problems. The internalizing subscale is made up of three of the eight syndrome scales: anxious/depressed, withdrawal/depressed, and somatic complaints. The externalizing subscales are comprised of two of the eight and include rule-breaking behavior and aggressive behaviors. The subscales of social problems, thought problems, and attention problems are not seen as internalizing or externalizing but are part of the empirically derived syndromes. When all eight syndrome scales (anxious/depressed, withdrawal/depressed, somatic complaints, social problems, thought problems, attention problems, rule-breaking behavior, and aggressive behavior) are combined, a total problem scale is formed (Achenbach, 2009; Achenbach, & Rescorla, 2001, 2015). Lastly, DSM-oriented scales are comprise of items that were evaluated by experienced psychologists and psychiatrists with a mean of 22 years of experience rated as being very consistent with the symptoms of the *Diagnostic and Statistical Manual for Mental Health Disorders, 5th edition* (Achenbach, 2014).

Standardization

The normative sample for the CBCL consisted of 4,994 children and associated parents by use of clinical and non-referred (via national survey) samples. Prior to the CBCL, very little research existed on how to determine if children were competent in behavioral, emotional, and social areas (Achenbach, 1978 as cited in Achenbach & Rescorla, 2001). Based on Achenbach's and Rescorla's (2001) findings and multiple approaches to testing, they were able to determine favorable characteristics that are the empirical basis for norms as displayed by percentiles and T-scores associated with the competency scales. Because of the rich empirical basis and various methods utilized for the standardization process for each scale of the CBCL, the readers should refer to the *Manual for the ASEBA School-Age Forms &*

Profiles (Achenbach & Rescorla, 2001) to see the complete findings for standardization and normalization of each scale.

Reliability and Validity

The *Manual for the ASEBA School-Age Forms & Profiles* (Achenbach & Rescorla, 2001) contains extensive information pertaining to the reliability and validity of the CBCL. It has inter-interview (p < .001) and test-retest (p < .001) reliability item scores. The CBCL/6–18 has been shown to have the highest test-retest reliability (Piper et al., 2014). Additionally, internal consistency was founded through factor analysis of the syndrome scales. Cronbach's alpha for the competency scales were moderately high, ranging from .63 to .79, and .78 to .97 were noted for the problem scales. Tavassolie et al. (2016) found Cronbach alpha averaged across girls and boys at .90 for internalizing scales, .93 for externalizing scales, and .96 for overall behavioral problems. Additionally, van der Ende, Verhulst, and Teimeier (2016) utilized the Dutch version of the CBCL and found Cronbach's alpha to range from .81 to .90 for internalizing scales and .81 to .92 for externalizing scales across informants.

Content validity has been strongly empirically supported for nearly the last four decades (Achenbach & Rescorla, 2001). Criterion-related validity established by use of multiple regression analysis were performed on the competence and adaptive functioning scales along with the problems scales. Overall, Piper et al. (2014) commented that the CBCL/6–18 form displays good agreement between maternal and other parental ratings. Construct validity has also been identified as compared to DSM-5 (American Psychiatric Association, 2013) symptom measures and correlations with the Conner's Scales ranging from .71 to .85 and BASC Scales with the highest correlations for the internalizing, externalizing, and total problem scales ranging from .74 to .89. Most recently, Gomez, Vance, and Gomez (2014) found further support for convergent and discriminant validity across the CBCL, TRF, and YSR forms of referred youth in a clinical setting. Cross-cultural replications have been conducted and founded similar results to that of the normative sample (Achenbach & Rescorla, 2001). A complete report of reliability and validity studies for the CBCL are beyond the scope of this chapter; for further information, the readers should refer to the various manuals published with ASEBA and continuous research studies related to the CBCL.

Administration

The CBCL was designed to be an easy and self-explanatory assessment to be filled out by parents (Achenbach & Rescorla, 2001, 2015). Master-level counselors with two years of practice are able to administer the CBCL/6–18. Administration takes approximately 20 minutes and can be given to parents prior to the initial session or filled out while in a waiting room. In addition to a brief demographic and basic information section pertaining to the child, it contains 112 items rated on a 3-point Likert scale ranging from "not true" to "very true or often true." When parents are not able to complete the forms alone, test items can be read aloud and then written down. When both parents are available, it is appropriate to have both of them complete the CBCL form for their child. This is helpful as sometimes parents have varying opinions or perceptions. When both parents complete the CBCL for the child, comparisons can be made to create a more accurate understanding or picture of the child's behaviors. When the assessment is given to parents for a child who has a disability, the test taker should be informed to rate the child based on the typical peers for the child's age (Achenbach & Rescorla, 2007).

Scoring Procedures

Computerized scoring is available for the CBCL through ASEBA-PC software (Achenbach & Rescorla, 2001; http://aseba.org/asebapc.html). If possible, computerized scoring is recommended because the hand-scoring is tedious and scorers are likely to make a few minor errors that can alter the loadings of the scales. More specifically the internalizing and externalizing scales are not a simple addition problem; thus computerized scoring is highly encouraged (Doll, Furlong, & Wood, 1998).

Should the counselor choose to hand-score the CBCL, they should be aware that separate scoring profiles exist for boys and girls and they should be utilized accordingly due to changes in loadings and T-scores (Achenbach, and Rescorla, 2001). Additionally, the computations for hand-scoring require raw scores to be converted to T-scores. Conversion figures are displayed on the profile scoring sheet and will not be repeated here to ensure the integrity of the instrument. T-scores for each scale are divided into normal ranges, borderline clinical range, and clinical ranges. The ranges vary per scale; thus the scorer should pay careful attention to ensure the appropriate clinical range is matched to the appropriate scale when writing the assessment report. Luckily for the scorer, the profile sheets provide separation marks indicating the various ranges of T-scores on the profiles (these separation marks are also visible for the computerized profiles).

Multicultural and Ethical Considerations

ASEBA (Achenbach & Rescorla, 2007) has provided additional supplements that address multicultural uses and instructions for administering the CBCL to various cultures. Most recently, Haack's, Kapke's, and Gerdes's (2016) study based on school-aged Latinos provided further evidence supporting the CBCL as a culturally appropriate measure of child psychological diagnoses with Latino families. To date, the CBCL/6–18 has been translated into over 80 languages and/or dialects and has withstood reliability and validity measures (www.aseba.org/ordering/translations.html). As a result of the extensive data and research, readers should refer to the *Multicultural Supplement to the Manual for the ASEBA School-Age Forms & Profiles* (Achenbach & Rescorla, 2007) for further information regarding the ethical use of the CBCL with multicultural populations.

Parent Stress Index

The Parent Stress Index was created from a theoretical model related to dysfunctional parenting (Abidin, 2012). This is not to say parents who are administered the PSI-4 are dysfunctional parents; however, this instrument acknowledges the stress components parents experience as they interact with the various aspects (or characteristics) unique to their child. The theoretical model can be viewed in Figure 7.1.

As gleamed from the previous sections and through the theoretical backing, the PSI-4 could provide some helpful information in regard to parental concerns and how a child's behavior may influence parental stress levels that in turn may affect the child (Cappa et al., 2011; Schoppe-Sullivan et al., 2007; Soltis et al., 2015). The instrument was designed to measure the amount of stress between the child-parent relationships. Abidin (2012) defines parenting stress as difficult interactions between the parent and child. These interactions can include multiple stresses such as emotional or behavioral difficulties, child rearing, financial obligations, etc. Additionally, because treating children often involves interactions and consultations with the parent(s), this type of assessment may be helpful to determine the

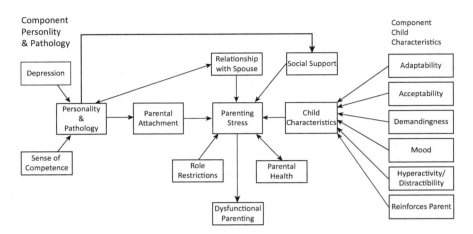

Figure 7.1 Parenting Stress Index

implications of family interactions and how the child may be affected as a result. The PSI-4 bases its four assumptions on stress based on the child's characteristics, parent's characteristics, and situational or demographic life stresses (Abidin, 2012). This does not mean to say the counselor who chooses to use the PSI-4 is making a recommendation on who the child should live with (this is not the counselor's role and in states such as Texas it can be a violation); simply put they may need to assess the parent's stress levels to evaluate how they are affecting the child's stress levels. Children's behaviors often trigger past issues their caregivers have faced. For this reason, it is also important for the counselor to evaluate the temperaments between the child and parent through use of the Parent Stress Index-4 (PSI-4).

The PSI-4 is comprised of 120 test items and two primary domains (child and parent) which combine to form a total stress score (Abidin, 2012). The child and parent domains are detailed in Table 7.2 along with their specialized subscales. The reader should refer to the testing manual for the full description of each subscale.

A short form (PSI-SF) is also available for use which consists of 36 items and three domains. The three domains on the short form of Parental Distress (PD), Parent-Child Dysfunctional Interaction (P-CDI), and Difficult Child (DC) combine to equal a total stress score. Begle et al. (2011) did indicate a high level of internal consistency with their study with a Cronbach's α = .91. For the purpose of this case study, the long version was chosen.

Normative Sample

The PSI-4 was standardized by utilizing a normative sample of 1056 adults comprising 522 fathers and 534 mothers. The sample consisted of diverse individuals from 17 states in the Southern, Northeastern, Western, and Midwestern regions of the United States with various levels of education and a mean age of 33.24 years (mothers) and 34 years (fathers).

The overall factor structure of the PSI-4 was examined in relation to the previous versions. The revision was conducted to evaluate the original factor structure with the newer normative sample used in the fourth edition. Varimax rotations were individually conducted for the child domains, parent domains, and total stress scale. The overall correlations between the PSI-3 and the PSI-4 domains fluctuated from .85 to .99. Additionally, all subscales were measured within their individual domain and were relatively strong, with child domain

Table 7.2 Outcomes of PSI-4

Domain	Purpose	Subscales
Child Domain	Recognizes the appraisal process involved during the stress experience	Distractibility/Hyperactivity (DI) Adaptability (AD) Reinforces Parent (RE) Demandingness (DE) Mood (MO) Acceptability (AC)
Parent Domain	Identifies parent characteristics that influence the ability to function as a caregiver	Competence (CO) Isolation (IS) Attachment (AT) Health (HE) Role Restriction (RO) Depression (DP) Spouse/Parenting Partner Relationship (SP)

subscales ranging from .75 to .92, parent domain subscales ranging from .76 to .92, and the overall correlation between child and parent domains being .81.

Reliability and Validity

Internal consistency for the PSI-4 were established by use of Cronbach's alpha on each subscale, domain, and the total stress score. The data obtained from the normative sample ranged from .78 to .88 on the subscales for the child domain and from .75 to .87 on the subscales for the parent domain. The reliability coefficients for the total stress score were .96 or greater (Abidin, 2012). Test-retest reliability was also obtained from 136 total participants (with more than 82 mothers), with administrations ranging from three weeks to three months after the initial administration. Overall, the test-retest reliability coefficients ranged from .55 to .82 on the child domain and from .70 to .91 for the parent domain. Only three of the four studies reported test-retest reliability coefficients which ranged from .65 to .96; however, the findings from the four studies suggested strong support for stability.

Literature supporting the use of the PSI can be found in approximately 250 research studies. Because of the depth of the studies and over 40 language translations the specific details are beyond the scope of this chapter. The PSI has shown predictive validity in studies involving African-American, Chinese, Portuguese, and French-Canadian populations and others. Ultimately, the PSI-4 testing manual suggested two important conclusions related to reliability and validity in that parenting is a universal construct and measuring parenting stress is useful across diverse populations (Abidin, 2012). Additionally, empirical findings have linked the PSI to specific areas related to parental stress including but not limited to anxiety and parenting, at risk children, attachment, ADHD, child abuse, family, forensic contexts, child–parent interactions along with observed behaviors, premature terminations and adherence to medical treatment, program evaluations, psychometrics, social support systems, substance abuse, and parental depression.

Administration

The PSI-4 is easy to administer and can be done by individuals who have not had formal training in counseling, psychology, social work, or related fields. However, individuals who do not have the formal training must have received instruction in the specifics of the PSI-4 and must be supervised. Individuals who qualify at the B or S level are able to administer the instrument without supervision. Prior to the administration of the test, the examiner should build rapport with the parent(s) to ensure they are comfortable. The test is comprised of a demographic section and a section in which the parents are asked to mark answers ranging from strongly agree to strongly disagree, mark specific response items numbered 1 to 4 or 5, and yes or no responses. Test takers are encouraged to mark only one answer per item and to mark out incorrect answers by putting an "X" through the response to change it. For multiple children, parents are asked to complete a separate assessment per child. After the test taker has finished, the examiner should review the answer sheet for any missing items and ask the taker to answer any remaining questions. If the test taker is not clear on the meaning of items, the administrator can provide guidance regarding definitions of terms or to address specific concerns.

Scoring

Scoring for the PSI-4 is straightforward. Many of the items are color coded for scoring purposes and only basic math skills are needed to make calculations for the domain scores (child and parent) and total stress score. Scores should note one color represents the possibility of "defensive scoring" and a score of < to 24 may indicate the test taker responded in a defensive manner (Abidin, 2012).

Multicultural and Ethical Issues

Parenting is seen as a universal construct along with parental stress, thus multicultural considerations are integrated into the instrument. To date, the PSI has been translated into over 40 languages while maintaining reliability, validity, and its factor structure through translations; thus, this testing instrument is considered culturally sound. Norms and specific psychometrics for the PSI have also been published by international publishers in seven other countries (Abidin, 2012). As a result of the universal construct of parenting and parenting stress, scoring modifications are not utilized for ethnicity and/or cultural differences. For further information pertaining to the ethical use with multicultural populations the readers is encouraged to refer to the testing manual or other relevant articles.

Reviewing Test Results

After the assessments are completed and scored but prior to communicating the results with parents or caregivers, it is imperative for the counselor to check to ensure errors were not made during the scoring process. Because the assessment process makes suggestions for sometimes life-changing events, one small error could affect the overall scores, recommendations, and well-being of the client. Thus, it is not only important for the counselor to review the assessment results and make sure they are valid, but it is also wise to check for any error in scoring (Drummond et al., 2016).

In the following section, we will refer back to the case of Charlie. Pay close attention to the considerations John makes in communicating the assessment results and his treatment recommendations for Charlie.

Communicating Results with Parents

John began with reviewing the purpose of the assessment as agreed upon in the informed consent then proceeded with discussing the results. Both Mark and Tiffany completed their own forms for the CBCL/6–18 and the PSI-4.

In scoring the CBCL both parents' ratings were within range, suggesting they are noticing many of the same problems. John informed Mark and Tiffany of Charlie's scores related to the competence scales, specifically the Activities (5), Social (5), and School (3) subscales. He further explained that Charlie fell into the clinical range for the Activities subscale and the borderline clinical range for the social and school subscales. Upon further discussion with parents, John indicated that Charlie's lack of participation in chores and organizations, clubs, teams, or groups (due to parents' non-enrollment) may have influenced the score a result.

In communicating the assessment results with Mark and Tiffany, John explained the differences of internalizing profiles and externalizing profiles. Charlie scored within the clinical range on the internalizing scale and within the normal range for externalizing behaviors. It was explained the clinical range on the internalizing behaviors may indicate anxiety (with a raw score from 17 to 18), symptoms of depression (with a raw score ranging 5 to 7), and symptoms related to somatic complaints (with a raw score ranging 10 to 12) which led to a T-Score of approximately 78. John further explained as a result of Charlie's developmental level and the inability to effectively communicate with words, all reported symptoms may be related to his current difficulties and possible tension or strains related to his adjustment process (due to the divorce).

In relation to the DSM-oriented scales it was reported Charlie's scores were categorized into the clinical ranges for Affective problems (12), Anxiety problems (15), and somatic problems (6), and the borderline clinical range for Oppositional Defiant problems (6). In relation to Attention Deficit/Hyperactivity problems and Conduct problems his scores were within the normal range. John suggested these scores may also be linked back to the adjustment struggles Charlie may be experiencing.

Prior to informing Mark and Tiffany the results of the PSI-4, John reminded them that the purpose of this assessment was NOT to determine who Charlie should live with and it should not be used for that purpose. He further explained the purpose was to evaluate how parental stresses influence the relationship between Charlie and themselves. John suggested he cover the results of the PSI-4 individually rather than with both of them together in the same room. He further explained that the purpose behind this was to communicate the individual results to them and if they wish to share their results with each other they can choose to do so. In John's documentation of the interaction, he justified this recommendation through noting that sharing results individually would create an additional safeguard (in addition to his previous reminder statement) from Mark and Tiffany attempting to utilize the results in a malicious way (which could affect Charlie's well-being) at a later date. However, John did indicate the results of both of their assessments were equally considered in making recommendations for treatment.

John's Conversation with Tiffany. John informed Tiffany that her results suggest she was not defensive when taking the assessment. Tiffany added to John's statement and commented because of her concerns for Charlie she wanted to make sure she was completely honest with her responses.

Tiffany's total stress score on the PSI-4 was 211, which indicates she falls within the normal range. Her life stress score of 5 also fell within normal limits, which indicates she does not have a significant number of major life stresses outside the child-parent relationship. This score is viewed as a positive factor in relation to her parenting role and carrying out her responsibilities related to parenting.

Overall, Tiffany's scores in the child domain were within normal limits with a total score of 97; however, the subscales of Adaptability and Mood were of clinical significance. Overall results of the subscales can be viewed in Table 7.3.

The clinical range in Adaptability indicates Tiffany may struggle in her roles as a parent as a result of Charlie's inability to adapt to the changes occurring in his current physical or

Table 7.3 Overall Results for Tiffany in the Child Domain

Child Domain Subscales	Score	Range
Distractibility/Hyperactivity	16	Low Range
Adaptability	31	Clinical Range
Reinforces Parent	6	Low Range
Demandingness	21	Normal Range
Mood	12	Clinical Range
Acceptability	11	Normal Range
Total Child Domain Score	97	Normal Range

social environment. As suggested by Tavassolie et al. (2016) and others (Schoppe-Sullivan et al., 2007), this may be compounded by the altering of effective parenting behaviors that may have occurred as a result of the marital conflict (separation/divorce proceedings). More specifically, this score indicates Charlie is likely to experience problems in changing from one task to another and may be prone to experience emotional upset, overreact to changes in sensory stimulation, avoid new people or strangers who enter his life, and experience difficulty establishing equilibrium when he becomes upset. Choe, Olson, and Sameroff (2013) suggest early maternal stress may contribute to the growth in a young child's adjustment problems; however, this is something John would need to explore further with Tiffany to be certain.

The clinical range in mood indicates Charlie may be experiencing dysfunction in his affective functioning. Additionally, he may be experiencing symptoms related to depression and unhappiness as a result of the situation. John further explained to Tiffany that it is important to consider Charlie's stage of emotional development here, as Charlie may be experiencing beliefs that he is somehow at fault for the divorce due to the conflict between her and Mark.

In the parent domain, Tiffany's overall score was within normal limits. The scores for the subscales of the parent domain can be viewed along with the range in Table 7.4.

The one area of clinical significance on the parent domain consisted of Spouse/Parenting Partner Relationship; however, the Depression subscale was only slightly below the clinical range; thus it is at moderate level of concern as well. The clinical score on Spouse/Parenting Partner Relationship suggests Tiffany feels a lack of emotional support in parenting Charlie and at times she may feel Mark is not willing to accept some of his parenting responsibilities. Because Tiffany scored slightly below the clinical range on the depression scale, symptoms of depression may be related to her relationship with Mark and the separation and upcoming divorce. When John informed Tiffany of this result, she expressed slight worry on her face. He then comforted her by noting van der Veen-Mulders et al.'s (2017) research findings in which mothers are more likely to rate themselves with depressive symptoms and additional parental stresses when compared to fathers. Her score indicates she may experience feelings of unhappiness or guilt related to the current situation and this in turn may affect her ability to be assertive and set a structured environment for Charlie. This result is consistent with what Tiffany indicated on the CBCL in that Charlie does not currently have chores at home nor does he participate in outside activities.

John's Conversation with Mark. Mark was informed that his results suggest he was not defensive while taking the assessment; at this time Mark commented, "Of course I wasn't, why would I be defensive—I was being honest." Mark did inquire if Tiffany's results came back non-defensive and John again explained it is up to Tiffany to decide whether she wants to share her results with him. Mark indicated his understanding.

Table 7.4 Overall Results for Tiffany in the Parent Domain

Parent Domain Subscale	Score	Range
Competence	28	Normal Range
Isolation	15	Normal Range
Attachment	9	Low Range
Health	9	Normal Range
Role Restriction	13	Low Range
Depression	24	Normal Range
Spouse/Parenting Partner Relationship	22	Clinical Range
Total Parent Domain	120	Normal Range

Table 7.5 Overall Subscales for Mark in the Child Domain

Child Domain Subscales	Score	Range
Distractibility/Hyperactivity	16	Low Range
Adaptability	33	Clinical Range
Reinforces Parent	8	Low Range
Demandingness	25	Normal Range
Mood	12	Clinical Range
Acceptability	11	Normal Range
Total Child Domain Score	105	Normal Range

Mark's total stress score was 211, which fell within the normal range. His life stress score was 3, which suggests he has very few stressors outside the child–parent relationship that may affect his parenting abilities. Overall his life stress score is seen as a positive factor.

Overall, Mark's scores in the child domain were within normal limits, with a total score of 105; however, the subscales of Adaptability, Demandingness, and Mood were of clinical significance. Overall results of the subscales can be viewed in Table 7.5.

The clinical range in Adaptability indicates Mark struggles in his role as a parent because of Charlie's inability to adapt to the changes occurring in his current physical or social environment. More specifically, this score indicates Charlie is likely to experience problems in changing from one task to another and may be prone to experience emotional upset, overreact to changes in sensory stimulation, avoid new people or strangers who enter his life, and experience difficulty establishing equilibrium when he becomes upset.

The clinical range in Demandingness suggests Mark feels Charlie puts additional demands on him as a parent. In discussing the results further, Mark indicated he has noticed Charlie started clinging to him when they "switch" because he is with his mother most of the time since their separation. John further explained, higher scores of Demandingness are linked to separation anxiety, which Charlie may currently be experiencing, as evident by the symptoms reported in Mark's responses on the CBCL and clinical interview. Furthermore, John explained that when parents experience demandingness from their child, they tend to rate the more externalizing behaviors as problems (van der Veen-Mulders et al., 2017), which was consistent with some of Mark's ratings on the CBCL scales.

The clinical scores in mood indicate Charlie may be experiencing dysfunction in his affective functioning. Additionally, he may be experiencing symptoms related to depression and unhappiness as a result of the situation. Just as John explained to Tiffany, he also informed Mark that it is important to consider Charlie's stage of emotional development, as

Table 7.6 Overall Subscales for Mark in the Parent Domain

Parent Domain Subscale	Score	Range
Competence	26	Normal Range
Isolation	12	Normal Range
Attachment	9	Low Range
Health	10	Normal Range
Role Restriction	18	Low Range
Depression	15	Low Range
Spouse/Parenting Partner Relationship	16	Normal Range
Total Parent Domain	106	Normal Range

Charlie may be experiencing beliefs that he is somehow at fault for the divorce due to the conflict between Mark and Tiffany and him being egocentric.

In the parent domain, Mark's overall score was within the lower normal limits. The scores for the subscales of the parent domain along with the range can be viewed in Table 7.6.

All of Mark's scores within the parent domain were in the lower normal range and the low range. Because his defensiveness score was not of concern, it is not likely that Mark was minimizing on the scales; however, this could still be a possibility.

John's Mental Note. Tiffany's parent domain scale may be higher than John's because Charlie spends most of his time with her versus Mark. This type of occurrence may have also influenced the scores on the child domain, such as the clinically significant Demandingness subscale on Mark's PSI-4. Ultimately, it appears Tiffany's current life stresses, depression, and feelings of lack of partner support in parenting Charlie may have further influenced her scores because of the amount of time she parents Charlie in comparison to Mark.

Rejoining the Parents

After individual discussions with Charlie's parents, John explained to Mark and Tiffany that ethically speaking he is not able to provide a diagnosis for Charlie until he is seen for counseling services. Charlie's parents indicated they appreciate John's honesty and inquired about the next steps in addressing their concerns. John indicated he had recommendations for Charlie and his parents for how to assist in the adjustment process. He informed them recommendations were based on the compilations of the background forms, clinical interview, and test results. These are detailed in the next section.

Treatment Recommendations for Charlie (and Parents)

Charlie's developmental level and cognitive abilities dictated John's recommendations for treatment. As a result of his age, John recommended play therapy for Charlie. Within play sessions, Charlie will be able to develop coping skills needed to adjust to his parents getting a divorce. Additionally, through play, Charlie will be able to learn how to begin identifying his emotions, which will assist him in communicating them to both Mark and Tiffany. Charlie will also be able to improve his confidence levels and esteem as a result of play techniques. Mark and Tiffany agreed about Charlie attending play therapy and indicated they would like John to provide this service.

John also suggested his parents participate in a program that will allow them to build a stronger relationship with Charlie. John explained that by building a better relationship with Charlie, he will feel more secure with each parent, which could assist in periods of separation from the other parent. John wanted to ensure this component was included within his recommendations because research by Soltis et al. (2015) and others (Begle & Dumas, 2011) suggested that, when parents are actively engaged in parenting programs, they have a higher level of satisfaction, efficacy, and reduced levels of parental stress, which in turn influences the child's coping competencies. In addition, this type of treatment protocol may also reduce the levels of Demandingness that Mark feels Charlie places on him, further help Charlie in the adjustment process, and help promote consistency in parenting between the two households (Tavassolie et al., 2016). As a result of Choe's, Olson's, and Sameroff's (2013) findings that parental behaviors affect child behavior more so than child behavior on parenting behavior, John's professional opinion is this treatment would be beneficial for all involved.

John informed Mark and Tiffany that he would like to refer Mark and Tiffany to a counselor who is a partner in his practice for this service. He further explained this would assist in ensuring that he does not develop a skewed vision of Charlie as a result of conducting both play therapy and relationship therapy. John informed both Mark and Tiffany he would check on their progress in relationship therapy and inform them of Charlie's progress in play therapy through scheduled parent consultations. Tiffany and Mark indicated understanding behind the reasoning that John did not want to provide all services and thanked him for his professionalism in helping them address their concerns for Charlie throughout the separation and eventually the divorce.

Lastly, a recommendation was made to Mark and Tiffany that related to Charlie's activities and socialization. Because his parents noted he is not involved in any outside organizations or clubs, which contributed to a score in the clinical range on the CBCL, John suggested Charlie be encouraged to participate in group activities outside of the family such as sports, boy scouts, etc. He noted that research (van der Ende et al., 2016) suggests poor social skills are closely linked to internalized behavior and often the sooner the intervention, the better the outcome. Tiffany noted this has been something they have been considering doing for a while but experienced hesitancy. Mark and Tiffany indicated the desire to do this to assist Charlie in developing better social skills with peers his own age.

John informed Charlie's parents that the CBCL and PSI-4 will be utilized periodically after the treatment begins to assess both Charlie's progress through play therapy and their levels of stress pertaining to parenting Charlie during this period of adjustment. He indicated that the PSI-4 may be administered as part of the relationship therapy (which will be conducted by his practice partner) and with their written permission results can be communicated back to him. John also suggested the TRF be used at a later date if deemed necessary and as a comparison method between home and school environments.

Summary

In assessing children in counseling, counselors must consider how the process varies from that of adults. Counselors should be mindful of the child's abilities and developmental level to ensure the appropriateness behind the tests and assessment interventions chosen. Additionally, because assessment is a continuous process throughout the counseling process, assessment protocols may be modified as the child grows and changes. Counselors should also be mindful that on occasion additional explanations, considerations, and safeguards should be put into place as the child alone cannot legally provide consent for counseling assessment. Thus, parents need to be adequately and ethically informed of the purpose of assessment prior to, during, and after the final assessment in counseling.

Test Your Knowledge:

1. In choosing a reliable and valid assessment test or instrument for a specific population type, what should be the primary consideration?
   a. The cost to the instrument
   b. The availability of the instrument
   c. The reason for referral
   d. None of the above

2. In utilizing the CBCL, scorers should be careful when hand-scoring because:
   a. Hand-scoring should never be used because computer scoring is available
   b. One or two minor errors can skew results on various profiles
   c. The computations are very complex and require skills beyond basic math
   d. Hand-scoring is no longer available for the CBCL

3. In communicating the results of the PSI-4 to Mark and Tiffany, what safeguards did John put in place to ensure the results would not be utilized in a custody dispute?
   a. John documented the reasoning behind him sharing the results individually
   b. John reminded Mark and Tiffany of the purpose of the assessment and how the results should and should not be used several times
   c. John discussed assessment results and the usage when reviewing the signed informed consent
   d. All of the above are correct

4. Individuals who use tests and assessments with children need to be aware of the specific training, qualifications, levels of experience, and any type of supervision required prior to utilizing specific testing instruments.
   T or F?

5. Which of the following was not considered in making treatment recommendations for Charlie?
   a. Results from the CBCL
   b. Results from the PSI-4
   c. Results from the TRF
   d. Information from the clinical interview

6. When choosing an instrument, the counselor should consider:
   a. Only the website of the test manufacturer
   b. Test in Print
   c. Mental Measurement Yearbook
   d. Both B and C are correct

7. Considerations for assessments with kids should include:
   a. The construct being measured
   b. The amount of time the child can "sit" for the test
   c. The cost
   d. Both A and B

8. Parents have the right to informed consent.
   T or F?

9. Parents may come to counseling with the idea, from their primary physician, that their child is diagnosable with a mental health condition.
   T or F?

10. Counselors are ethically mandated to consider any additional special training required to use tests and assessments with children and teens before they use such instruments.
    T or F?

Discussion Questions/Prompts:

1. In providing counseling assessment for Charlie (and his parents), discuss the steps and considerations John acknowledged throughout the assessment process.
2. How did Charlie's developmental level weigh into how John chose to proceed with the assessment process?
3. In choosing assessment types for children, what must the counselor consider?
4. Discuss some of the ethical obligations involved in the assessment of children.
5. What role can and do parents/guardians play in the process of assessment of a child/teen?

8 Assessment of Psychological Conditions

Stephanie S.J. Drcar

In a clinical landscape that is increasingly focused on the provision of evidence-based practice, it is incumbent on counselors to fully identify any and all psychological conditions that one's client may be experiencing in order to inform the provision of appropriate clinical interventions (Morrow, Lee, Bartoli, & Gillem, 2017). However, in the real, messy world of clinical work, clients often bring a myriad of concerns and parsing these out to identify which particular psychological conditions may be present can be a daunting task. Of course, a well-done clinical interview can elucidate many of the difficult circumstances and psychological symptoms that a client is experiencing; however, the provision of targeted, objective assessment can provide another level of information to clarify the diagnostic picture, inform conceptualization, and determine which approaches to treatment are warranted. The challenge for counselors is determining both *when* assessment of psychological conditions is warranted as well as *how* to go about the process (i.e., what assessments could be used, what level of qualification and training is needed, where do counselors obtain such assessments).

One of the primary factors to consider in the use of formal assessments by counselors is determining which assessments one can ethically administer, score, and interpret based on their qualifications and training. The commonly used system in the realm of mental health assessment is the "ABC" qualification level ranking method (American Educational Research Association, 2014). "A" level assessments do not require any special training or order to administer, score, and interpret. "B" level assessments require a higher level of training and experience compared to "A" level assessment and a master's degree in the field of counseling, along with formal training in the ethical administration, scoring, and interpretation of clinical assessments. These assessments typically fulfill the baseline levels of competence needed to administer, score, and interpret such assessments. Lastly, "C" level assessments require the highest level of training and experience and usually require a doctoral degree and the appropriate additional, formal training. For the purposes of this chapter, given that most counselors fall under the "B" level, "B" level assessments will be the primary focus, although some "C" level assessments will be discussed, when relevant.

The goal of this chapter is to introduce readers to commonplace and easily accessible objective assessments that are appropriate to the training and needs of counselors, explore the clinical scenarios and client presentations that warrant their use, and discuss the strengths and weaknesses of each assessment. Certainly, excellent texts and book chapters exist that discuss some of the forthcoming assessments with greater detail and we refer readers to those when further information is desired. Additionally, the manuals provided by the publishers of each of these tests provide essential information regarding test construction, reliability, validity, scoring, interpretation, etc. and should be fully read and understood prior to use of any following assessments. This chapter will first introduce readers to foundational knowledge regarding the assessment of common psychological conditions and under what conditions assessment is typically warranted. Next, this chapter will review some assessments that are capable of measuring symptoms associated with a broad range of psychological conditions. Following the exploration of broad-ranging assessments, narrow-focus assessments for specific psychological conditions will be discussed (i.e., those appropriate for disorders of mood, anxiety, trauma, eating, and psychosis). Lastly, a case study will be presented to explore the real-world application of such an assessment and how an appropriate assessment is selected, administered, scored, and interpreted, and how feedback is provided and treatment is impacted.

The Assessment of Psychological Conditions

The sheer number of assessments available to mental health clinicians can be overwhelming enough to make routine use of assessments feel inaccessible to those who are not familiar with the use of assessment as a clinical intervention. Before discussion of assessments that can be utilized for a variety of psychological conditions, first a review of the types of assessments available is necessary. The first distinction that can be made among assessments is regarding the scope of their assessment of psychological conditions: assessments may be broad or narrow focus. Broad-focus assessments are beneficial when a clinician needs to obtain a large amount of data regarding the presence, severity, and type of psychological conditions that a client is reporting. Such broad-focus assessments are typically longer and take more time to complete compared to narrow-focused assessments. Examples of such broad-focus assessments include the Minnesota Multiphasic Personality Inventory-2 (MMPI-2) and the Personality Assessment Inventory (PAI). The MMPI-2 and PAI contain hundreds of items and may take an hour or more to complete. Additionally, the MMPI-2 and PAI are classified as "C" level instruments, meaning that a doctoral degree and/or advanced training is necessary before one can ethically administer, score, and interpret such an assessment. Certainly, assessments such as the MMPI-2, PAI, and others provide invaluable clinical data; however, these are typically provided as a part of a larger psychological assessment battery and a counselor is not typically involved in such a process. The Behavior Assessment System for Children, Third Edition, (BASC-3) is a "B" level instrument that is often utilized when a counselor seeks to obtain a wide-reaching picture of a child's behavioral functioning. Given that comprehensive measures for adults are typically "C" level assessments, a counselor is more likely to find themselves utilizing narrow-focus assessments that aid in diagnosis clarification, case conceptualization, treatment planning, and progress/outcome tracking. Narrow-focus assessments typically are shorter and their content is specific to the symptoms, behaviors, and associated personality characteristics from a particular diagnostic category (i.e., Major Depressive Disorder, Generalized Anxiety Disorder, and Posttraumatic Stress Disorder).

There are a variety of time points and situations that warrant use of narrow-focused, objective assessments, although assessments vary in their capacity to be useful for all time points or events. Some common time points in the therapeutic process in which assessments could be utilized include upon initial contact with a counselor/agency during the intake process, early in therapeutic work, throughout therapy to track progress, and at the end of therapy to assess the overall change from the initial baseline. Common situations that warrant the use of assessment include difficulty clarifying a diagnostic picture, improving case conceptualization, and subsequent treatment planning, or when therapy seems to have little to no impact on the client or progress has plateaued. Regardless of the situation or time point, a therapist should always ask themselves, "What can this assessment provide for me?" and, "Are there other ways of obtaining the outcome of this assessment in a more efficient and/or cost-effective manner?" These questions are not to imply that assessments are inherently a poor use of time or cost-prohibitive; however, all clinical interventions (assessments included) have benefits and drawbacks that must be balanced. Sometimes, a well-done clinical interview or other means of tracking can appropriately accomplish the intended goal as opposed to the use of formal, objective assessment. The counselor must consider the time taken to administer, score, and interpret the particular assessment and determine if it is worth the client's and counselor's time considering the type of information that the assessment can provide. Many times, counselors will find that the right assessment at the right time is an invaluable tool in their clinical tool belt. Assessments should not be seen as a panacea to difficult intake sessions, clients who are not progressing, or difficult diagnostic pictures because assessment simply provides another source of clinical data. The clinical data they provide can be indispensable; however, they should be selected because the balance of what they can provide in a particular situation outweighs any drawbacks and is the appropriate choice when compared to other methods.

Counselors are typically in the "ball park" regarding their initial understanding of the psychological conditions that their clients are experiencing. An initial session with a client provides the attuned counselor with a myriad of information (i.e., client's description of symptoms, client presentation and behavior, and potentially previous clinical records) and counselors usually leave the session with a sound hypothesis of what psychological concerns exist. However, hypotheses are best confirmed when multiple sources of information support them and as such the utilization of narrow-focus assessments can provide another piece of evidence to confirm the counselor's diagnostic hypothesis. It is important to note that an objective test result is not necessarily the be-all and end-all piece of data when determining the psychological conditions present for a client; it is simply another piece of information that can provide valuable data on the client's experiences compared to those of the test's norming sample. Test results should always be interpreted in light of other sources of data such as counselor observations, collateral data, and client self-report. It is important to remember that tests are simply a tool in the clinician's tool belt; tests do not have a brain of their own and it is incumbent on the clinician to place the results in context with other sources of data.

Mood Disorders

Mood disorders, particularly unipolar depression and related disorders, remain one of the most common psychological conditions that counselors assess and treat among their clients (Substance Abuse and Mental Health Services Administration, 2015). Although the symptoms common to Major Depressive Disorder and Dysthymia are a part of both the clinical and lay-person lexicon, this doesn't remove the utility of narrow-focus assessments of mood disorder symptoms. Given that a major depressive episode, for example, can include a wide range of cognitive, behavioral, and emotional symptoms, narrow-focus assessments can elucidate both the severity of such symptoms as well as which symptom clusters are most prevalent for a particular client. Additionally, some of the tests specific to depressive symptoms are brief and are incredibly useful in establishing a baseline of symptoms so that the effectiveness of clinical work with the client can be tracked over the course of therapy.

Beck Depression Inventory-II

The Beck Depression Inventory-II (BDI-II; Beck, Steer, & Brown, 1996) is an accessible, common-sense, and quick test to administer (i.e., ~5 minutes), score, and interpret. The brevity and face validity of the BDI-II also make it manageable for clients to complete, often on a reoccurring basis for the purposes of symptom tracking. The BDI-II consists of 21 items, each item containing a list of four statements regarding a particular symptom, ranging in severity so that clients can select the sentence that best describes their experience (in the previous two-week time frame). The items assess symptoms that align well with the *Diagnostic and Statistical Manual of Mental Disorders, 5th edition* (DSM-5; American Psychiatric Association, 2013) symptoms for a major depressive episode. The raw score is easily calculated and then the appropriate qualitative descriptor is determined using the associated manual (Beck, Steer, & Brown, 1996).

One of the advantages of the BDI-II, its face validity, is also a potential drawback if a client wishes to inaccurately portray their symptoms. It is quite easy for a client to understand what the BDI-II is assessing for and to potentially "fake good" or "fake bad." There are no validity scales within the BDI-II and the counselor must rely on the client to be an accurate reporter of their experience. The BDI-II can be used in several fashions: as a screening instrument at intake, a tool to quickly identify the presence and severity of a range of depressive symptoms to clarify diagnosis and inform treatment, and to track symptoms throughout the course of treatment. The BDI-II is appropriate for clients age 13–80, who have at least a 5th grade reading level capacity, and are not under an assessment circumstance in which they have motivation to misrepresent their symptoms (i.e., competency evaluation, etc.). For clients younger than 13, the Beck Youth Inventories-2 (BYI-2) contain five inventories, one of which assesses depressive symptoms, and the BYI-2 is appropriate for children ages 7–18. The depression inventory of the BYI-2 is similar to the BDI-II in content but the items are set up differently: each item contains a statement of a depressive symptom and the child reports how frequently that statement has been true for them in the previous two weeks.

Given that a potential symptom of depressive episodes is suicidal ideation, it is expected that the BDI-II (and the BYI-2) assess for the presence and intensity of suicidal ideation. Given that the BDI-II can be used in a variety of scenarios (i.e., screening, tracking, etc.), it is absolutely necessary to review the response to the item regarding suicidal ideation before a client departs from the session so that the counselor can follow-up and appropriately assess, and engage in collaborative safety planning, if necessary. However, the BDI-II should not replace inquiring about a client's potential suicidal ideation during the course of a session. For a variety of reasons clients may not accurately report their level of suicidal ideation on the BDI-II and it is the counselor's responsibility to use both the BDI-II *and* their clinical skills within a session to fully assess suicidal ideation.

Mood Disorder Questionnaire

The assessment of bipolar I or bipolar II disorder involves determining if there is presence of symptoms that encompass a manic or hypomanic episode, respectively, in addition to the presence of a previous/current depressive episode(s). Unfortunately for counselors, fewer assessment tools exist for measurement of bipolar disorders compared to depressive disorders and some of the existing assessments (e.g., Millon Clinical Multiaxial Inventory-IV, Minnesota Multiphasic Personality Inventory-2) that assess for manic/hypomanic symptoms are "C" level, requiring a doctoral degree and/or advanced clinical training. Fuller exploration into assessment tools for bipolar disorders also exist (cf. Miller, Johnson, & Eisner, 2009). An accessible and appropriate assessment tool for counselors is the Mood Disorder Questionnaire (MDQ; Hirschfeld et al., 2000) which can be used as a screening tool and can guide a counselor's further in-session exploration of which manic/hypomanic symptoms are of the greatest concern. The MDQ asks clients to respond to 15 items, 13 of which are common manic/hypomanic symptoms in which the client answers "yes" or "no" as to whether they have experienced that symptom. The final two items on the MDQ inquire if these symptoms have occurred within the same time frame and the client's perception of how much of a problem these symptoms caused them. The scoring of the MDQ is quite simple and the creators determined that the endorsement of seven or more symptoms is the optimal cut-off to detect the likely presence of a current or past manic/hypomanic episode.

The most prominent advantages of the MDQ are accessibility (i.e., it is publicly available), face validity, and ease of scoring. However, much like the BDI-II, the MDQ's advantages also serve as its drawbacks. The face validity of the MDQ allow for misrepresentation of symptoms, whether intentional or unintentional. The other main drawback of the MDQ is that it is only appropriate to be used as a screening tool. The MDQ can certainly assist counselors by providing guidance of what manic symptoms the client has experienced so that the counselor can further discuss the experience and context of these symptoms within session. This follow-up of endorsed items from the MDQ is crucial as many of the items can be alternatively explained by situations that are not a manic/hypomanic episode. For example, one item is the statement "you were much more interested in sex than usual," which assesses for hypersexual behavior that is sometimes present in manic/hypomanic episodes; however this behavior could also be explained by a more normative event such as beginning a new dating relationship with a partner. The MDQ is appropriate for clients aged 18–80 and for the purposes of screening only. Given that the MDQ is not to be used to determine the presence or absence of a bipolar disorder, it is inappropriate to use this as a diagnostic tool, particularly because the results of the MDQ without the context of other assessment procedures could lead to inaccurate conclusions regarding a bipolar disorder diagnosis.

Anxiety Disorders

Anxiety disorders come in many forms, including Specific Phobias, Social Anxiety Disorder, Panic Disorder, and Generalized Anxiety Disorder, among others (American Psychiatric Association, 2013). Given the overlap between symptoms of these various conditions, counselors may find the process of identifying the specific constellation of symptoms and coinciding diagnosis to be easier when formal measures are integrated into the assessment process. Several brief and common-sense assessments exist for the measurement of symptoms common across anxiety disorders, including the Beck Anxiety Inventory (BAI; Beck & Steer, 1993), the State-Trait Anxiety Inventory (STAI; Spielberger, Gorsuch, Lushene, Vagg, & Jacobs, 1983), the Hamilton Anxiety Rating Scale (HAM-A; Hamilton, 1959), and the Panic and Agoraphobia Scale (PAS; Bandelow, 1999). Given that the BAI has a similar format to the previously discussed BDI-II, the current section on the measurement of anxiety disorders will focus on the STAI and the PAS instead. Of note though regarding the BAI, it is to be used a screening instrument only, not a diagnostic tool.

State-Trait Anxiety Inventory

The STAI (Form Y) differentiates itself from other assessments of psychological conditions because it assesses both an acute/temporary experience (i.e., state) of anxiety as well as a longstanding/pervasive experience (i.e., trait) of anxiety. The STAI contains 40 items, 20 measuring state anxiety and 20 measuring trait anxiety, which the client responds to regarding the frequency of the particular experience on a 4-point scale ranging from "Almost Never" to "Almost Always." The STAI is easily scored and results provide information on the level of both acute and longstanding experiences of anxiety.

The brevity and simplicity of the STAI make it ideal for the purposes of screening, diagnostic clarification, and tracking. Additionally, the two-pronged focus of the items allow counselors to differentiate acute experiences of anxiety to longstanding predispositions to experience anxiety. An additional benefit of the STAI is that it has been translated into a variety of languages making it a great option for counselors working with diverse clientele. Similar to many of the previously discussed tests in this chapter, the STAI does not contain any validity scales and it is face valid, so once again it provides an opportunity for clients to misrepresent their symptoms, if they wish. The STAI is appropriate for individuals who are 16 years of age or older and who have at least a 6th grade reading level.

Panic and Agoraphobia Scale

The experience of a panic attack is a distinct and separate clinical syndrome that is separate from the generalized sense of anxiety seen in Generalized Anxiety Disorder (American Psychiatric Association, 2013). It is not uncommon for the term "panic attack" to be used by lay persons and mental health professionals to describe an experience of heightened anxiety but that does not meet the criteria for a panic attack, as defined in the DSM-5. Therefore, the assessment of Panic Disorder is facilitated by the use of the Panic and Agoraphobia Scale (PAS; Bandelow, 1999), a brief and simple measure of symptoms associated with Panic Disorder. The PAS contains 13 items in which the client reports the presence/level of intensity of each particular symptom. Client responses allow the counselor to measure the experience of a panic attack, anticipatory anxiety, agoraphobic avoidance, level of impairment caused by the symptoms, and concerns over one's health. The PAS comes in both self-rated and observer-rated forms and is simple to score and interpret.

The PAS is an ideal tool for diagnostic clarification and tracking purposes due to its brevity and simple format. Additionally, it is available in a variety of languages. However, as previously discussed regarding the MDQ, endorsed items should be further discussed within session as the context in which the potential symptom occurred may clarify if the symptom is indeed evidence of a panic attack or if it is better explained by other circumstances. The PAS is appropriate for clients aged 15 and older who are able to reliably report their experiences of anxiety.

Trauma Disorders

Trauma Symptom Inventory-2

The timely and accurate identification of Posttraumatic Stress Disorder (PTSD) or a related diagnosis is critical given that a variety of effective treatments exist for the treatment of PTSD, as identified by the International Society for Traumatic Stress Studies (Foa, Keane, Friedman, & Cohen, 2008). Once again, the symptoms of PTSD overlap with other psychological conditions (i.e., Major Depressive Disorder, Generalized Anxiety Disorder, Panic Disorder) and some clinicians may find themselves overwhelmed by multifaceted diagnostic criteria laid out in the DSM-5. Although it is usually clear to both the client and counselor when criterion A has been met (e.g., exposure to a traumatic event), fully assessing for symptoms of intrusion, persistent avoidance, negative alternations in mood and cognition, and hyperarousal require keen familiarity with the diagnosis. Compared to the tests that have been discussed so far in this chapter, the Trauma Symptom Inventory-2 (TSI-2; Briere, 1995) is longer and more comprehensive in its ability to measure a variety of symptoms and experiences associated with trauma-related disorders. The TSI-2 contains 136 items that assess for the presence of posttraumatic symptoms associated with a variety of traumatic events (e.g., physical and sexual assault, combat, motor vehicle accidents, intimate partner violence, etc.) and takes about 20 minutes for a client to complete. Clients report the frequency of each particular symptom, in the past six months, on a four-point scale ranging from "never" to "often." The TSI-2 contains 12 clinical scales and associated subscales and two validity scales. Clinical scales include: anxious arousal, depression, anger, intrusive experiences, defensive avoidance, dissociation, somatic preoccupations, sexual disturbance, suicidality, insecure attachment, impaired self-reference, and tension reduction behavior. Additionally, the TSI-2 measures four overarching factors: self-disturbance, posttraumatic stress, externalization, and somatization. Validity scales allow for the measurement of potential under/over-endorsement and random/inconsistent responding. The TSI-2 is computer scored in which raw scores are converted to T-scores to facilitate detection of elevated clinical scales.

A clear advantage of the TSI-2 is the measurement of a broad range of symptoms related to a diagnosis of PTSD, which allows a counselor to have a comprehensive understanding of the sequelae of trauma for the client. Additionally, the TSI-2's validity scales provide a clinician with normed guidelines to better evaluate the potential for under- or over-reporting of symptomology. Although not as brief compared to previously discussed measures in this chapter, the TSI-2 can still be used to track the effectiveness of clinical interventions. A potential drawback is the necessity for a client to accurately report a variety of symptoms, some of which can be difficult to accurately report given the nature of the symptom (e.g., disassociation).

The TSI-2 is appropriate for clients 18–88 years of age who have experienced a traumatic incident. Companion versions of the TSI-2 exist for younger populations: the Trauma Symptom Checklist for Children (TSCC) for children 8–16 years of age and the Trauma Symptom Checklist for Young Children (TSCYC) for children 3–12 years of age. The TSCC and TSCYC contain fewer items compared to the TSI-2 and the TSCYC is filled out by a caretaker of the child client. Similar to the BDI-2, the TSI-2 and companion child versions contain items related to suicidal ideation. These items should always be followed up upon within session and never be solely relied upon as an infallible report of a client's suicidal ideation.

Eating Disorders

Eating Disorder Inventory-3

The timely detection of eating disorders such Anorexia Nervosa and Bulimia Nervosa is essential, given the potential for grave physical and psychological consequences of the diagnoses. Additionally, individuals with such diagnoses typically have a period of changed eating behavior prior to fully meeting DSM-5 criteria for such disorders (American Psychiatric Association, 2013), which can allow clinicians to engage in early detection and intervention. The Eating Disorder Inventory-3 (EDI-3; Garner, 2004) and associated Checklist (EDI-3 SC) are self-report measures that assist counselors in the identification of a variety of behaviors connected to DSM-5 criteria for various eating disorders as well as patterns of behavior that are theoretically associated with eating disorders. The EDI-3 takes about 20 minutes to complete and contains 91 items in which the client reports the frequency of each particular behavior. The EDI-3 is computer scored and results in three validity scales, 12 clinical scales (i.e., Drive for Thinness, Bulimia, Body Dissatisfaction, Low Self-Esteem, Personal Alienation, Interpersonal Insecurity, Interpersonal Alienation, Interoceptive Deficits, Emotional Dysregulation, Perfectionism, Asceticism, and Maturity Fears), and six composite scale scores. The EDI-3 SC is taken separately and asks clients to report the frequency of various behaviors (i.e., self-induced purging behaviors, binge eating, etc.) to assist the counselor in determination of an appropriate DSM-5 diagnosis.

The benefit of using the EDI-3 and EDI-3 SC when working with a client with eating disorder symptoms is the ability to identify which particular eating disorder behaviors are most prevalent as well as overarching behavioral patterns (i.e., Overcontrol, Interpersonal Problems, etc.) that likely will benefit from clinical intervention. Certainly, the EDI-3 and EDI-3 SC rely on clients to be forthcoming and accurate historians of their behavior and, as such, a client could choose to misrepresent their experiences while self-reporting. However, given that the EDI-3 contains three validity scales, such misreporting (i.e., over-reporting, under-reporting) will likely be identified by these scales. However, the EDI-3 SC does not contain validity scales and the counselor must rely on the client to accurately report the frequency of various behaviors.

The EDI-3 and EDI-3 SC are appropriate for clients aged 13 through 53 and who have at least an 8th grading reading level and are most beneficial when a counselor would like to know how various eating disorder behaviors and related thoughts coalesce into behavior and thought patterns to be targeted within therapy. Given that the EDI-3 takes around 20 minutes to complete, it is not the best measure to be used in a screening fashion. However, the EDI-3 Referral Form (EDI-3 RF) is an abbreviated form that takes between five and 10 minutes to complete and can assist counselors in screening for potential eating disorder behaviors and associated psychological symptoms.

Psychotic Disorders

Counselors looking for brief, self-report measures that assess symptoms associated with schizophrenia and other psychotic disorders will be disappointed to learn that such measures are not common or easily accessible. Within broad-focus measures such as the Minnesota Multiphasic Personality Inventory-2 (MMPI-2) and the Personality Assessment Inventory (PAI), that are of the "C" level of classification, various scales measure the presence of self-reported experiences, behaviors, and thoughts associated with psychotic symptoms. The challenge for counselors is that they may not have the needed education and training in order to administer, score, and interpret the MMPI-2 or PAI for the purposes of better understanding a client's experience of psychotic symptoms. Further, the assessment of symptoms associated with psychosis is complicated because reduced insight into symptoms and functioning is a common feature of schizophrenia, for example, which leads these individuals to misestimate their symptoms when compared to clinician ratings (Durand et al., 2015). Due to these constraints (i.e., reduced client ability to accurately self-report and prevalence of "C" level measures), the author presents the option of the Brief Psychiatric Rating Scale (BPRS; Ventura et al., 1993). Of note, the Positive and Negative Syndrome Scale (PANSS; van der Gaag et al., 2006) is another widely used, clinician-report measure that is similar to the BPRS.

Brief Psychiatric Rating Scale

The BPRS (Version 4.0) contains 24 items that assess the presence and level of severity of various behaviors associated with psychosis in a semi-structured interview format. The clinician rates the presence/severity of each behavior in the past several days, on a seven-point rating scale that contains behavioral anchors to improve rater reliability and validity. Areas of assessment include hostility, hallucinations, self-neglect, blunted affect, and other behavioral, cognitive, and affective experiences associated with psychosis. Some of the areas require inquiry into the client's experience and others can be rated through behavioral observation alone. The clinician may also inquire with family/friends/close contacts of the client to further clarify the presence of various behaviors. Higher scores indicate the presence of more and/or greater severity of various symptoms associated with psychotic behavior. Completing the BPRS may take between 20 to 45 minutes, depending on the client's level of disclosure.

The BPRS is unique among the other measures presented in this chapter because of the observer-rater format. This format and the area of focus (e.g., psychotic disorders) requires additional training and experience prior to use because the ability to identify and rate behaviors accurately requires knowledge of common behaviors associated with psychosis such as the ways in which people experience ideas of reference, common delusions, the use of neologisms, and stereotyped mannerisms. A clear advantage of the BPRS is the semi-structured interview format with behavioral anchors within the rating scales which facilitate depth of symptoms exploration while balancing this with a format that ensures strong reliability. Additionally, the use of behavioral observation and observer completion is appropriate given documented difficulties with insight and accurate self-rating within the population of individuals with psychotic disorders. The drawback of the observer rating format though is that completing the BPRS takes more time compared to traditional, self-report measures and may take up to an entire session to complete. Additionally, although research suggests that individuals with a less clinical experience can utilize the BPRS in a reliable and valid fashion, particularly when using a structured interview guide, additional training and supervision is needed before using the BPRS (Crippa, Sanches, Hallak, Loureiro, & Zuardi, 2001).

The BPRS is appropriate for adults where there is evidence of psychotic symptoms. Given time constraints that most counselors face, the BPRS is best used to identify and clarify the presence of various psychotic symptoms to assist in diagnosis, case conceptualization, and treatment planning. With practice and a well-formed therapeutic relationship, the BPRS could also be given in an expedient manner to support a counselor in tracking progress in the reduction of symptoms throughout the course of therapy.

Case Study

The following fictional case study is an opportunity to review circumstances of a prototypical outpatient clinical case and explore how objective, narrow-focus assessment would be selected, administered, scored, interpreted, and integrated into the clinical work. This case study example will focus on Natasha, a 20-year-old, cis-female, African American college student who is seeking therapy at a local community mental health agency.

Referral Reason

Natasha self-referred to a community mental health agency upon recommendation from her academic advisor at her community college. Ms. Ramirez, Natasha's academic advisor, provided Natasha with a pamphlet about the local community mental health agency after Natasha disclosed some of her current life stressors during a routine academic advising session.

Current and Historical Circumstances

Natasha is currently enrolled in the nursing program at the community college near her home. Natasha had planned to pursue nursing after high school and had originally looked at out-of-state colleges; however, Natasha's parents encouraged her to consider staying local for her college education so that she could live at home and support her family, emotionally and physically. Natasha's father had been struggling with several chronic illnesses in the past 10 years and Natasha took on many roles as her father's health declined, such as caring for the home and lending financial support to her family. Additionally, Natasha's cousin, Farrah, and Farrah's one-year-old daughter recently moved in with Natasha and her parents due to conflict between Farrah and Natasha's aunt. Natasha finds herself caring for Farrah's daughter on a regular basis, on top of working, school, caring for her father, and caring for the family home.

Natasha had maintained high marks in her courses during her first year in college, however, the previous two semesters her grades have been declining, and she failed a foundational nursing course that is a prerequisite to several other nursing courses. While meeting with her academic advisor, Ms. Ramirez, Natasha casually disclosed the various other obligations outside of school that were making it difficult for her to find time to study and attend class. Ms. Ramirez suggested Natasha considering "taking care of herself so she can better care for her family and progress through the nursing program" and attend individual therapy. Natasha initially balked at the suggestion and shared that she simply needed to "set better boundaries" and "manage time more effectively." However, after several more stressful weeks at home, Natasha reconsidered the suggestion and thought it would be helpful to have someone "outside" of the family to talk to.

At Natasha's intake appointment, she discussed the stressors in her life and discussed how she wanted to learn how to cope with life stressors more effectively. The intake counselor remarked how "composed" Natasha was considering all that she was balancing and that she would "probably only need a few sessions of therapy" to help get her back to her prior level of functioning. Natasha then began meeting with Greg, her counselor, on a bi-weekly basis. The first sessions were spent building rapport and providing Natasha with a space to feel heard and understood. However, after three months of regular appointments, Natasha hesitantly voiced concern with Greg that life "didn't seem to be getting any easier" and that she found herself still entrenched in familiar patterns with her schoolwork that had led to poor grades in the past. Greg was somewhat surprised himself; he had initially viewed Natasha as an "uncomplicated" client, due to the lack of previous mental health concerns, lack of family mental health history, and the relatively short duration of her current difficulties. Greg had based his treatment plan and case conceptualization around the initial information collected by the intake therapist, who has assigned a diagnosis of Adjustment Disorder, Unspecified and assumed that psychoeducation on time management and boundary setting, along with assertiveness training, would help resolve her difficulties.

Feeling "stuck" and wondering if he was "missing something," Greg considered that Natasha may be experiencing symptoms of a major depressive episode. At their next appointment, Greg introduced his hypothesis that Natasha may be "depressed" and Natasha audibly laughed at the suggestion and stated, "Look at me and all that I get done in a given day, that's not what 'depressed people' are like." Greg validated Natasha's experience and also suggested that "depression can look different for different people" and he began considering if the use of a formal, objective assessment was appropriate for the current clinical situation.

Application of Assessment

Greg shared with Natasha that counselors have different ways to understand the experiences of their clients and that counselors occasionally use "questionnaires" to better understand how their clients are feeling and how their experiences compare to other people. Greg shared that he would like Natasha to take a brief questionnaire about her thoughts, emotions, and behaviors so that he could better understand Natasha's experience and that, after taking it, they would discuss the results and explore how they may impact their work together. He asked Natasha if she was open to the process and what questions she may have. Natasha replied that she was happy to take the questionnaire and reported that she did not have any questions.

Greg selected the Beck Depression Inventory-II (BDI-II) as the most appropriate assessment for the purpose of obtaining a better understanding of Natasha's potential depressive experiences and so that it could be used to track progress in therapy to better understand how their work in therapy impacted her potential depressive symptoms. Additionally, Greg would be able to ethically administer the BDI-II given his master's degree in Clinical Mental Health Counseling, which included relevant coursework in appraisal and assessment and due to his internship experiences where he regularly administered, scored, and interpreted the

BDI–II under the supervision of his internship supervisor. Lastly, the BDI–II was practical given that his agency had purchased the BDI–II and that it would only take a brief amount of time to administer (~5 minutes) so that Greg and Natasha would not take up their valuable time in-session with assessment administration.

At their next assessment appointment, Greg reminded Natasha of the plan to take the "questionnaire" and once again reminded Natasha that there were "no right or wrong answers" and that she should answer honestly because it helped Greg better understand her experiences. Natasha took the BDI–II and, when she completed it, Greg asked Natasha what questions and reactions she had after taking it. Natasha reported that she had none, that it seemed "pretty straightforward," and that today she wanted to focus on a recent issue at home with Farrah and her mother, who got into a heated argument the night before. Greg shared that he would score the assessment before their next session and discuss the results then; however, before Greg put the assessment away on his desk, he glanced at the item related to suicidal ideation and noted that she selected "0" for that item, indicating that she had not had thoughts of killing herself in the previous two weeks. Greg and Natasha continued on with their session as planned and he also checked in with Natasha about any current or recent thoughts of suicide. Even though she has responded that she had not on the BDI–II, Greg knew that clients did not always feel comfortable putting such experiences into written form, so he knew that he should also ask in the context of their current conversation within the session. Natasha confirmed her BDI–II response and reported that she had not had any suicidal idea that day or recently.

Later that day, Greg scored Natasha's BDI–II by adding up the raw score based on her responses and then finding the appropriate table in the Beck Depression Inventory-II manual (Beck, Steer, & Brown, 1996) so he could determine the qualitative descriptor associated with her self-reported level of symptoms. Natasha's raw score was 22 with an associated qualitative descriptor of "moderate depression." Greg was somewhat surprised; given his interactions with Natasha, he did not suspect she would fall into a "moderate" category. Greg reviewed Natasha's individual answers on the BDI-II to determine which items she scored the highest on. Greg noted that she reported her highest scores on items such as "I get very little pleasure from things I used to enjoy," "It's hard to get interested in anything," and "I find I can't concentrate on anything." Greg observed that she reported moderate to severe levels (e.g., scores of 2 or 3) on items related to anhedonia, irritability, concentration, fatigue, and sleep. Greg observed that she did not endorse items related to suicidal ideation, crying, or sadness, and surmised that this is why Natasha initially was perplexed by Greg's inquiry into potential depressive symptoms, as Natasha's conceptualization of "depression" may be dominated by the symptoms that many lay people associate with depression (i.e., feeling sad, thinking about suicide, crying, etc.).

At their next appointment, Greg reminded Natasha of the assessment and suggested they spend the first part of their session discussing the results. What follows is an excerpt from their dialogue from this part of the session.

Greg:	So, I had a chance to score the questionnaire that you filled out during our last session and I thought we could discuss that today in session. The questionnaire asked you about your experiences and they were all related to the common types of experiences people have when they experience depression.
Natasha:	Oh, that's what I figured because some of those questions were kind of obvious, like … are you crying a lot or whatever. But other questions were just kind of … normal I guess, or at least about stuff that is normal for me.
Greg:	What type of questions felt "normal" for you?

Natasha:	There was a question about not finding things fun anymore, I think? Something like that. Buy yeah, it made me think about how I used to love working out with my mom, we would go to the gym most mornings together. But I kind of stopped going with her because I just wasn't having fun with it anymore, not to mention I've felt so much more tired lately, it's been hard to just get going in the morning anyways. Oh yeah, and school used to be lots of fun for me, I loved going to class and learning new things. Now I really just feel uninterested in it all.
Greg:	You've lost enjoyment of working out with your mom and school and you've been feeling more drained lately it sounds like. What else resonated with your experiences from the questionnaire?
Natasha:	There was a question about sleep too . . . I've been sleeping pretty badly lately. At first I thought it was just because Farrah and her baby live with us, but the more I thought about it, I realized that I've been having problems falling asleep long before they moved in. And then sometimes I wake up in the morning, earlier than I planned to get up and I just can't get back to sleep. But then I'm still exhausted all day long!
Greg:	What you're sharing with me right now resonates with the results of the questionnaire, your responses on the questionnaire suggested that you're actually experiencing a moderate level of depressive symptoms, compared to other adults. What is your reaction to hearing that?
Natasha:	Hmph, really? Like I said, I'm not crying or thinking about killing myself or anything . . . I guess I'm just exhausted and bored . . . and like my brain just isn't working right. Like, when I sit down to read the assigned textbook chapters for class, it's like my brain can't retain any information. I read a page again and again and it's like nothing is sticking in here.
Greg:	What I hear you saying is that you don't feel like you fit the mold of a person who is feeling "depressed," but that you have noticed this pattern of experiences, like fatigue, feeling uninterested, trouble sleeping, and having a hard time concentrating.
Natasha:	Yes, exactly . . . I mean, is that depression? I thought that was just a normal reaction to life.
Greg:	Certainly people can experience fatigue and the other things you just mentioned, however, the results of this assessment suggest that you're experiencing a variety of different things on a consistent basis that aligns with the experience of depression. What are your reactions to hearing this?
Natasha:	I mean . . . I dunno. Like I said, I don't think of myself as "depressed." You said something last time, like "different people are depressed in different ways" or something like that. I guess what you're saying is that I'm depressed? It's just a different way of feeling depressed?
Greg:	Yes, in a way, I suppose what this assessment and our conversation right now is telling me is that you're experiencing a variety of symptoms associated with depression, and even though they may not be the "prototypical" symptoms like crying or feeling sad, you're certainly experiencing symptoms that are probably making your life more difficult to navigate right now, particularly with all the stressors lately.
Natasha:	Well . . . that sucks for me. There's a weird comfort in hearing this though, it's like . . . it's not just me not trying hard enough or something. Sometimes I feel that way, like if I just tried harder, then I wouldn't be having such a hard time getting school stuff done and helping with my family.

Greg: What you're saying is that this is validating for you?

Natasha: Yes, it is . . . what does that mean for therapy though?

The session continued on and Greg discussed how he was already finding their conversation to be productive and to help him better understand Natasha's experiences. Greg spent the remainder of the session further exploring her experiences of depressive symptoms regarding their onset and impact. Greg later updated Natasha's diagnosis and updated her treatment plan to reflect her updated diagnosis of Major Depressive Disorder, Moderate. Greg's treatment plan for Natasha shifted from a solution-focused approach to coping with her current stressors to examining Natasha's underlying thought patterns and how experiences of resentment toward her family were impacting her and how the separation–individual process felt "stuck" for her. Natasha continued to attend therapy and began implementing changes in her life based on discussions from therapy and found that she was having an easier time focusing in school and she had more energy on a daily basis.

Test Your Knowledge:

1. Which of the following is not a narrow-focus assessment?
   a. Mood Disorder Questionnaire
   b. Behavior Assessment System for Children
   c. Beck Anxiety Inventory
   d. Brief Psychiatric Rating Scale

2. The PAI and MMPI-2 are both:
   a. "A" level assessments
   b. "B" level assessment
   c. "C" level assessment
   d. Unclassified assessments

3. Which of the following assessments is given in a semi-structured interview format?
   a. Trauma Symptom Inventory
   b. Beck Depression Inventory
   c. Panic and Agoraphobia Scale
   d. Brief Psychiatric Rating Scale

4. The Beck Depression Inventory-II provides subscales to further understand client experiences of depression.
   T or F?

5. Which of the following assessments is only appropriate to be used as a screening tool?
   a. Mood Disorder Questionnaire
   b. Beck Depression Inventory
   c. Trauma Symptom Inventory
   d. State-Trait Anxiety Inventory

6. Which of the following is *not* a difference between the Trauma Symptom Checklist for Young Children (TSCYC) and the Trauma Symptom Checklist for Children (TSCC)?
   a. The TSCC is appropriate for teens up to 16 whereas the TSCYC is appropriate for children up to 12
   b. The TSCYC is to be filled out by a caretaker whereas the TSCC is self-report

    c.   The TSCYC contains validity scales and the TSCC does not

    d.   The TSCYC is appropriate for children as young as 3 whereas the TSCC is appropriate for children as young as 8

7. The EDI-3 is appropriate to use as a screening tool.
T or F?

8. What is the most important reason to review the results of the BDI-II before a client departs from the session?

    a.   Clients want to know the "results" as soon as possible

    b.   To ask the client what questions or difficulties they had when completing the assessment

    c.   To review the response for items related to suicidal ideation as a part of the routine process of assessing risk

    d.   Out of curiosity to see what the client reported

9. Which of the following is a reason why the BPRS utilizes an observer report format?

    a.   Clients with psychotic disorders may have reduced insight into their own behaviors, cognitions, and emotions

    b.   Clients with psychotic disorders do not like completing self-report assessments

    c.   Counselors who work with clients with psychotic disorders prefer observer report styles

    d.   The BPRS only inquiries about observable behavior

10. The Panic and Agoraphobia Scale is useful because some individuals report having "panic attacks" when, rather, they experienced a time of heightened anxiety that does not constitute a DSM-5 description of a panic attack.
T or F?

Discussion Questions/Prompts:

1. What clinical situations and times are you mostly likely to use objective, narrow-focus assessment and why? What clinical situation and times are you least likely to use objective, narrow-focus assessment and why?

2. Given your current clinical work, what types of objective, narrow-focus assessments are you most likely to utilize? Do you have access to these and, if not, how would you obtain access?

3. How would you introduce the topic of conducting assessment with a client such as Natasha? Role play with a colleague how you would introduce the topic and have your colleague ask common questions about the assessment process.

4. If you were Natasha's counselor, what ethical, multicultural, and practical aspects would you consider before deciding upon the best assessment to use in the situation?

5. How confident do you feel regarding your ability to utilize objective, narrow-focused assessment when it is appropriate? What steps can you take to increase your confidence in this clinical skill area?

9 Intelligence Testing
WISC-V

Tyler Wilkinson

For centuries humans have been interested in measuring human intellectual ability (Neukrug & Fawcett, 2015). Some of the earliest tests of individuals focused on measuring mental abilities and intelligence (Gregory, 2013; Neukrug & Fawcett, 2015). In 1905 Alfred Binet invented the first modern intelligence test with his colleague Theodore Simon (Neukrug & Fawcett, 2015) in Paris to respond to new French laws mandating Universal education (Gregory, 2013). The French administration wanted a standardized method to help identify children who may have difficulties learning from typical instructional methods (Wechsler, Raiford, & Holdnack, 2014). The development of this type of test has been considered the beginning of the special education classroom (Gregory, 2013).

This chapter will provide a brief overview of the history of intelligence testing and specifically of the development of the Wechsler Intelligence Scale for Children-Fifth Edition (WISC-V; Wechsler, Raiford, & Holdnack, 2014), one of the most frequently used measures of intelligence. After an overview of the instrument a case study will be presented that will help contextualize the results and provide the reader an opportunity to interpret results within a presenting context. The reader will be provided cursory results of a fictitious client in which quantitative and qualitative data of the WISC-V will be given. Finally, the results will be integrated with the case study in order to provide the reader with an understanding of how to develop feedback and clinical considerations when using the WISC-V.

Intelligence Testing Overview

Since the emergence of intelligence testing in the early 20th century, it has quickly become a highly researched and debated area in the field of psychology and counseling (Gregory, 2013). After the publication of the Binet-Simon test of intelligence in 1905, the use of intelligence testing expanded quickly to the United States due in part to Henry Goddard, who translated the Binet-Simon test (Gregory, 2013) in order to identify immigrants who may be classified as "feebleminded" (see Farreras, 2014). However, it wasn't until Lewis Terman introduced the concept of the intelligence quotient (IQ) and revised the Binet-Simon scales in 1916 that the test become popularized (Gregory, 2013; Neukrug & Fawcett, 2015; Wechsler, Raiford, & Holdnack, 2014). When Terman the revised the test in 1916 the test took on the name as it is currently known, the Stanford-Binet scales, as Terman was a professor at Stanford University (Neukrug & Fawcett, 2015).

As research regarding theories of intelligence developed, David Wechsler recognized a need for more discrete measures of intelligence (Wechsler, Raiford, & Holdnack, 2014) that included performance-based measures of intelligence (Kaplan & Sacuzzo, 2001). Wechsler (1940) felt that the measures of intelligence at that time did not appropriately assess how well an individual is able to deal with the environment, which he called "non-intellective" measures of intelligence. As such, he developed his original intelligence test, the Wechsler-Bellevue Intelligence Scale, in 1939 (Wechsler, Raiford, & Holdnack, 2014). Today, there are three different types of Wechsler intelligence tests that are designed for various age groups (Whiston, 2017): the Wechsler Preschool and Primary Scale of Intelligence-Fourth Edition (WPPSI-IV; Wechsler, 2012) for individuals ages 2 years, 6 months through 7 years, 7 months; the Wechsler Intelligence Scale for Children-Fifth Edition (WISC-V; Wechsler, Raiford, & Holdnack, 2014) for individuals ages 6 years, 0 months through 16 years, 11 months old; and the Wechsler Adult Intelligence Scale-Fourth Edition (WAIS-IV; Wechsler, 2008). Today, the Wechsler scales are some of the most widely used measures of intelligence (Neukrug & Fawcett, 2015). In fact, according to a recent survey of counselors (Peterson, Lomas, Neukrug, & Bonner, 2014), the WISC was identified as one of the top 10 assessments used by all counselors and one of the top five assessments used by school counselors, in particular. Because of the frequency of use of the WISC-V in educational contexts and the extensive research surrounding this test, many counselors should have a basic understanding of how to understand the results. It should be noted that the Wechsler series of instruments are quite complex and typically require extensive training. Often, these tests are administered by psychologists and anyone using this instrument should make sure they are doing so under the supervision of someone qualified to administer it (Whiston, 2017).

Wechsler Intelligence Scale for Children, Fifth Edition (WISC-V)

The Wechsler Intelligence Scale for Children, Fifth Edition (WISC-V; Wechsler, Raiford, & Holdnack, 2014) is an intelligence test administered to children between the ages of 6–16. The WISC-V has been demonstrated to be a useful tool in the identification of specific learning disabilities, intellectual disabilities, and placement in specialized programs (e.g., gifted programs; Wechsler, Raiford, & Holdnack, 2014; see Table 9.1).

The study of intelligence and its theories is an extensive field that goes beyond the scope of this chapter. A brief review over theories that have influenced the WISC-V development will be discussed; however, readers are encouraged to review other sources (e.g., Gregory, 2013; Whiston, 2017) for further information on the various theories of intelligence. The WISC-V is developed around various structural theories of intelligence (Whiston, 2017) such as Spearman's general factor of intelligence (Spearman, 1904) and the Cattell-Horn-Caroll framework (CHC; Gregory, 2013; Neukrug & Fawcett, 2015). The CHC framework introduced an understanding of broad and narrow abilities within the general factor of intelligence, such as fluid intelligence (Gf) and crystallized intelligence (Gc), that has led many professionals to consider the CHC to have the strongest empirical foundation for any theory of intelligence (Gregory, 2013). Moreover, the CHC framework has greatly influenced the development of the WISC-V, which has led to the current structure of the scales and the specific types of cognitive abilities assessed (Wechsler, Raiford, & Holdnack, 2014). Additionally, modern understanding of cognitive abilities, neurodevelopment, and statistical analysis, such as factor analysis, have influenced the WISC-V development (Whiston, 2017).

Table 9.1 Key Characteristics of WISC-V

Type of Instrument	Strengths	Weaknesses	Ideal Populations	Typical Referral Questions
Individual Intelligence Test	Psychometrics are well researched Multiple levels of information	Complex to interpret Requires specialized training Can be expensive	Children aged 6–16	Cognitive Abilities Intellectual Aptitude Specific Learning Disabilities Placement in specialized education

The WISC-V does not merely provide a measure of general intelligence (*g*). Rather, the WISC-V consists of four levels of interpretation: Full Scale IQ (FSIQ), Primary Index Scales, Ancillary Index Scales, and Complementary Index Scales. Each level of interpretation is composed of multiple scales and each scale is a combination of different subtests (Wechsler, Raiford, & Holdnack, 2014). The WISC-V consists of a total of 21 different subtests that make up the different scales for the different levels of interpretation (see Figure 9.1 for a framework). There are 10 primary subtests: Block Design, Coding, Digit Span, Figure Weights, Matrix Reasoning, Picture Span, Similarities, Symbol Search, Visual Puzzles, and Vocabulary; six Secondary Subtests: Arithmetic, Cancelation, Comprehension, Information, Letter-number Sequencing, and Picture Concepts; and five complementary subtests: Delayed Symbol Translation, Immediate Symbol Translation, Naming Speed Literacy,

Full Scale IQ (FSIQ) and Primary Index Scales				
Verbal Comprehension Index (VCI)	Visual Spatial Index (VSI)	Fluid Reasoning Index (FRI)	Working Memory Index (WMI)	Processing Speed Index (PSI)
Similarities*	Block Design*	Matrix Reasoning*	Digit Span*	Coding*
Vocabulary*	Visual Puzzles	Figure Weights*	Picture Span	Symbol Search
NOTE: Subtests with * are used to derive FSIQ; the other subtests are used to find Primary Index Scales				

Ancillary Index Scales				
Quantitative Reasoning Index (QRI)	Auditory Working Memory Index (AWMI)	Nonverbal Index (NVI)	General Ability Index (GAI)	Cognitive Proficiency Index (CPI)
Figure Weights	Digit Span	Block Design	Similarities	Digit Span
Arithmetic	Letter-Number Sequencing	Visual Puzzles	Vocabulary	Picture Span
		Matrix Reasoning	Block Design	Coding
		Figure Weights	Matrix Reasoning	Symbol Search
		Picture Span	Figure Weights	
		Coding		

Complementary Index Scales				
	Naming Speed Index (NSI)	Symbol Translation Index (STI)	Storage and Retrieval Index (SRI)	
	Naming Speed Literacy	Immediate Symbol Translation	Naming Speed Index	
	Naming Speed Quantity	Delayed Symbol Translation	Symbol Translation Index	
		Recognition Symbol Translation		

Figure 9.1 Overall WISC-V Framework

Naming Speed Quantity, and Recognition Symbol Translation (Benson, 2014; Wechsler, Raiford, & Holdnack, 2014). The authors of the WISC-V recommend that the 10 primary subtests be administered as a comprehensive assessment of general intellectual ability (Wechsler, Raiford, & Holdnack, 2014). If more information is needed in the clinical decision-making process, the clinician can administer any of the six secondary subtests or five complementary subtests. The 10 primary subtests will yield the FSIQ, the Primary Index Scales, and three of the five Ancillary Index Scales. The reader should note that only seven subtests are used to derive the overall FSIQ. The secondary subtests may be used to derive the FSIQ if one of the primary subtests is missing or invalid. The substitution procedure is complex and reduces reliability of results. Familiarity with this process is needed prior to engaging the process (Wechsler, Raiford, & Holdnack, 2014). The secondary subtests are also used to derive the remaining Ancillary Index Scales. Finally, the complementary subtests are only used to find the Complementary Index scores.

The results of the WISC-V are provided using two types of age-corrected scores: scaled scores and standard scores. Scaled scores on the WISC-V have a mean of 10 and a standard deviation (*SD*) of 3. Raw scores on the specific subtests yield scaled score results. Standard scores on the WISC-V have a mean of 100 and *SD* of 15. Results of the FSIQ, the Primary Index Scales, the Secondary Index Scales, and the Complementary Index Scales all yield standard scores. These results can also be converted to percentile ranks so the individuals can be compared to others their same age. The range of possible standard scores on the FSIQ is between 40 and 160; this lower limit may be a possible limitation if one is assessing an individual with a potential moderate to severe intellectual disability (Benson, 2014). In addition, the WISC-V manual (Wechsler, Raiford, & Holdnack, 2014) suggests qualitative descriptors to attempt to describe the individuals' level of performance (see Table 9.2).

Standardization

Normative data of the WISC-V was collected over an approximate 12-month period with a final sample consisting of 2,200 children (Benson, 2014). Stratified random sampling was utilized using 2012 US Census data across the following variables: age, sex, race/ethnicity, parental educational level, and geographic region (Wechsler, Raiford, & Holdnack, 2014). There were 200 children divided across 11 different age groups (Whiston, 2017) in developing the sample to match proportions found in the Census. Additionally, a representative proportion of students with various special education classifications was included at each age level (Benson, 2014).

Reliability/Validity

The WISC-V technical and interpretive manual (Wechsler, Raiford, & Holdnack, 2014) includes extensive information on the reliability and validity of this particular instrument.

Table 9.2 Qualitative Descriptors of Scaled Scores

Composite Scaled Score Range	Qualitative Descriptor
130 and above	Extremely High
120–129	Very High
110–119	High Average
90–109	Average
80–89	Low Average
70–79	Very Low
69 and below	Extremely Low

The internal reliability estimates of the WISC-V are provided for every subtest and indices. The split-half method with a Spearman-Brown correction formula (Neukrug & Fawcett, 2015) was used to find the internal reliability estimates of the WISC-V (Wechsler, Raiford, & Holdnack, 2014). The internal consistency estimate for the FSIQ is .96. The Primary Index Scales have internal consistency coefficients that range from .88 to .93 while the subtests have estimates of internal consistency ranging from .80 to .94 (Benson, 2014; Wechsler, Raiford, & Holdnack, 2014; Whiston, 2017). Test-retest stability of the WISC-V was obtained through two administrations of the instrument to a sample of 218 children (Wechsler, Raiford, & Holdnack, 2014). The interval of time between the two administrations ranged between 9–82 days, with a mean interval of 26 days (Benson, 2014; Wechsler, Raiford, & Holdnack, 2014). The test-retest stability coefficients ranged from .71 (Picture Concepts) to .90 (Vocabulary) for the subtests (Benson, 2014). The Primary Index Scales have estimates ranging from .75 to .94. and the FSIQ has a stability estimate of .92 (Wechsler, Raiford, & Holdnack, 2014).

The technical and interpretive manual provides robust data for evidence of validity (Benson, 2014). The WISC-V provides evidence of validity with its internal structure as indicated by results from confirmatory factor analysis (CFA, Benson, 2014; Whiston, 2017). The technical and interpretation manual (Wechsler, Raiford, & Holdnack, 2014) provides evidence of convergent and discriminate validity with other instruments. There is some evidence for relationships with the WISC-V and other measures of intelligence, achievement, and adaptive behaviors (Benson, 2014), such as the Wechsler Intelligence Scale for Children-Fourth Edition (WISC-IV), the Wechsler Primary and Preschool Scale of Intelligence-Fourth Edition (WPPSI-IV), the Wechsler Individual Achievement Test-Third Edition (WIAT-III), and the Vineland Adaptive Behavior Scales-Second Edition (Vineland-II; Wechsler, Raiford, & Holdnack, 2014). For example, there is a correlation ($r = .86$) between the FSIQ results on the WISC-V and the previous revision of the instrument, the WISC-IV. Though the technical and interpretative manual provide evidence of correlations with other instruments (e.g., the Kauffman Assessment Battery of Children-Second Edition), some (Benson, 2014; Whiston, 2017) caution individuals regarding validity as the instrument is still new and the evidence of validity is just beginning to emerge. More research is needed on evidence to support the validity of interpretations and use of test scores from predictive and concurrent validity analyses (Benson, 2014).

Administration

Administration of the WISC-V requires extensive training and coursework before one should engage in the process (Whiston, 2017). Moreover, individuals can't purchase the WISC-V without providing the test publisher evidence of specialized training in assessment and testing (Pearson Clinical, n.d.). As previously mentioned, counselors are not typically responsible for administration of the WISC-V, as this is typically done by a psychologist (Whiston, 2017). The test takes approximately one hour to administer and derive the five primary index scores and the FSIQ (Carlson, Geisinger, & Jonson, 2014). The WISC-V can be administered via paper-pencil format or a new digital format through Q-interactive (Pearson Clinical, n.d.; Whiston, 2017). The digital format allows the WISC-V to be administered to a child using two iPads connected via Bluetooth. The test administrator can score and record responses, and control visual stimuli using one iPad. The child can use the other iPad to view and respond to stimuli in real time (Weiss, Saklofske, Holdnack, & Prifitera, 2016). This new technological advancement is being implemented in an effort to reduce administration errors (Weiss, Saklofske, Holdnack, & Prifitera, 2016).

Scoring Procedure

The scoring procedure for the WISC-V is complex (Whiston, 2017) and the details of these procedures go beyond the scope of this chapter. Entire publications (see Weiss, Saklofske, Holdnack, & Prifitera, 2016) are devoted to administration and scoring the WISC-V, where readers are directed for more information. The questions of the WISC-V are organized in order of difficulty as the individual progresses through the items (Whiston, 2017). The administrator is responsible for scoring the items of the subtests and the procedure varies based on the subtest. The administrator must be aware that one typically does not begin with the first item of the subtest. Each subtest has its own rules regarding the starting item; additionally, reversal rules and discontinuation rules exist, as the administrator has to establish basal levels and ceiling levels for each subtest (Weiss, Saklofske, Holdnack, & Prifitera, 2016; Whiston, 2017). Once the administration is completed, the administrator is responsible for the *clerical task* (Weiss, Saklofske, Holdnack, & Prifitera, 2016) of summing scores and converting them to standard scores. It is critical that when engaging in this *clerical task* that the administrator works to minimize error. It has been estimated (Hopwood & Richard, 2005) that administrator clerical error can impact FSIQ results by as much as 5.5 points per error.

Ethical Considerations

The WISC-V has been standardized with a stratified random sample across the variable of race/ethnicity, age, sex, parental level of education, and geographic location (Whiston, 2017). This sampling procedure assumes an approximation to the US Census based on the variables mentioned. Individuals should be mindful of how the norming data may be utilized when assessing individuals from groups that may not be clearly represented in the norm sample. For example, if a child presents from a racial or ethnic group that is underrepresented in the norming group, the clinicians would need to decide how to utilize this information when making interpretations.

Cultural differences in overall IQ scores have been a source of considerable attention for many decades (Neukrug & Fawcett, 2015), which has led to discussion in the literature on bias in testing (Weiss, Saklofske, Holdnack, & Prifitera, 2016). This has led to an emphasis in more recent literature for the discussion of test fairness. The *Standards for Educational and Psychological Testing* (American Educational Research Association, American Psychological Association, and National Council on Measurement in Education, 2011) makes very clear the importance of test fairness and ensuring that the clinician consider contextual factors to ensure that test administration and interpretation is done fairly. It has been demonstrated that FSIQ and primary index scores differ across demographic groups; some have noted that socioeconomic status (SES) and parental level of education have a significant impact on children's scores (Weiss, Saklofske, Holdnack, & Prifitera, 2016).

A final ethical consideration is the training of the administrator. The WISC-V is a complex instrument that requires the clinician to be familiar with the elaborate scoring procedure of this assessment. Additionally, the administrator should make note of how the individual answers different items in each subtest to provide qualitative data that can be used in the final interpretation. The individual making interpretations will need to be familiar with the presenting concern and contextual factors of the individual being assessed so that rich descriptions can be utilized. Moreover, the WISC-V is often used within a school or academic environment, which usually requires knowledge of federal and state laws associated with special education such as the Individuals with Disabilities Education Improvement Act (IDEA, 2004).

Case Study

Presenting Concern

Kevin, a 7-year-old Caucasian male, was administered the WISC-V after his 2nd grade teacher Ms. Walker reported difficulties with Kevin remaining in his seat and finishing his coursework. The teacher reported that Kevin will pull out crayons during a time when students are being asked to complete math problems after she has given verbal instructions to complete the assignment. Kevin is reported as becoming "increasing irritable" when the teacher has attempted to redirect his attention to complete coursework. His teacher reported that Kevin "daydreams" during individual assignments. She stated that if asked why he isn't doing the assignment, Kevin will often reply that "he forgot" that he was supposed to be doing work. Moreover, he has frequently stated that he "can't remember" what he was going to say when called on in class to answer a question. The teacher requested an evaluation for Kevin after several incidents of throwing various school supplies and crying while attempting to have him complete his work. The teacher has indicated that this behavior has been increasing in intensity since the beginning of the school year.

His teacher acknowledged that Kevin "excels" when they are focusing on reading assignments with her help. Ms. Walker reported that Kevin's verbal aptitude is "advanced" for someone of his age. She stated that Kevin has "good" relationships with his peers although she did acknowledge that he seems to prefer playing in smaller groups or by himself.

Family Background

Kevin is the oldest of two children. He has one sister who is approximately 20 months younger. His parents have been married for approximately 10 years. Kevin's father is employed as a mechanical engineer. His mother works in human resources at a local hospital.

Client Background

Kevin's parents reported that he is a "normal" child who is "sometimes shy with others." His mother stated that she had a straightforward pregnancy without any complications. Both parents indicated that they have not had any concerns about his development until recently when the teacher expressed her concerns. His mother stated that he has "always been verbal," Kevin began talking around 10 months and "picked up" words quickly.

His parents stated that Kevin enjoys coloring and playing with building blocks and cars when he is at home. He tends to play well with his sister but his parents indicated that he does seem to prefer to play by himself. His parents reported that, during the last year, they have had to repeat themselves "more frequently" when asking Kevin to finish chores or to stop playing with his toys. Kevin "generally does well following directions"; however, his parents reported that "he has had difficulty with tasks such as putting away his toys." They indicated that he seems to get easily distracted.

Kevin has played soccer and baseball on recreational teams since he was four years old. His parents described him as an "average" player. His father indicated that he seems quiet around other children. The father indicated that Kevin "sometimes seems to be daydreaming and not focusing on the play" on the athletic field.

Medical History

Kevin has not had any significant medical issues in his life. His parents reported that he had tubes places in his ears when he was approximately 2 years old at the recommendation of a pediatrician due to regular ear infections. Kevin's parents reported that he has always seemed taller than his peers but they do not consider this to have impacted Kevin in any way.

Kevin has never had any previous psychological evaluations. His parents have considered having him assessed for ADHD, though they have not yet done this.

Results

Laws such as IDEA (2004) make it clear that, when evaluating children, it is especially important to utilize multiple sources of information when making diagnostic impressions and intervention recommendations for parents and teachers. This can include the use of multiple instrument, ongoing observations in various contexts, and reports from many different individuals in a child's life. For the purposes of this case study, only the WISC-V will be interpreted here.

Kevin was administered the 10 recommended subtests of the WISC-V. Table 9.3 contains his FSIQ and Primary Index Scale results. As indicated previously, the WISC-V provides a highly detailed level of results. As such, only the overall composite scores of the FSIQ and Primary Index Scales will be presented and discussed. Readers interested in more detailed information on the administration and interpretation of WISC-V data are encouraged to obtain further training.

Testing Behaviors

Kevin arrived on time for the test session accompanied by his mother. He was appropriately dressed and groomed. He was oriented to person, place, time, and situation. He showed an appropriate level of energy. However, he had difficulty maintaining eye contact and at times seemed to be staring off. He asked the clinician multiple times to clarify or repeat instructions. On the digit span subtest Kevin seemed to demonstrate some frustrations. He asked the clinician to repeat the second number sequence of the subtest; Kevin stated that he "didn't want to do this anymore" and sunk in his seat after the clinician told him to "take your best guest, I can only say it once."

Interpretation

Full Scale IQ (FSIQ)

The FSIQ is seen as a global indicator of one's cognitive abilities that has been demonstrated to have strong correlations with academic achievement, work performance, and memory functioning; however, the relationship to academic achievement has been demonstrated

Table 9.3 Composite WISC-V Results

Scale	Composite Score	Percentile Rank	95% Confidence Interval	Qualitative Descriptor
Verbal Comprehension (VCI)	133	99	123–143	Superior
Visual Spatial (VSI)	119	90	109–129	High Average
Fluid Reasoning (FRI)	99	49	89–109	Average
Working Memory (WMI)	88	22	78–98	Low Average
Processing Speed (PSI)	98	45	88–108	Average
Full Scale IQ (FSIQ)	113	81	107–119	High Average

to be one of the strongest correlates with FSIQ (Weiss, Saklofske, Holdnack, & Prifitera, 2016). Due to these demonstrated relationships, the degree of utility one should provide to the FSIQ is often debated, with some practitioners (Canivez & Watkins, 2010) seeing it as a useful measure of one's overall cognitive ability; however, others argue that the FSIQ isn't the best measure of intellectual functioning and focus should be given to the Primary Index Scales (Hale, Fiorello, Kavanagh, Holdnack, & Aloe, 2007). Weiss, Saklofske, Holdnack, and Prifitera (2016) argue that a balanced approach utilizing the individual's presenting concern should guide the clinician's use of the FSIQ.

Kevin's FSIQ resulted in a score of 113, which falls at the 81st percentile. This indicates that Kevin scored at or above 81% of the other children his age who took this test. This result indicates that his overall intellectual functioning is higher than average. Exploring the results on the individual index scores will provide the clinician with greater clinical utility and understanding of Kevin's cognitive functioning (Weiss, Saklofske, Holdnack, & Prifitera, 2016).

Verbal Comprehension Index (VCI)

The VCI is a measure of verbal reasoning and measures one's ability to retrieve, access, and apply acquired word knowledge (Wechsler, Raiford, & Holdnack, 2014). This index measures one's ability to retrieve knowledge that has been acquired throughout the lifetime; as such, it deals with long-term memory recall. Kevin's composite score of 133 (99th percentile) indicates superior functioning on this index. The results indicate that Kevin is probably able to recall events, memories, and already acquired knowledge with ease. He probably demonstrates a strong ability to remember verbal terms.

Visual Spatial Index (VSI)

The VSI measures one's visual working memory and one's ability to deal with visual details and spatial relationships (Wechsler, Raiford, & Holdnack, 2014). An individual who scores high on this index is able to see how different shapes or designs can work together in space. Kevin's VSI score, 119, indicates high average functioning at the 90th percentile. Individuals with these results may be able to imagine how certain shapes fit together quite readily, readily analyze visual details, and have a well-developed mind's eye.

Working Memory Index (WMI)

The WMI measures one's ability to manage acquired knowledge, gain new knowledge, and work toward a decision. This index is influenced by how well one is able to keep attention to new information and hold this information in one's conscious awareness (Wechsler, Raiford, & Holdnack, 2014). Kevin's composite score of 88 (22nd percentile) indicates low average functioning on this particular index, meaning he scored at or above 22% of his peers on this index. Individuals with these results may have a difficult time prioritizing incoming stimuli and making decisions on how to address new information. Individuals with low scores on the WMI may have a hard time holding new information in the working memory to make decisions on how to act; as such, Kevin may have a difficult time following audible instructions or may require being told instructions multiple times.

Processing Speed Index (PSI)

The PSI measures one's speed and accuracy of processing visual information. Scores on the PSI are related to concentration, visual scanning, and visual discrimination (Wechsler,

Raiford, & Holdnack, 2014). Kevin's composite scores on the PSI of 98 (45th percentile) indicate average functioning on this index.

Fluid Reasoning Index (FRI)

This index measures one's ability to solve everyday problems in which previous experience may not have yet occurred. The FRI assesses one's ability to solve abstract problems using inductive and quantitative reasoning (Wechsler, Raiford, & Holdnack, 2014). Kevin's composite score of 99 (49th percentile) indicates average functioning on this result.

Decision-Making

It has been recommended to not merely consider the overall index scores in and of themselves, but rather to consider them in relationship to each other (Weiss, Saklofske, Holdnack, & Prifitera, 2016). In this case, the overall ability level (FSIQ) of Kevin indicates he is someone who is of higher than average intellectual functioning with a score of 113. However, relative to this score, the WMI demonstrates an index score (88) that provides the clinician information about an area of weakness for Kevin as well as an index score on the VCI (133) that shows an area of strength for Kevin. Additionally, Kevin's results on FRI and PSI, 99 and 98 respectively, indicate average functioning in these domains. Because it has been recommended (Wechsler, Raiford, & Holdnack, 2014) to consider the relationship of scores ecologically, a discussion of the relationship with WMI, FRI, and PSI will follow.

The FRI, PSI, and WMI together indicate how one acquires new, abstract, and novel information and subsequently makes decisions from it. Kevin's results and information from his case indicate that his difficulties in the academic context seem to occur when receiving new information. Research has indicated that low scores on WMI relative to other scores may be indicative of someone who meets the criteria for Attention Deficit/Hyperactive Disorder (ADHD) or a traumatic brain injury (TBI; Weiss, Saklofske, Holdnack, & Prifitera, 2016). Though the WISC-V is not a diagnostic tool, the WMI composite score of Kevin indicate a relative deficit in holding attention to certain stimuli. It may be that when certain stimuli are no longer present, Kevin will have a harder time acting upon it. It is recommended that further analysis is conducted on his working memory. The clinician would be wise to conduct a thorough history of any recent head trauma. Also, children are best observed in multiple contexts to fully understand their functioning. The clinician would be wise to consider having Kevin assessed for symptoms of ADHD in which feedback from both parents and teacher can be utilized. The Conner's Rating Scale is an excellent tool for this. Multiple assessments are needed when making academic and clinical decisions with children.

Feedback

It is generally recommended to report the FSIQ first (Wechsler, Raiford, & Holdnack, 2014). A strengths-based approach would highlight Kevin's cognitive strengths first. It would be important to communicate to Kevin's parents that the results of this assessment indicate that his overall intellectual aptitude is a 113, which is considered high average; data regarding the relationship between FSIQ scores and academic success could be shared. Kevin demonstrates a superior ability to retrieve information from his crystallized intelligence and long-term memory, as indicated by the VCI. Additionally, he demonstrates a high average descriptor regarding visual spatial functioning. Kevin is probably able to work well with geographic ideas and "see" images in his mind's eye well. This may be demonstrated in school or at home during creative assignments or play—such as building with blocks.

The presenting concern by Kevin's teacher is that he seems to have difficulties following verbal instructions, which has led to a greater awareness from the teacher of Kevin's "day-dreaming." Kevin demonstrates average functioning on fluid reasoning and processing speed. However, Kevin's composite score on working memory is much lower than his highest score (approximately three *SD*s). Thus, relative to his other results, the WMI indicates low average ability within this cognitive domain. It is not uncommon for children who score low on the WMI relative to other index scores to demonstrate difficulty staying focused on certain tasks or being "forgetful" (Weiss, Saklofske, Holdnack, & Prifitera, 2016). The relationship of the WMI to the PSI indicates that Kevin may have a difficult time manipulating information in the short-term memory once the stimulus is removed (Wechsler, Raiford, & Holdnack, 2014). The parents should be referred to a clinician to further assess the possibility of any recent head trauma, a diagnosis of ADHD, or a specific learning disorder. Additionally, the parents and teachers can begin to work directly to help develop Kevin's working memory. Some basic interventions include:

- Give short, simple instructions
- When possible, break instructions into discrete steps
- Be willing to repeat instructions
- Encourage Kevin to ask for assistance when he forgets
- Have Kevin repeat back instructions to help him stay focused on the information
- Utilize memory aides when possible to help with learning (e.g., Please Excuse My Dear Aunt Sally to teach order of operations in math—Parenthesis, Exponents, Multiplication/Division, Addition/Subtraction)
- Allow Kevin to use these aides in the classroom
- Use daily schedules in class

Kevin's parents should work with the teacher, school counselor(s), and school administration to develop additional interventions as needed for academic success. Finally, Kevin's parents would benefit from a referral to a clinician who can work directly with him to develop his working memory through dedicated sessions. Kevin's parents can find trained clinicians who use a program called Cogmed to address working memory. Cogmed is a computer program with self-adjusting "games" (Kerr & Blackwell, 2015) that has demonstrated some efficacy in developing individuals' working memory over time (Weiss, Saklofske, Holdnack, & Prifitera, 2016).

Summary

The WISC-V is considered to be a robust measure of intellectual ability (Wechsler, Raiford, & Holdnack, 2014; Weiss, Saklofske, Holdnack, & Prifitera, 2016) and the Wechsler series of tests has been widely used since 1939 (Gregory, 2013). The WISC-V can provide an overall global score of intellectual ability with the FSIQ; however, more emphasis is placed on the clinical utility of the index scores and ancillary scores (Weiss, Saklofske, Holdnack, & Prifitera, 2016). This allows the clinician to be more descriptive and thorough in making clinical decisions with individuals. The previous revision, the WISC-IV, has been used quite frequently to assess cognitive ability with children (Peterson, Lomas, Neukrug, & Bonner, 2014). It would be expected that the WISC-V will continue to be used at a similar rate. The WISC-V has made shifts in the scoring to place more emphasis on the use of index scores. The reliability of the instrument is thoroughly discussed in the technical and interpretation manual (Wechsler, Raiford, & Holdnack, 2014); however, the instrument is still relatively new and research on the predictive validity of the WISC-V is still being conducted (Whiston, 2017). As demonstrated in the case study presented earlier in this chapter, the results of the WISC-V can be especially useful when applied within the context of presenting concern. The index scores can provide further insight into the relationship of different cognitive processes, which allows the clinician to make recommendations specific to the needs of the individual. When used by a qualified administrator, the WISC-V can be a helpful instrument in assessing children's intellectual and cognitive functioning.

Test Your Knowledge:

1. What is the mean (M) and standard deviation (SD) of the FSIQ and Index Scales?
   a. M = 115; SD = 20
   b. M = 100; SD = 15
   c. M = 10; SD = 3
   d. M = 100; SD = 20

2. Who developed the first intelligence test?
   a. David Wechsler
   b. Robert Yerkes
   c. Alfred Binet
   d. Theodore Simon

3. What are the appropriate ages for someone to be administered the WISC-V?
   a. 4 years–18 years
   b. 5 years–17 years
   c. 6 years–16 years
   d. 3 years–18 years

4. How many subtests are recommended to be administered in a typical WISC-V administration?
   a. 10
   b. 5
   c. 7
   d. 8

5. When did David Wechsler develop his original intelligence scales?
   a. 1915
   b. 1990
   c. 1939
   d. 1952

6. The WISC-V is influence by the CHC Theory of Intelligence.
   T or F?

7. When was the first intelligence test created?
   a. 1905
   b. 1916
   c. 1939
   d. 1940

8. Which of these is an ethical consideration when administering the WISC-V?
   a. Considering a client's cultural background
   b. Understanding the implications of the interpretation
   c. Being mindful of test fairness
   d. All of the above

9. The WISC-V is recommended to be used within a cultural context.
   T or F?

10. Which of the following is not an intended use of the WISC-V?
   a. Assessing working memory
   b. Assessing academic achievement
   c. Assessing spatial reasoning
   d. Assessing processing speed

Discussion Questions/Prompts:

1. After reading this chapter, describe and discuss the depth of intricacy involved in measuring IQ.
2. Discuss what causes the test manufacturer to require additional training for the administration of the WISC-V.
3. Discuss "test fairness" in relation to IQ testing.
4. How would YOU share the data of the case with both the child and his parents/guardians?
5. Describe the difference in IQ testing now versus when the concept first emerged.

10 Assessments in Rehabilitation Counseling

Suneetha B. Manyam and Jonathan D. Brown

Assessment is the key component of the rehabilitation process in the life of a Person with Disability (PWD). Through vocational assessment, a rehabilitation client's strengths, weaknesses, vocational interests, and preferences are identified; their functional limitations are carefully plotted; their residual capacities are acknowledged; and appropriate interventions are planned by integrating this information for the client's optimal vocational adjustment. American Educational Research Association (AERA), American Psychological Association (APA), and National Council on Measurement in Education (NCME) in 2011 defined assessment as "any systematic method of obtaining information from tests and other sources, used to draw inferences about people, objects or programs" (p. 6). The goal of rehabilitation assessment is client empowerment. Assessment should be focused on making beneficial recommendations for client services through obtaining relevant data from all possible sources (Rubin & Roessler, 2008). Common assessment sources in the rehabilitation counseling field include (but are not limited to) interviews, standardized tests, interest inventories, projective techniques, observations, psychosocial and medical evaluations, vocational analysis, job tryouts, work samples, etc.

This chapter will focus on the role of assessments in the rehabilitation counseling field, basic components of comprehensive rehabilitation assessment, and the seven categories of common assessments and tests used in the rehabilitation process. Then, an overview of an original case study is presented with the demographic information along with detailed assessments used for vocational appraisal. The information gathered through the client's psychological and vocational evaluations is discussed in detail with appropriate research evidence. Followed by that, the authors will present the results from the instruments, including the rehabilitation counselor's decision process. The major conclusions that were communicated to the client along with the feedback process are discussed at the end of this chapter.

Role of Assessment in Rehabilitation Counseling Field

As mentioned earlier, assessment plays a vital role in the client's rehabilitation process starting with the initial stage of client referral, to the eligibility determination, to diagnosis (in the assessment of residual capacities, vocational exploration, and evaluation), to writing the individual plan for employment (IEP), to the final stage of job placement. According to Rawlins-Alderman, Dock, Steele, and Wofford (2015), rehabilitation assessment is a multifaceted, individualized, and ongoing process for a successful IEP. They further state that "the appropriateness of the vocational methods used in each unique evaluation will depend on the functional strengths, limitations, past experiences, educational background, and specific needs of the consumer" (p. 19).

Basic Components of Comprehensive Rehabilitation Assessment

Although research suggests that rehabilitation counselors use a variety of tools and assessment instruments to measure the unique interests and vocational needs of rehabilitation clients (Betters & Sligar, 2015), this chapter focuses on the four basic components of comprehensive rehabilitation assessment process that are described by Lee and Ditchman (2012). According to these authors, the rehabilitation assessment begins with the intake interview followed by medical, psychological, and vocational evaluations. The purpose of the intake interview is to establish rapport with the rehabilitation client in addition to exploring the demographic information, family history, and reason for rehabilitation. Further, the counselor also initiates the diagnostic process; explains the need for medical, psychological, and vocational evaluations; and explains its purpose toward the end of the interview. The medical evaluations are performed by medical experts and specialists with an aim of screening the type, frequency, and severity of the disability. The client is also educated on his current health as well as future implications of his/her disability, and any residual functioning capacities that may impact their ability to perform certain jobs (Lee & Ditchman, 2012). Psychological evaluations focus on gathering clients' data related to their interests, aptitudes, achievements, personality, and any other relevant vocational adjustment information that might help the counselor in identifying the functional limitations, in challenging the client's unrealistic vocational goals, and sometimes in deciding the eligibility for cognitive and psychiatric disabilities (Rubin & Roessler, 2008). Lastly, vocational evaluations assist the rehabilitation counselor in gathering information regarding the client's current vocational potential, type of jobs suitable for him, training or interventions needed to regain gainful employment, discovering the appropriate community resources, identifying the family support systems, and placing the client in a feasible work environment (Lee & Ditchman, 2012).

Common Assessments and Tests in Rehabilitation Counseling Field

Based on the extensive review of literature regarding assessments and tests used in the field of rehabilitation counseling (West, Armstrong, & Ryan, 2005; Weed & Hill, 2008; Lee & Ditchman, 2012; Power, 2013; Betters & Sligar, 2015; Grasso, Jitendra, Browder, & Harp, 2004; Rawlins-Alderman, Dock, Steele, & Wofford, 2015; Smedema, Ruiz, & Mohr, 2017), the common vocational assessments are discussed under the following seven categories. The first five categories fall under standardized tests and inventories that are normed with specific populations with appropriate psychometric properties such as reliability and validity constructs. The measures of work readiness and assessments of physical functioning are used mostly for the vocational and job analysis purposes during the rehabilitation process of a PWD.

1. *Intelligence Tests:* Used to measure the psychological construct of intelligence. In the rehabilitation counseling field, the intelligence tests are typically used to assess the intellectual functioning (verbal and nonverbal), cognitive, and reading abilities of PWD. Table 10.1 lists 13 different intelligence tests used by the vocational evaluators and counselors.
2. *Aptitude Batteries:* Assesses client's skills and abilities. They are also used to predict the probability of learning or mastering a new skill required for a specific vocation. Common aptitude factors measured include verbal, numeric, spatial aptitudes, clerical perception, code speed, etc. Table 10.1 depicts six widely used aptitude batteries in the rehabilitation counseling field.
3. *Achievement Tests:* These are used to measure client's knowledge from formal learning and life experiences (Power, 2013, p. 269). Common areas of achievement tests that

Table 10.1 Common Instruments Used in the Rehabilitation Counseling Field

Type of Instrument	Ideal Populations	Typical Referral Questions
Intelligence Tests		Intellectual functioning
1. Wechsler Adult Intelligence Scale	Adults aged 16–90 Mental retardation Learning disabilities	Learning disabilities Cognitive abilities
2. Wechsler Intelligence Scale for Children (WISC)	Children aged 6–16 Mental retardation Learning disabilities	Intellectual functioning Cognitive abilities
3. Wechsler Preschool and Primary Scale of Intelligence (WPPSI)	Children aged 2.5–7 Mental retardation Learning disabilities	Intellectual functioning Cognitive abilities
4. Stanford-Binet Scales	Individuals aged 4–adulthood Mental retardation Learning disabilities	Verbal intellectual abilities Cognitive abilities
5. Slossan Intelligence Test	Individuals with visual impairment, reading difficulty, and physical disabilities	Oral verbal intelligence test Cognitive abilities
6. Bender Gestalt Visual Motor Test	Individuals with mental retardation, learning disabilities, neurological impairment	Attention to detail Approaches to organization Visual motor functioning
7. Halstead-Reitan Test	Individuals with brain damage	Behavior and cognitive functioning capacities
8. Haptic	Individuals with visual impairment	Intellectual functioning
9. Leiter	Individuals with hearing impairments, aphasia, or mental retardation	Nonverbal intelligence scale, cognitive abilities
10. Luria-Nebraska	Individuals with brain damage Persons with traumatic brain injury	Behavior and cognitive functioning capacities
11. Hisky Nebraska	Deaf population	Learning aptitude
12. Shipley Institute of Living Scale	Elderly	Decline in intellectual functioning due to aging
13. Raven's Progressive Matrices	Individuals with Asperger's and Autism Spectrum Disorders	Test of reasoning Intellectual functioning Progressive puzzles to solve
Aptitude Batteries		
1. General Aptitude Test Battery (GATB)	Individuals aged 16 and older	Nine types of vocational aptitude including general intelligence for occupational aptitude patterns
2. Non-reading Aptitude Test Battery (NATB)	Disadvantaged or semi-literate adults and individuals from 9th–12th grades	Vocational aptitude in nine areas
3. Apiticom TM	English- or Spanish-speaking disadvantaged job applicants, high school or special education students, rehabilitation clients	Combined assessment program Quick vocational assessment in aptitudes, interest, and educational level Computer based and gives instant results
4. Differential Aptitude Tests (DAT)	8th–12th grade students, and adults	Eight different types of aptitude measurement Educational and vocational guidance Career planning program
5. Armed Services Vocational Aptitude Battery (ASVAB)	Youth ages 16–23 who want to enter into the military service	Vocational aptitude Test score information

(Continued)

Table 10.1 (Continued)

Type of Instrument	Ideal Populations	Typical Referral Questions
6. McCarron-Dial (MDS)	People with mental retardation; neurological impairments; physical, mental, or emotional disabilities	Vocational and clinical evaluation, for special education and rehabilitation purposes
Achievement Tests		
1. Wide Range Achievement Test (WRAT)	For diagnosing approximate educational level Level 1 used for persons with low intellect	Reading, arithmetic, and spelling capability testing
2. Peabody Individual Achievement Test (PIAT)	For diagnosing approximate educational level	Reading, reading comprehension, mathematics, spelling, and general information testing
3. Tests of General Educational Development (GED)	Individuals seeking high school equivalency certificates	Testing in social sciences, natural sciences, and correctness of expression
4. Basic Occupational Literacy Test (BOLT)	Educationally deficient adults	Basic reading and arithmetic skills testing
5. Woodcock Johnson Psychoeducational Battery (WJ)	Clients with learning disabilities	Cognitive abilities Academic achievement testing
Interest Inventories		
1. Strong Interest Inventory® (SCII)	8th graders and up including adults	Occupational interest exploration in different fields, world-of-work information, and general occupational themes
2. Self-Directed Search (SDS)	Individuals who don't need or have direct access to career counseling services	Holland's theory, minimal counselor involvement
3. Enhanced Career Assessment Inventory (CAI)	Non-college clients who want to enter into the labor force	Direct placement and short-term training clients, occupational extraversion and introversion, questions on activities, school subjects, and occupational titles
4. Kuder Occupational Interest Survey (KOIS)	High school students, dropouts, college freshman, adults needing career planning and job placement services	Occupational preferences, vocational exploration, and vocational decision-making
5. Minnesota Importance Questionnaire (MIQ)	Youth and adults exploring their vocational needs	Vocational needs and values of clients
6. Reading Free Vocational Interest Inventory	Individuals with limited reading ability, persons with mental retardation and learning disabilities	Vocational preferences exploration, vocational interests through 55 triads of illustrations
7. Salience Inventory (SI)	Individuals in different cultures	Work values, relative importance of five major life roles
8. Geist Picture Interest Inventory	Individuals with limited reading levels, nonverbal/non-expressive clients	Pictures of work interests
9. My Vocational Situation (MVS)	Individuals needing career development	Career maturity and career development instrument, Vocational identity
Personality Tests		
1. Minnesota Multiphasic Personality Inventory (MMPI)	Adults 18 and above	10 personality factors related to vocational needs such as schizophrenia, depression, psychasthenia, etc.; psychological adjustment of rehabilitation clients

Type of Instrument	Ideal Populations	Typical Referral Questions
2. 16 Personality Factor Questionnaire (16 PF)	Adults 18 and above Form E is for clients with reduced reading level	16 primary personality characteristics, computer-generated personal career development profile
3. Myers-Briggs Personality Type Indicator (MBTI)	Adults 18 and above	Carl Jung's psychological types, clients classified as one of two preferences from four dimensions
4. Rorschach Ink Blot Test	Children, youth, and adults	Psychological evaluation, personality appraisal, 10 ink blots
5. Thematic Apperception Test (TAT)	Children, youth, and adults	31 pictures of life situations, projective technique of psychological evaluation and personality appraisal
6. Draw-A-Person test	Children, youth, and adults	Projective technique, rich information on self-concept, personality style, and conflict areas
Measures of Work Readiness		
1. Work Adjustment Rating Form (WARF)	Clients with mental retardation	Identification of functional limitations, residual capacity, assessment through eight subscales
2. Vocational Behavior Checklist (VBC)	Adults and persons with disabilities	338 vocationally relevant skill objectives, skill mastery
3. Work Samples: Valpar and TOWER	Clients requiring vocational evaluation system, individuals with severe disabilities, and special populations	Work samples of physical functioning
Assessments of Physical Functioning		
1. Vineland Social Maturity Scale	Non-institutionalized individuals with mental retardation	Adaptive behavior
2. Barthel Inventory of Self-Care Skills and Mobility Skills	Individuals with disabilities and special populations	Physical functioning in medical rehabilitation, client's mobility independence, activities of daily living
3. PULSES Scale of Severity of Disability	Individuals with disabilities and special populations	Six broad areas of disability such as physical conditioning, upper limb self-care functions, lower limb mobility functions, etc.

rehabilitation counselors need for diagnosis include verbal, numerical, and reading abilities. Five widely used achievement tests are described in Table 10.1.

4. *Interest Inventories:* Assesses client's preferences, interests, and vocational choices that might help them in making informed vocational decisions for greater job satisfaction. Most of these assessments are based on Holland's occupational code or R-I-A-S-E-C typology (Lee & Ditchman, 2012). Table 10.1 lists the nine most commonly used interest inventories by the vocational evaluators. Some of these instruments, such as Self-Directed Search, are self-administered, which can be a strength or a weakness for a client with disability. Some of these inventories are administered through computers and can be a challenge if the client or rehabilitation counselor is not technologically savvy.

5. *Personality Tests:* Assesses person's emotional, motivational, interpersonal, and attitudinal characteristics (Anastasi & Urbina, 1997). They often measure mental health traits such as depression, paranoia, schizophrenia, etc. or personality constructs such as extroversion,

introversion, thinking, sensing, perceiving, judging, intuition, etc. Six commonly used personality tests are discussed in Table 10.1.

6. *Measures of Work Readiness:* Used to assess if the PWD is ready for reentering the job. Typically, these measures are utilized in the vocational training facilities or workshops. According to Lee and Ditchman (2012), client skill mastery, aptitude, and vocational potential is assessed through work samples (activities involving the tasks, materials, and tools similar to the actual job environment). There are three common measures of readiness that vocational evaluators use that are described in Table 10.1.

7. *Assessments of Physical Functioning:* These are utilized to assess the level of self-care, independence in mobility, and activities of daily living for the PWD. This assessment

Table 10.2 Assessments Used for the Current Case Study

Type of Instrument	Strengths	Weaknesses	Ideal Populations	Typical Referral Questions
The World Health Organization Disability Assessment Schedule 2.0 (WHODAS 2.0)	Allows for the incorporation of third-party (i.e., family or caretakers) view of functioning	The ability to self-administer could lead to misrepresentation of information	All adult populations being assessed for level of disability	What is the client's level of disability according to the six domains of functioning?
The Wechsler Abbreviated Scale of Intelligence (WASI-II)	Quick to administer, not as intensive as WAIS Determines whether more intensive and comprehensive intelligence assessment needs to be conducted	Although there are two administration options, a shorter option can lead to a loss of relevant information necessary for the counselor decision-making process	Individuals aged 6–90	What is the client's current level of intellectual functioning?
Wide Range Achievement Test-4 (WRAT-4)	Allows for adjustments dependent upon client age Has been standardized on 3,000 individuals nationally	Given that the spelling and math subsets can be given in groups, if necessary, there is a possibility of external factors influencing client scores	Individuals aged 5–94	At what level is the client's academic functioning?
Preliminary Estimate of Learning (PEL)	Utilization of a shorter scale allows for quicker assessment of verbal ability	Since the PEL is taken from the Preliminary Diagnostic Questionnaire, a restricted view of intelligence is determined by testing verbal ability	Individuals with a disability seeking employment	What is the client's level of intelligence based on verbal ability?
Career Scope Interest Inventory	Provides the counselor with the client's perceived areas of interest Aids the counselor and client in determining area of employment suitability	Possibility of client purposefully skewing interest to match their own desired interest, rather than responding openly	Individuals planning their career and educational futures	What are areas of interest for the client that would be beneficial to the decision-making process?

is important to identify functional limitations and residual capacity of the individual with disabilities. Table 10.1 describes three commonly used assessments of physical functioning.

Table 1 lists various types of instruments that rehabilitation counselors use for the vocational analysis of PWD under each of these seven categories. Furthermore, Table 10.1 depicts the ideal populations and typical referral questions for each of these instruments.

In addition to these measures, vocational counselors and job analysts often use labor market information and occupational information systems such as Dictionary of Occupational Titles (DOT), Occupational Information Network (O★NET), Standard Occupational Classification System, etc. Further, situational and ecological assessments such as observing the client's job performance in a controlled work environment (workshop or training facility) or in a natural setting are also common during the rehabilitation process. Sometimes, employers are required to offer supported employment (ensuring work site accommodations) based on the on-the-job evaluations (Lee & Ditchman, 2012).

Table 10.2 lists the assessments utilized for the original case study presented in the later section of this paper. Authors present this table to illustrate crucial significance of assessments in the rehabilitation process. It is evident from Table 10.2 that rehabilitation assessment is comprehensive and involves all four basic components of assessment described in this section by using a variety of instruments.

Specialized Training Needed for Administering the Assessments

The majority of the assessments discussed thus far—such as intelligence, aptitude tests, personality inventories, etc.—requires extensive training and is usually administered by psychologists or certified vocational evaluation experts. Special certification is needed for administering measures such as WISC, WAIS-IV, GATB, ASVAB, etc. Moreover, test administrators and vocational experts should be thoroughly trained in making appropriate interpretation of test results. Power (2013) reported that vocational evaluators should be competent in test administration, scoring, and interpretation of various instruments and need to be familiar with both the federal and state laws related to the assessment of PWD. Further, the administrators should be culturally sensitive in selecting appropriate assessment measures. The experts also need to be mindful of the client's disability and unique needs, as well as choose appropriate assessments that accurately reflect their vocational potential. Betters and Sligar (2015) add that vocational experts should be up to date with the technological advances, as some of these assessments are administered through computers, tablets, and iPads.

Ethical and Multicultural Considerations

Commission on Rehabilitation Counselor Certification (CRCC) outlines the ethical and legal considerations for rehabilitation assessment and requires all of the rehabilitation counselors to follow those guidelines related to the test selection, administration, and interpretation. Lee and Ditchman (2012) suggests the following ethical considerations for the rehabilitation counselors and test administrators:

1. Test selection should be based on the needs and traits of the consumer to avoid overuse or indiscriminate use of testing. Consumers' disability-related considerations should be carefully accommodated. For example, a person with serious cognitive or emotional problems may have low attention span and shorter tasks may be more appropriate. The

descriptive appraisal of the client should reflect the consumer's accurate and current level of functioning.

2. Test taker rights should be explained clearly before the testing begins. Testing accommodations are necessary depending on the client's disability. Important decisions such as eligibility determinations should not be based on the results of a single test.
3. Proper measures should be taken to protect the consumer's privacy and confidentiality.
4. Potential test biases (test items that favor one person or group over the other) should be carefully monitored. Test administrators, interpreters, and counselors should be multi-culturally sensitive.

Overview of the Case

In this section, authors discuss a real case study of Ms. Amy (pseudonym is used to protect the client's privacy and confidentiality) and her rehabilitation journey with an emphasis on the vocational assessment. The client's permission was obtained through informed consent in addition to seeking authorization to access her file from the local Vocational Rehabilitation Agency.

Demographic Description and Presenting Problem

Ms. Amy is a 46-year-old African American female with two children, a 7-year-old boy and a 15-year-old girl, reportedly living in Section Eight housing. She reported her primary disability as Dyslexia and a secondary disability of Diabetes. Ms. Amy came to Vocational Rehabilitation Agency to seek assistance in obtaining gainful, competitive employment. She stated that she grew up with her mother and step-father. Although Ms. Amy did not have a relationship with her biological father, she has a great relationship with her parents.

Medical History

Ms. Amy has a reported medical history of Diabetes, which caused her to be hospitalized five times due to complications, as well as having and recovering from a stroke. To work through the physical abuse endured at the hands of her ex-husband, Ms. Amy was referred to a psychiatrist and attended sessions for six months. She reported being prescribed Zoloft but did not continue to take it for more than two weeks. Ms. Amy stated that she experienced depression when thinking about her financial situation, experiencing anxiety, and sometimes feeling easily overwhelmed by life stressors.

Ms. Amy reported that she did experience some difficulties learning while in school. However, she never failed or had to repeat a grade and did not receive special education services in school. It was not discovered that she lived with Dyslexia until after her graduation from high school. Over the years, Ms. Amy obtained various degrees ranging from cosmetology to culinary arts, some of which were obtained through funding from a state Vocational Rehabilitation Agency. Although Ms. Amy achieved academic success, she had not obtained gainful, competitive employment. Past employment opportunities for Ms. Amy include working in a nursing facility and a hair salon. Financially, Ms. Amy does not receive disability income. She currently utilizes the Supplemental Security Income (SSI) received for her daughter, who lives with a psychological disability and son, who lives with a physical disability, to support her family. Ms. Amy revealed that she has been married and divorced twice. The first marriage ended after five years because of reported physical abuse. The second marriage ended after 10 years because of extensive distance and separate living arrangements. Ms. Amy presented as very entrepreneurial and sought assistance from Vocational

Rehabilitation (VR) to obtain gainful, competitive employment, and assistance with opening her own restaurant.

The Vocational Rehabilitation Process

Ms. Amy's case began at status 00–Referral, attempt to contact and take VR application. Ms. Amy was self-referred to the VR agency. During this period, known as the intake session, a VR Application for Services was completed. The application for services documented Ms. Amy's demographic information, reported disability, previous work experiences, educational and medical history, and current sources of income. The intake form also included Ms. Amy's referral question, or purpose for seeking Vocational Rehabilitation Services, in which she stated the need to obtain gainful, competitive employment and assistance with opening her own restaurant.

Vocational Assessments and Diversity Considerations

The completion of the VR Application for Services moved Ms. Amy's case to status 02. Her case was then assigned to a rehabilitation counselor. The counselor receiving the case was responsible for determining Ms. Amy's eligibility for Vocational Services. To make Ms. Amy eligible for services, the counselor needed a current assessment that reflected she did have Dyslexia since it was reported as the primary disability. The Client Services Policy Manual dictates that counselors can utilize evaluations and assessments for eligibility purposes. However, the assessments and evaluations must be facilitated by specific professionals, depending upon the reported disability. Cultural awareness must be present while conducting assessments. As discussed by Fouad (1993),

> it is important for counselors to clarify expectations in this phase because the process of self-analysis and introspection may be unfamiliar to minority clients. They may be uncomfortable with self-disclosure, and may be concerned with how the information will be used.
>
> (p. 2)

The assessment process begins with the vocational counselor. The counselor must ensure they are culturally competent while working with clients. While it may become rather routine to request assessments and evaluations for clients, the effective preparation may be needed on behalf of the client. Minority clients may feel uncomfortable sharing personal details with individuals they are not familiar with, although the information is necessary for successful Vocational Rehabilitation. The initial meeting between the vocational counselor and Ms. Amy was important to the vocational process. The initial meeting "is a valuable assessment strategy for both actively involving the client in exploring interest, preferences, and past activities and providing the counselor with important information regarding the client's general level of career maturity and knowledge of occupations" (Leahy, 1995, p. 300). After having this meeting with Ms. Amy, the vocational counselor could provide to the vocational evaluator the information gathered. The information received during the meeting can be compared to the outcome results of the vocational evaluation, making it easier to develop an effective individualized plan for employment. It is also to be noted that evaluations and assessments requested by vocational counselors are typically written at a lower reading level, as copies are given to the client.

The rehabilitation counselor requested that a Vocational Evaluation and Psychological Assessment be done to aid in determining Ms. Amy's eligibility for services. According to the Client Services Policy Manual for the Vocational Rehabilitation Agency (2014), the following professionals can conduct assessments and evaluations of Learning Disabilities for eligibility purposes:

- Licensed psychologist
- Psychologist or psychometrist who has been countersigned by a licensed psychologist
- Psychologist or psychometrist employed by the state Department of Education who is certified as either school psychologist (doctorate level), associate school psychologist (specialist level), or school psychometrist (master's level)
- Psychiatrist with the ability to individually administer and interpret general intelligence tests
- Licensed clinical social workers skilled in the diagnosis of learning disorders
- Pediatricians skilled in the diagnosis of Attention Deficit/Hyperactivity Disorders (for ADHD only)

Psychological Evaluation

Ms. Amy's psychological evaluation was conducted by a local licensed psychologist who works as a vendor, an individual external to the agency that provides services for clients for the agency. A psychological evaluation was necessary to receive an official professional's certification that Ms. Amy did indeed suffer from a learning disability for eligibility of services purposes. Also, included in the evaluation were details regarding Ms. Amy's psychological well-being, which would serve as necessary information for the counselor to utilize while interacting with Ms. Amy. The evaluation covered many details regarding the client's background information, levels of functioning, and evaluative outcomes. Given Ms. Amy's referral question, the areas of greatest importance were levels of functioning, testing results, and diagnostic impressions.

Results of Vocational Assessments

The levels of functioning obtained from the intake, medical, and psychological evaluations indicated that Ms. Amy can perform daily functions, such as personal hygiene, cooking, cleaning, driving, and utilizing public transportation. It was also noted that Ms. Amy could manage her personal finances independently. The Bender Visual Motor Gestalt Test-II indicated high-level visual-motor integration skills (standard score = 123; T-score = 65; 93.74th percentile). Ms. Amy's score indicates that she does not have a neuropsychological impairment.

WHODAS 2.0

The World Health Organization Disability Assessment Schedule 2.0 (WHODAS 2.0) provides an assessment of disability based on the International Classification of Function, Disability, and Health (ICF) (World Health Organization, 2014). There are six domains of functioning assessed: cognition, mobility, self-care, getting along, life activities, and participation. Ms. Amy reported marked distress in each of the six domains. She reported having issues with extended periods of concentration and remembering to do important things, interpersonal issues, taking the time to do things pleasurable or relaxing things for herself alone, difficulty engaging in community activities, and being affected emotionally regarding her physical health and the strain it placed on her financially.

WASI-II

The Wechsler Abbreviated Scale of Intelligence (WASI-II) was conducted to evaluate Ms. Amy's intellectual functioning. Ms. Amy's scores are reported in Table 10.3.

The scores presented by the evaluation were compared to the scores of other individuals along the same chronological age as Ms. Amy. It should be noted that the evaluator did not consider the received scores to be an accurate representation of Ms. Amy's abilities. However, the reason behind this notion could not be determined. Although Ms. Amy's obtained IQ score is 77, given that the perceived scores may understate her abilities, the evaluator concluded there was a 95% chance that Ms. Amy's true IQ score may fall between 73 to 83.

Diagnostic Impressions

The psychological evaluator provided the following diagnoses for Ms. Amy:

DSM Code   Diagnosis

311   Unspecified Depressive Disorder
V62.89   Borderline Intellectual Functioning

Specific Learning Disorder:

315.00   With impairment in reading
315.1   With impairment in mathematics

The psychological evaluation concluded that Ms. Amy functions at the borderline level intellectually. Ms. Amy can do basic work functions, understand and execute directions, and follow a standard work schedule. Reflecting on Ms. Amy's referral question, the evaluator believed that Ms. Amy would be able to open her own restaurant. Future recommendations included literacy and writing ability classes, and to learn how to effectively cope with the stressors of life through psychological intervention.

Vocational Evaluation

Ms. Amy's Vocational Evaluation was conducted by a trained vocational evaluator, who also worked as a vendor for the agency. The purpose of the evaluation was to assess Ms. Amy's vocational potential and capabilities regarding any jobs or training she may engage in. The results of the evaluation provided the counselor with an understanding of which vocational opportunities Ms. Amy would be better suited for and recommended training that would benefit her. A vocational evaluation was vital to Ms. Amy's case, or any client, as it renders a vocational profile of her to be utilized by the rehabilitation counselor.

Table 10.3 Representation of Ms. Amy's WASI-II Scores—Quantitative Data

Composite and Index Scores	IQ	Percentile	Category
Verbal	81	10th	Low Average
Performance	78	7th	Borderline
Full Scale IQ	77	6th	Borderline

A point to note is that vocational and psychological evaluations share similar material within the documented reports. Some of the shared data are background information, tests of verbal intelligence, educational and vocational background, and medical information. Although they share slight similarities in the material included, it is important to understand their differences. A psychological evaluation is utilized to obtain a diagnosis of various mental health and illness issues, whereas a vocational evaluation provides a vocational profile of the client. This profile gives the rehabilitation counselor the knowledge necessary to help the client determine areas of gainful, competitive employment. The obtained information also helps to formulate the client's Individualized Plan for Employment. Reflecting on Ms. Amy's referral question to seek gainful, competitive employment, and to open her own restaurant, the focus of the vocational evaluation sought to determine whether her chosen career path would be feasible. Also, if Ms. Amy's preferred vocational goal was not feasible, other areas of possible employment were recommended.

WRAT-4

To test Ms. Amy's basic academic capabilities, the vocational evaluator administered the Wide Range Achievement Test-4 (WRAT-4). Ms. Amy received the results displayed in Table 10.4.

The results provided an indication of Ms. Amy's academic capabilities and the respective grade level, noted by GE, of each score. The WRAT-4 was given orally, with pencil and paper being provided for use if necessary.

Preliminary Estimate of Learning (PEL)

The PEL was given to Ms. Amy to determine her verbal ability. The PEL correlates within 6 points of the Wechsler Intelligence Test and is derived from the Preliminary Diagnostic Questionnaire (PDQ) (Moriarty, Minton & Spann, 1981). Ms. Amy's score of 97–103 revealed she was of average intelligence. It is important to note that Ms. Amy was given two capabilities tests to evaluate her intelligence. The Wechsler Full Scale Intelligence Test stated Ms. Amy was of borderline intelligence, whereas the Preliminary Estimate of Learning Test stated she was of average intelligence. A possible limitation to assessments in Vocational Rehabilitation is the lack of standardization. Since different offices utilizes different vendors, there is no single instrument used for testing things such as intelligence. A lack of standardization in testing and assessment could lead to an unnecessarily skewed view of the client's vocational capabilities.

Vocational Interest

Ms. Amy was administered the Career Scope Interest Inventory to determine what her highest interest areas were, as listed in Table 10.5.

Table 10.4 Representation of Ms. Amy's WRAT-4 Scores—Quantitative Data

Word Reading (Word Recognition)	78	4.8 GE
Measure:	Standard Score:	Grade Equivalency:
Sentence Comprehension	94	12.5 GE
Math Computation	106	> 12.9 GE
Spelling	79	5.9 GE

Table 10.5 Client's Vocational Interests from Career Scope Interest Inventory—Quantitative Data

1 (86%)	*01 Artistic:* an interest in creative expression of feeling or ideas through literary arts, visual arts, performing arts, or crafts (e.g., writer, painter, actor, editor, dancer, singer, designer)
2 (50%)	*12 Physical Performing:* an interest in physical activities performed before an audience, such as sports or daring physical feats (e.g., athlete, coach, movie stunt performer, juggler, sports illustrator)
3 (50%)	*06 Industrial:* an interest in repetitive, concrete, organized activities in a factory setting (e.g., machinist, assembler, baker, welder, laborer)
4 (50%)	*04 Protective:* an interest in using authority to protect people and property (e.g., police officer, firefighter, security guard, bodyguard, park ranger, prison guard)
5 (50%)	*05 Mechanical:* an interest in applying mechanical principles to practical situations using machines, hand tools, or techniques to produce, build, or repair things (e.g., electrical engineer, architect, carpenter, chef, mechanic, ambulance driver, project manager)

Reflecting on Ms. Amy's referral question, to obtain gainful employment and receive assistance to open her own restaurant, it was noted that her 5th interest area included the occupation of a chef and her 3rd interest included baker. This information is vital in aiding the rehabilitation counselor in determining whether Ms. Amy's preference for employment is feasible. Given the results of the Career Scope Interest Inventory, Ms. Amy's stated desire to become a chef of her own restaurant could be supported by the rehabilitation counselor.

Vocational Appraisal

After conducting the vocational evaluation with Ms. Amy, the vocational evaluator developed a table of Ms. Amy's vocational assets and possible employment barriers (see Table 10.6).

The vocational evaluator recommended that Ms. Amy was capable of competitive employment with the assistance of accommodations for her Dyslexia if needed. As part of the evaluation, the evaluator provided feasible jobs for Ms. Amy through ONET related to her reported reason for referral and the outcome of the assessments:

- Chefs and Head Cooks
- Cooks, Restaurants
- Cooks, Institution and Cafeteria
- Dining Room and Cafeteria Attendants and Bartender Helpers
- Bakers
- Food Preparation Workers
- Combined Food Preparation and Serving Workers, Including Fast Food
- Hosts and Hostesses, Restaurant, Lounge, and Coffee Shops

Rehabilitation Counselor Decision Process

Assessments in Vocational Rehabilitation are necessary as they often confirm what a person thinks s/he knows, and give options as well as a place to start toward research on career and educational decision-making (Lewis & Sabedra, 2001). Now that Ms. Amy's counselor has received all the necessary evaluations and assessment, the case can be moved to status 10. A case in status 10 means that the client has been deemed eligible for services. Effective documentation of Ms. Amy's reported primary disability of Dyslexia was necessary to deem her eligible for services. The psychological evaluation conducted by the licensed psychologist sufficed to validate Ms. Amy's reported disability and make her eligible for services.

Table 10.6 Results of Client's Vocational Appraisal

Vocational Assets:	Possible Employment Barriers:
• Grooming/hygiene • Worked to completion • Math comprehension > 12.9 GE (WRAT 4) • Average verbal intelligence—SS 97 to 103 (PEL) • Average abstract reasoning ability—SS 98 (Raven) • Often did math in her head • Sentence comprehension—12.5 GE (WRAT 4) • Aptitudes match stated and tested interest	• Dyslexia • Diabetes • Spelling—5.9 GE (WRAT 4) • Word recognition—4.8 GE (WRAT 4) • 10 minutes late for appointment

The next step of Ms. Amy's case was to reach status 12. This was achieved by Ms. Amy working with her rehabilitation counselor to develop an Individualized Plan for Employment. This plan will contain all the services provided to Ms. Amy that the Vocational Rehabilitation Agency deemed necessary for her successful obtainment of gainful, competitive employment. Also included are all the services provided to aid Ms. Amy in opening her own restaurant. It is important that Vocational Rehabilitation funding determinations be based on valid assessment data that reflect the actual needs of the individual with developmental disabilities with respect to instruction and behavioral supports in the workplace (Grasso, Jitendra, Browder, & Harp, 2004). Thus, the importance of a vocational counselor utilizing assessments and evaluations conducted by specific, regulated professionals is a vital key in the Vocational Rehabilitation process. Having the appropriate information provided in the assessments aided the counselor in effectively determining the appropriate supports for Ms. Amy to effectively meet her goal or referral question.

The rehabilitation counselor utilized the information provided in the psychological and vocational assessment to determine the necessary services for Ms. Amy. The rehabilitation counselor, with approval from the agency, supported Ms. Amy's goal to open a restaurant. This decision was made based on the data received from the vocational and psychological evaluation.

The vocational evaluation provided results indicating Ms. Amy possessed the abilities necessary to run and open her own restaurant. It was important to note that Ms. Amy has experience operating her own entrepreneurial pursuits. To effectively support her, the rehabilitation counselor takes Ms. Amy's vocational and educational background into account, in conjunction with the evaluation results.

List of Conclusions to Communicate to the Client

As the rehabilitation counselor reviewed Ms. Amy's background information and evaluation results, there were a few conclusions to communicate with her:

- The findings of the WHODAS 2.0 effectively address the marked distress Ms. Amy reported feeling and how the distress could affect employability or further success.
- Address what was possibly seen as a conflict of information between the WASI-II and the PEL regarding Ms. Amy's intelligence score.
- Give an overview of the Career Scope Interest Inventory to show Ms. Amy how her results aligned with her vocational goals.
- Discuss Ms. Amy's personality and learning type with her and how they can be utilized in the workplace.
- Consider ways to effectively deal with the possible barriers to employment noted in the vocational evaluation.

- Have a candid discussion on the possibility of seeing an outside therapist, psychologist, or other mental health professionals to learn effective ways of coping with life's stressors.

Feedback Process

The information received in the psychological and vocational evaluations provided the rehabilitation counselor with data that can aid in the feedback process. For example, Ms. Amy registered high as an auditory learner and low as a visual learner. This understanding, combined with knowing Ms. Amy did better on the verbal sections of the assessments, prompted the counselor to engage Ms. Amy mostly verbally. Since the client was given a copy of her evaluations, it is imperative that the counselor does auditory reviews of the documents with Ms. Amy. This ensures that the client has a full breadth of knowledge regarding the case. Also included in Ms. Amy's vocational evaluation was her personality type, ENTJ. Having the client's personality distinction can aid the vocational counselor in "structuring the counseling relationship and in selecting specific interventions for that client" (Whiston, 2009, p. 241). A possible limitation to the utilization of assessment in Vocational Rehabilitation is overworked and understaffed offices. Many counselors have large caseloads and may not have the time to dedicate to extensively review each client's evaluation with said client.

After having a thorough conversation with the counselor, Ms. Amy completed and signed her Individualized Plan for Employment, moving her case to status 12. For Vocational Rehabilitation to continue to support Ms. Amy's goal or referral question, she was required to develop a business plan and blueprints for the restaurant. Ms. Amy completed both tasks and has been approved to receive funding, through the Vocational Rehabilitation Agency, to assist in opening a dream restaurant. Ms. Amy's case progressed smoothly and should soon be in status 26, which is the status for a successful closure.

Summary

Assessment plays a crucial role in the vocational evaluation and rehabilitation of a PWD. It is unique to every client and should be tailored to their customized vocational needs, functional potentials, and limitations with a goal of client empowerment through successful job placement. Vocational assessment is complex, with four key components and seven different categories of assessments and tests. Since there are numerous vocational tools and assessment measures, the use of these instruments requires expert training and collaboration among the team of professionals working with each case. Like in Ms. Amy's case presented in this chapter, rehabilitation counselors should carefully choose the assessments based on the referral questions and specific needs of each client with a focus on the ethical, legal, and multicultural considerations.

Test Your Knowledge:

1. John is a 19-year-old high school dropout. He recently had a minor knee surgery and is ready to get back to work after full recovery. He is confused about his occupational preferences and the type of job that he wants to apply for. He reports to his counselor that he becomes overwhelmed and anxious if he has to make a decision about his career. Which of the following is an interest inventory that John's counselor needs to consider?
   a.   Self-Directed Search
   b.   Kuder Occupational Interest Survey
   c.   Salience Inventory
   d.   Strong Interest Inventory®

2. _____ are developed to assess rehabilitation clients' abilities and skills.
   a.   Achievement tests
   b.   Intelligence tests
   c.   Aptitude batteries
   d.   Interest inventories

3. All of the following are intelligence tests used by vocational evaluators EXCEPT:
   a.   Luria-Nebraska
   b.   Wechsler Adult Intelligence Scale
   c.   Raven's Progressive Matrices
   d.   Draw-A-Person test

4. According to Lee and Ditchman (2012), comprehensive rehabilitation involves how many components?
   a.   2
   b.   5
   c.   3
   d.   4

5. Which of the following is used as a measure of work readiness?
   a.   Vineland Social Maturity Scale
   b.   Vocational Behavior Checklist
   c.   Self-Directed Search
   d.   Dictionary of Occupational Outlook

6. Which of the following assessments is a self-administered interest inventory based on Holland's career theory?
   a.   Self-Directed Search
   b.   Salience Inventory
   c.   Strong Interest Inventory®
   d.   Reading Free Vocational Interest Inventory

7. _____ is an achievement test used for assessing the cognitive functioning of an individual with learning disabilities.
   a.   Peabody Individual Achievement Test
   b.   Woodcock Johnson Psychoeducational Battery
   c.   Tests of General Educational Development
   d.   Basic Occupational Literacy Test

8. Your new rehabilitation client reports that she remembers scoring very high on depression and psychasthenia on a test that she took a couple of years ago, but cannot recall the name of the test. Which personality test do you think she took?
   a.   16 Personality Factor
   b.   Myers-Briggs Personality Type Indicator
   c.   Minnesota Multiphasic Personality Inventory
   d.   Rorschach Ink Blot Test

9. According to Power (2013), vocational evaluators should be competent in test administration, _____, and interpretation.
   a. development
   b. scoring
   c. both of the above
   d. none of the above

10. CRCC code of ethics requires the rehabilitation counselors to be multiculturally sensitive in test selection and should consider clients' disability-related issues.
   T or F?

Discussion Questions/Prompts:

1. For what reasons might a mental health or school counselor need to understand the rehabilitation assessment process?
2. Discuss the importance of using a holistic approach to assessment in rehabilitation cases.
3. Describe and discuss the "measures of work readiness."
4. Why are "assessments of physical functioning" so critical with this population?
5. How would you work with Ms. Amy in making her assessment results meaningful?

11 Suicide Assessment

Kathryn C. MacCluskie and Debra A. Tkac

Introduction

Of all the occasions on which you may be called to assess a client, there may be no other time when the stakes are as high as they are when you assess for suicidality. You may not remember the name of the client or exactly what was said in session. You will, however, remember the sinking feeling in the pit of your stomach and the racing of your heart the first time someone discloses to you that they no longer wish to be alive. When a situation of this nature arises, a thorough clinical assessment of the client's safety is essential! The assessment procedures may include the use of formal instruments, informal assessment instruments (i.e., mnemonics), and clinical consultation. All components of the assessment process assist in determining the level of risk and the resulting steps to ensure safety. Each work setting has their own expectations about proper procedure during a suicide assessment and in the subsequent treatment planning.

This chapter may be a bit of a red herring in comparison to the other chapters of this book that cover specific assessment procedures. An assessment of suicide risk is a completely different undertaking than a standardized assessment of a person's academic achievement or personality. There are aspects of this assessment that look totally different to an observer; one is the time frame in which the suicide assessment occurs. Often, the clinician may only have an hour or two in which to establish rapport, gather a host of data, and arrive at a sound decision about the best clinical course of action to deliver help. There is often some element of time pressure which certainly has potential to escalate the degree of stress a counselor experiences as he or she strives to make the best decision.

Another aspect that differs from standard assessment procedures is that we believe the suicide assessment process itself is ideally one of dynamic, relational dialogue, a dialogue that is interactive on a far different level than other standardized assessments. Whereas many standardized instrument administration manuals actually provide a script and seating directions for the person administering the instrument, a suicide assessment more closely resembles a counseling session.

Please note that all the material and information contained in this chapter pertains to work with young adult and adult clients. Suicide assessment of children and teens (minors) involves some differences in terms of how to gather information, legal considerations, and what factors need to be considered in a dispositional decision for the child, all of which lie beyond our current scope in this discussion.

The Conceptual Foundation of Suicide Assessment

As mentioned in the previous section, in the realm of suicide assessment, theoretical knowledge and clinical skills supercede the use of standardized instruments. Sullivan and Bongar

(2006) observed that in lieu of standardized tests, "most clinicians rely primarily on the clinical interview and certain valued questions and observations to assess suicide risk" (p. 177). The process of risk assessment is extremely complex and comprehensive, requiring a thorough evaluation of objective risk factors in conjunction with the client's self-report *and* clinical presentation. Referring to some basic statistical concepts, the challenge of any assessment is avoiding the commission of Type I or Type II errors. Related to this concept, Pokorny (1983) observed that the clinical task is not prediction of potential suicide but rather the assessment of suicide risk. In this context, a Type I error would be erroneously identifying someone as high risk for a suicide attempt when in reality they are at a low risk, while a Type II error would be represented as erroneously deeming someone as a low risk when in fact a suicide attempt is imminent. The consequences of committing a Type I error in this case clearly carry less serious implications than the consequences of a Type II error.

Accurate prediction of a likely suicide attempt is considered by the courts and by society in general to be among the most serious and important tasks of mental health professionals (Sullivan & Bongar, 2006). As we reviewed the professional literature about methods of assessing for suicidality, we found an interesting range of approaches. While we expected to find mainly objectively scored and normed inventories, we found literature supporting semi-structured interviews that are also empirically sound and offer quantifiable results to either support or refute a counselor's diagnostic impression of and treatment planning for a client who is suicidal.

Before we examine a selected number of instruments used to assess suicidality, we will touch briefly upon 12 principles that Granello (2010) advocates as the conceptual basis for the process. These principles represent broad, overarching caveats that form the foundation for suicide assessment, regardless of whether it is done through a structured interview or with a more standardized instrument. For the purpose of this discussion, the principles have been grouped as pertaining to items of clinical objectivity, and items pertaining to the relationship between the counselor and the client who is suicidal.

The principles related to clinical objectivity hold that suicide assessment is:

- unique—each person presents with different circumstances. While the uniqueness of an individual is always a present factor in score interpretation, the idiosyncrasy of each individual person takes on another level of importance when considering the dangers of using norms to predict the level of someone's risk for an attempt.
- complex—there are myriad factors related to the first point that must be considered.
- conservative—maintaining a cautious stance in arriving at recommendations or taking action is always advisable.
- dependent on sound clinical judgment—use of sound clinical judgment is absolutely critical.
- responsive to *all* threats—being dismissive of verbalized intent is inadvisable.
- comprehensively and accurately documented.

There are six additional principles that relate more to the relationship aspects of the suicide assessment. The relationally related principles posit that suicide assessment is also:

- collaborative—the assessment process can involve other individuals besides the client, mainly those collateral individuals who hold a position of emotional significance to the client.
- inquisitive and receptive to exploration of difficult subjects (self-harm)—despite the anxiety and discomfort that may be elicited for the counselor, frank discussions about suicidal ideation and intent are an integral aspect of assessment.

- focused on discerning and understanding the motivation for considering suicide— Granello (2010) recommends attempting to uncover the underlying message which most often is to either communicate, control, or avoid.
- deeply culturally embedded—the meaning attached to suffering and suicide varies widely across cultures, and is a critical aspect of understanding the individual's motivation.
- a continuous, ongoing process—in many cases, level of suicidality is dynamic and continuously changing, as a function of other situational factors. It is erroneous to assume that because a person's suicidality at one session is low, it will remain a negligible threat.
- a form of treatment; the assessment process itself can and should be therapeutic—the conversations and empathic responding that happen in a competent assessment of suicidality can offer a great deal of relief for individuals who have been unable to express their thoughts and feelings about wanting to die.

Two of the instruments we will be discussing, the IS PATH WARM mnemonic and the Relational Risks and Resources Guide, are not normed instruments, but rather are semistructured models to guide a suicide assessment interview. We mention them here because both of those models are consistent with Granello (2010) in their emphasis on the importance of the therapeutic relationship as a component of the assessment.

Let's take a brief look at each of the instruments specified in Table 11.1 before choosing some and illustrating a case application. The Columbia Suicide Severity Rating Scale features many versions of the instrument, all of which are free. There is a downloadable form that can be used by friends and family members at http://cssrs.columbia.edu/wp-content/uploads/Community-Ace-Card-2017-v2.pdf and enables a mental health professional to potentially enlist the support of others in the client's support system to monitor the suicidal ideation on an ongoing basis.

Table 11.1 Instruments

Type of Instrument	Strengths	Weaknesses
Columbia Suicide Severity Rating Scale	Free Brief version is just six easy questions that can be accessed by friends and family online Objectively scored Extensively researched and empirically validated	Full version is lengthy Neglects questions about protective factors
Burns Depression Inventory	Easy to administer Free—available online	Not developed specifically for suicide risk assessment
Beck Scale for Suicide Ideation (Beck, Kovacs & Weissman, 1979; Beck & Steer, 1993)	Evaluates wish to live/wish to die	Old
Reasons for Living Inventory (Linehan, Goodstein, Nielsen & Chiles, 1983)	Looks at the protective factors	Old Unclear how to actually use it unless you agree to register on their site
Relational Suicide Assessment (Flemons & Gralnik, 2013)	Interactive, semi-structured interview Identifies risks and resources, client and client's significant others—very comprehensive	No norms or quantification that could be a challenge for inexperienced clinicians
IS PATH WARM (Juhnke, Granello, & Lebron-Striker, 2007)	Easily remembered	

The Burns Depression Checklist is an easily administered set of 25 questions that cover emotional, cognitive, and behavioral aspects of depressive symptoms, with the last three stimulus items querying specifically about suicidal intent. One disadvantage of this instrument is that it assesses depressive symptoms in general but doesn't hone in on, or give additional stimulus items for, assessing suicidality in detail. Closely related is the Beck Depression Inventory which, like the Burns, assesses the three components of feeling, thinking, and behaving, which represent Beck's predominant theoretical emphasis upon the cognitive-behavioral aspects of depressive symptoms. Neither the Beck nor the Burns assess strengths or protective factors; these are weaknesses when considering either of these instruments for assessing suicidality.

Cognitive rigidity and beliefs about the hopelessness of one's situation are noted to be important mediators of suicidal behaviors (Linehan et al., 1983). The Reasons for Living (RFL) Inventory (Linehan et al., 1983) is an outstanding contribution to the literature on assessment because it looks at reasons for wanting to stay alive, which is the obvious counter-balance to reasons for wanting to die. These reasons to stay alive may come back to a sense of hope, but there are additional categories of reasons to live. The RFL Inventory was developed by field testing a model that assessed a variety of respondents' answers to questions about what kept them going at the point in their lives when they were most likely to consider suicide. The categories that evolved from their statistical analysis were Survival and Coping Beliefs, Responsibility to Family, Child-Related Concerns, Fear of Suicide, Fear of Social Disapproval, and Moral Objections. Interestingly, these same categories of information could potentially represent avenues for intervention as foci in addition to a focus on developing cognitive flexibility and room for hope in the person's narrative. The RFL is available free online, and after a person takes the test their responses can be viewed, with higher numbers suggesting a higher level of optimism. It did not appear to be easy to determine how to get a score print out with levels of responding on each of the six factors; this is somewhat of a disadvantage of this instrument.

The last two assessment techniques in Table 11.1 are both guidelines for structuring a clinical interview and intervention, rather than specific instruments per se. The first one is called Relational Suicide Assessment (RSA) (Flemons & Gralnik, 2013). Those authors aptly made the observation:

> Suicide assessments are relational conversations, interactive dialogues that trace back and forth across the sometimes too thin line separating death from life—back and forth between giving up and going on, between pulling away and reaching out, between hopeless certainties and faint-hope possibilities.
>
> (p. 1)

Thus, whereas other aspects of psychological assessment, such as cognitive functioning, lend themselves more readily to standardized assessment, suicide assessment is in some respects a completely different process, one that more intensely involves dialogue and interaction with the person who is suffering. There are several advantages to the RSA approach. Perhaps the most central strength is that it emphasizes empathic connection with the client, which can itself be highly therapeutic for a person who is feeling isolated and alienated. Another value of using an RSA approach is that, like the Linehan RFL instrument, it features particular topics and foci that are relevant not only for assessment but also for treatment. The four categories of assessment are 1) Disruptions and Demands, 2) Suffering, 3) Troubling Behaviors, and 4) Desperation. Within each of these categories, the clinician is provided with empirically based risk factors and protective factors, pertaining to the client as well as to the client's significant others. Thus, it is more broadly comprehensive and balanced than an instrument that only assesses for depressive symptoms.

Finally, IS PATH WARM is a mnemonic device developed by Juhnke, Granello, and Lebron-Striker (2007), with each of the letters representing a category of information to be gathered. Following are the categories and the associated questions:

- I(deation)—how frequently and intensely the person thinks about suicide
- S(ubstance Abuse)—is there excessive use of mood-altering substances?
- P(urposelessness)—how clearly the person feels a sense of meaning or purpose in his or her life
- A(nger)—how much rage or uncontrolled anger the person experiences; harboring resentment toward specific others?
- T(rapped)—how able is the person to see alternatives or avenues beyond the immediate problem; does death look like the only escape from the problem?
- H(opelessness)—how able is the person to see ahead to better times?
- W(ithdrawal)—has the person drawn away from significant others?
- A(nxiety)—does the person experience an inability to relax? Is there a disruption of normal sleep, with either hypersomnia or insomnia?
- R(ecklessness)—is there evidence of engaging in risky behaviors without taking precautions?
- M(ood change)—are there dramatic changes in mood with some rapidity?

Simply as a procedural recommendation, we suggest that if you are intending to use paper-and-pencil instruments to assess suicidality, keep those materials readily available in your office or wherever you are seeing your clients. A suicide assessment can become the focus of any counseling intake or session at any point; sometimes a client with whom you have worked for some time already will come to a session with suicidal ideation and the day's appointment immediately becomes one of suicide assessment. It can be a stress reducer to have any instruments you intend to use readily accessible at a moment's notice.

Specialized Training

The American Association of Suicidology offers certification training programs in forensic suicidology. Forensic suicidology refers to being qualified to testify as an expert witness in legal cases involving suicide. Additionally, there are multiple other, less intensive, opportunities for training and continuing education for mental health workers. Considering the likelihood for needing these assessment skills, readers are encouraged to obtain additional training. A study of social workers' decisions about case disposition showed that although the participants varied broadly in their recommendations, ranging from immediate inpatient psychiatry admission to no hospitalization, all participants were equally confident in their own decision (Regehr et al., 2016). These findings suggest two things about training—it is definitely important to stay current with assessment skill, and, most important, regardless of how seasoned a therapist you are, it's a very good idea to consult with a colleague to discuss your decision-making process. No matter how careful we are it is possible to miss something or make an assumption that is incorrect. There are frequently continuing education courses offered in assessing suicidality and given the gravity of the topic, any counselor working with people in distress does need to possess some rudimentary skill in identifying individuals who are at elevated risk for a suicide attempt.

Ethical Considerations

If you have completed a course in legal and ethical issues in counseling, you already know that legal mandates and ethical codes are two related, but separate, considerations. Counselors are considered to be mandatory reporters of abuse, and also are mandatory reporters for suicidal or homicidal intent. The term "mandatory reporter" means that counselors are required by law to report a person who poses an identifiable, imminent threat to self or others. As you will see when we examine our case example, the assessment of imminent threat is rarely if ever clear cut; there will always be a ratio between protective factors and risk factors that requires clinical judgment.

The other consideration in this type of assessment lies in the realm of professional ethics; again, another murky area in many real-life situations. The ethical principles of autonomy, beneficence, non-maleficence, fidelity, and justice certainly play a huge role in this suicide assessment process with clear relevance to beneficence and non-maleficence. A less obvious, but also relevant, ethical dilemma arises in the realm of client autonomy; suicide assessment runs the risk of pathologizing the wish to die, while ultimately the decision about whether to live or to die is the most personal, private decision any person can make. It is each person's right to make that decision. The real ethical dilemma comes in when we consider the legal term "of sound mind and body"; at what point do we ascertain that the suicidal intent is symptomatic or indicative of a treatable mental illness? This is a very difficult question to answer in some cases, and one that by necessity must be considered on a case-by-case basis. Careful consideration of the completely unique details of each person's history relates back directly to one of the 12 principles posited by Granello (2010) about each suicide assessment being unique and specific to that individual.

We could work from the assumption that because suicidal behavior is atypical in society, it represents a psychological disturbance. And yet, there may be some individual life circumstances in which the person making the choice is fully mentally competent, not depressed, and also is not interested in going on living. However, often if a person can pull through a suicidal episode and recover, he or she is able then to see that the suicidal intensity was a state that did in fact pass with time. One clinical adage taught to me (KM) by a supervisor many years ago is, "Suicide is a permanent solution to a temporary problem." Interestingly, the relevance of recognizing the transience of suicidal intent is confirmed from a volunteer who works with suicidal people; a TED Talk was given in March 2014, by Sergeant Kevin Briggs, a firefighter who specializes in de-escalating suicidal emergencies. Sergeant Briggs has spoken with many people who are over the railing and poised to jump from the Golden Gate Bridge (www.ted.com/talks/kevin_briggs_the_bridge_between_suicide_and_life#t-831390). Of the hundreds to whom he has spoken, only two have jumped. The lethality of this method is extremely high; only 1% to 2% of people who jump survive. Two pieces of information about his experiences are of high relevance. One is that he attributes his high rate of success not to his ability to influence another person's choices, but rather his ability to just listen without trying to fix, reframe, or blame: *non-judgmental active listening*. This description of the most salient aspect of the intervention supports our previous point about the relational aspect of assessment. The other highly compelling piece of information Sergeant Briggs shared is that in very few cases (1–2%), the people who jump somehow survive the fall and he has had the opportunity to speak with those individuals. He said that in every case the person reported that the moment they let go of the rail and jumped, they knew they had made a mistake.

Yet, if a person does in fact decide after a prolonged period of time that suicide is actually the best option, that is his or her choice. Thus, on a very fundamental level the argument *could* be made that defining suicidality as pathological is a violation of that person's autonomy. Nevertheless, new therapists and students are often advised to explain limits of confidentiality to clients, with the first limit being, "If you tell me you plan to hurt yourself I must take steps to make sure you stay safe." This limit is a legal mandate, so counselors have no choice about whether to report to others, or have hospitalized, those individuals who disclose they are suicidal. Counselors who are not licensed to independently diagnose and treat people with mental and emotional disorders must immediately consult with either their direct supervisor or another senior mental health clinician when a client presents with active suicidal ideation. Often, the decision about how actively a counselor needs to intervene with a client can be murky, with some advantages and disadvantages to taking steps to have a person hospitalized. Regardless of whether the clinician is independently licensed, in the interest of self-care we recommend frequent consultation and debriefing with trusted colleagues or supervisors in order for the clinician him or herself to benefit from support of others.

Case Description

As a clinician, you will encounter numerous situations in which you will be asked to complete a suicide risk assessment, make a recommendation, and implement a plan (i.e., hospitalization, psychiatric evaluation) within a very brief period of time. Most clinical environments (i.e., community mental health centers, private practices, schools) have procedures and protocols for such instances. This may include the utilization of a suicide assessment screening tool, as reviewed earlier in the chapter. Screening tools however are only one part of this multifaceted assessment. A working knowledge of your client, strong rapport, clinical intuition, and supervisor/colleague consultation are also an integral part of this important assessment. As Rudd (2014) reports:

> The core of any assessment for suicide risk is a careful and thorough assessment of suicidal thinking and behavior, with an accurate understanding of suicide intent. It is important to recognize that intent is very much fluid in nature, with suicide warning signs providing observable markers consistent with potential elevations in intent to die. The presence or absence of suicidal thinking is not particularly useful in formulating risk; it is the nature of the suicidal thinking, the specificity, duration, and related features that help the clinician gauge intent to die.
>
> (p. 326)

We have created a client profile that is comprised of elements from numerous people with whom we have worked. The complexity of the client history and safety planning is a close approximation to how people often present when suicidal ideation is a concern.

History of the Referral

Jan is a 32-year-old bi-racial female (Caucasian and Native American). She enters mental health treatment as the result of a "recommendation" for her Children and Family Services case plan. The Children and Family Services worker had concerns about Jan's mental health. Jan has been working with you for three months and has just recently started to share meaningful information. As she begins disclosing information about past suicide attempts and current depression, the question of whether immediate hospitalization or an imminent suicide attempt is indicated.

Current Symptoms and Functioning

Jan presents this date with a restricted affect and irritable mood. She is somewhat disheveled and displays marginal hygiene. You have her complete a Burns Depression Checklist before you begin your session. She brings her two youngest children with her to the appointment (4 years old and 18 months old). Jan's children are very active and display a good amount of energy. Jan appears somewhat disengaged with the children emotionally, but does not let the children out of her sight. She has been married for 12 years, and her children are a 15-year-old daughter, a 9-year-old son, a 4-year-old son, and an 18-month-old daughter. She currently works part-time as a waitress and her husband works in a factory. They are financially struggling and she expresses they are having difficulty "making it" from paycheck to paycheck. Jan reports that Children and Family Services was contacted because their 9-year-old son reported to a teacher that he was frightened by his mother's and father's "fights." He also frequently comes to school with poor hygiene and no lunch money.

Jan acknowledges that she has difficulty attending to her day-to-day responsibilities. As you assess her emotional functioning, she reports the following issues. Jan states she feels "tired all the time" but has difficulty sleeping. Her diet is poor and she comments that she is "not able to eat." She confirms a 12-pound weight loss within the past few weeks "without trying." Jan states she is sad "all the time," she "cries for no reason," and finds it tough to make decisions. Jan feels "helpless" in her situation and often wonders if her children "might be better off without her." Jan confirms frequent suicidal ideation, but denies current intent this date. She admits to past attempts to overdose and a history of self-injury using cutting behaviors. Jan relays that with all the current stressors her depression continues to "get worse." Although you have attempted to refer, Jan has not been receptive to participating in a psychiatric consultation to discuss the potential effectiveness of medication for her issues of depression.

Psychosocial History

In further assessing Jan's psychosocial history, she acknowledges a history of sexual abuse as a child and sexual assault (rape) as an adult. Jan states she "does not trust anyone" and is very "overprotective" of her children. She confirms episodes of "zoning out" and isolating from others. She reports trauma-related nightmares, rumination, anxiety, and "feeling on edge." In light of Jan's symptoms, she has been diagnosed with Major Depression and PTSD.

In regard to her childhood, Jan was the oldest of three girls. She describes an "abusive" household. She indicates that her parents were "on and off" in their relationship. Her father frequently abused alcohol and had verbal and physical altercations with her mother. Jan experienced a profound trauma at the age of 12 when she witnessed her father "choke" her mother. Jan does remember calling 911 and waiting for the ambulance to arrive, but little else about that evening. Jan indicates her mother died as the result of that episode. She relayed that she has not seen her father since that day; Jan and her sisters were placed with a maternal aunt who provided them with food and shelter but minimal nurturance. Jan reports that she "never recovered" from this incident. She remembers in the months following her mother's death, "staying in bed all day" and "feeling guilty that the ambulance did not get there fast enough." Jan became the emotional caretaker for her two younger sisters. She relayed that she still sees her aunt occasionally but does not view her as an active support. Jan views her youngest sister as her primary support. She reports however that she rarely sees her sister (one time per year) and speaks with her sporadically due to her sister's other commitments. Jan indicates that she "cannot" rely on either sister, or any other family member, in times of need.

Jan reports that she met her husband when she was 16 years old. He was six years her senior and she was flattered by his attention. Her first sexual experience with her husband was not consensual. Jan commented that following the rape she "did not think anyone else would want her" so she continued to date him. After one year of being together, she became pregnant and she and her husband moved into a house together. Jan relayed that it was at this time that she recognized that he had a "drinking problem." She states that shortly after they began living together, he became verbally and physically abusive toward her when he would drink. Jan reports that, at first, this frightened her but she refused to report the nature of her injuries to others because she "had no place to go." Jan indicated that she eventually decided she would "not put up" with the abuse and "started to fight back." Their current arguments often include verbal and physical altercations. Jan reports that although they are married, they spend little time together outside of parenting the children. She reports he is an "adequate provider" but continues to "drink." Jan relays that her husband does not understand her depression, and during times of conflict will taunt her by saying, "go ahead and kill yourself." Jan states she is frequently overwhelmed with her household responsibilities and parenting her children. Jan indicates that she recently called her sister to request that her sister watch her children for a weekend over the next few weeks. They are currently trying to make arrangements for this to happen.

In relation to Jan's family history of substance abuse and mental health issues, she reports a history of alcoholism on both the maternal and paternal side of her family. Jan indicates that she believes her mother had a history of depression prior to her death. She recalls that one of her mother's sister's committed suicide when she was young, but is unaware of the circumstances surrounding this event. Jan comments that she does not know much about her father's extended family, with the exception of her paternal grandmother being "a worrier." Jan acknowledges "drinking" and "smoking marijuana" daily to calm herself down. She reports increased amounts and frequency (multiple times per day) to achieve the same calming effect.

In regard to Jan's physical health, she reports a history of heart disease and alcoholism in her family of origin. She indicates she is having "dizzy spells" at times, but has not been to see a doctor because of the cost. Jan seemed to have difficulty reading the papers presented to her to sign. She had to frequently hold them close to her face.

Jan reports that she persevered and completed her high school degree. She indicates that she struggled with learning and often experienced difficulty "thinking outside of the box." She expressed an interest in the medical field and indicated that at one time she dreamed of becoming a "nurse." She reports that, with her financial and parenting responsibilities, she was never able to return to school. She has had several jobs in the service industry, but has often been "let go" as the result of her volatile interactions (physical and verbal fights) with others. Jan comments, " I don't know why I try . . . it really doesn't matter."

Jan expressed limited social support, aside from her youngest sister, who is not readily available. She indicated that she does not "trust others" and minimally socializes. When she does interact, she prefers to socialize with men. She reports that people fall into one of two categories: they are either on her "good side" or on her "bad side." She indicates that she used to be involved with a Christian neighborhood church, but has "not gone in years." She reports she is embarrassed to go back to the church because she has utilized the church's food pantry. Jan relays that she still has a strong religious belief but does not practice this in a formalized manner.

Jan reports that she often does not feel like she "fits into" any cultural group because of her bi-racial background. Jan reports feeling comfortable with her native culture, but has limited knowledge of it. She relays she knows "very little" about herself culturally. Recalling the preliminary information in this case, the referral question is, what is the extent of the imminent risk for Jan to make a suicide attempt in the next several weeks? Is hospitalization indicated?

Application of Assessment Strategies

We move now to a review of several clinical components of Jan's case to assist us with identifying her level of suicide risk. As her clinician you recognize that Jan's presentation this date warrants cause for concern. She appears disheveled and does not engage with you as she has previously (i.e., low energy, limited eye contact, poor hygiene). As you review her Burns Depression Checklist, you become increasingly concerned; her overall score places her in the "extreme" range of depressive symptoms. As you scan the document you notice several items that signal you to continue to assess her level of intent for suicide. Jan has endorsed the following checklist items with the highest rating (4 = extremely experiences the symptom in the past week): feeling discouraged; feeling hopeless; feeling worthless; blaming yourself; loss of pleasure or satisfaction in life; having suicidal thoughts, ending your life; and plan for harming self. A preliminary step in the suicide assessment is to do an item analysis of that checklist; in this case, "item analysis" would consist of selecting some of those critical items and asking her to elaborate. You might phrase it like this: "So Jan, I noticed that on this questionnaire there was a question about hopelessness and you indicated strong agreement. I'd really like to hear more about that." In response you receive no eye contact and only a shrug with the comment, "What does it matter?" You become increasingly aware that there is cause for concern related to Jan's safety and well-being. You ask Jan to rate her level of depression on a Likert scale. You identify a rating of 1 as being indicative of "feeling slightly blue" and 10 as being indicative of a "plan to kill myself." Jan rates herself as a "9." When you ask if she has a plan or current intent, she indicates "not today . . . but if I did, I would go with pills . . . they hurt less than cutting." Although Jan denies current intent, she has acknowledged a plan, confirms that she has access to pills, displays an increased level of depression, is making arrangements for the care of her children (weekend stay with sister), and appears hopeless. You recognize that further exploration of her suicidal ideation is clinically indicated.

To further assess her risk factors you utilize the mnemonic IS PATH WARM. This stands for the following: Ideation, Substance Abuse, Purposelessness (no sense in life), Anxiety, Trapped (by circumstances), Hopelessness, Withdrawal (from friends, family, society), Anger, Reckless behavior, and Mood (change in mood). Taking into account Jan's psychosocial history and style of presentation this date, you are able to confirm the following risk factors:

- **I(deation)** Jan confirms suicidal ideation both verbally and through the Burns Depression Checklist. She rates herself as a 9/10 on a Likert scale with 10 indicating a "plan to kill myself." Jan also has two prior suicide attempts and a family history of suicide completion (maternal aunt).
- **S(ubstance Abuse)** She has confirmed daily alcohol and marijuana use. Jan reports an increase in the quantity of substances to achieve the same effect. There is also a history of substantial substance abuse in the family and in her immediate environment (husband).
- **P(urposelessness)** Jan reports limited meaning and motivation in her life, aside from the care of her children. She indicates limited plans for the future and decreased motivation to work toward goals (i.e., nursing certification).
- **A(nger)** Jan describes feeling irritable and reports a history of verbal and physical altercations with others (i.e., work settings, husband).
- **T(rapped)** Jan acknowledges difficulty "thinking outside of the box" and is not able to problem solve alternative courses of action. **This has been exhibited in her remaining with the children's father, through issues of domestic violence and emotional abuse.**
- **H(opelessness)** Client marked her level of hopelessness as "extreme" on the Burns Depression Checklist. Throughout the interview she also commented "what difference does it make" and her children "might be better off without her." Jan also confirms difficulty letting go of thoughts.
- **W(ithdrawal)** Jan is socially isolated and exhibits limited interest in expanding her social network. She was involved in a spiritual community in the past but has discontinued these ties.

- **A(nxiety)** Jan indicates current anxiety and agitation. She reports "drinking and smoking daily to calm down." She also has a history of PTSD symptoms.
- **R(ecklessness)** Jan relays that she actively fights with her husband and uses substances even while caring for her children.
- **M(ood Change)** Jan confirms a marked increase in her symptoms of anxiety and depression.

As we take these factors into consideration, we notice that in addition to her elevated Burns depression score, she is either endorsing, or exhibiting, numerous other indicators as defined by the IS PATH WARM model. This constitutes further evidence of elevated risk for a suicide attempt. Jan continues to present as high risk related to her suicidal ideation. It's very important to note that the literature on suicide assessment addresses the importance of protective factors in a client's successful navigation of suicidal ideation/behaviors, with a recognition that both risks and protective factors represent a ratio that will influence the dispositional outcome (Flemons & Gralnik, 2013; Simon, 2002; Linehan et al., 1983). Generally speaking, protective factors include, but are not limited to:

- easily accessible support system
- coping and problem-solving skills
- active participation in treatment
- presence of hopefulness
- children in the home
- pregnancy
- religious commitment
- connection to others
- life satisfaction
- intact reality testing
- fear of social disapproval
- fear of suicide or death

The presence, or absence, of these factors provide ongoing data to this complex assessment process. In reviewing all the available data about Jan, we are able to ascertain the following risk analysis.

Jan's protective factors include:

- access to mental health services;
- has children in the home;
- religious beliefs.

Jan's risk factors include:

- high levels of hopelessness (commenting "what does it matter," "children may be better off without me," "don't know why I try");
- expression of ideation;
- plan (take pills, making arrangements for children to spend time with her sister);
- accessibility to means (knows where to get "pills");
- mental health diagnosis (MDD and PTSD); substance abuse; anxiety;
- feeling trapped;
- isolation (lack of trust in others);
- increased symptoms of depression;

- lack of receptiveness to medication management;
- lack of problem-solving;
- anger;
- past suicide attempts;
- family history of completed suicide;
- history of trauma (mother's death, rape, domestic violence);
- lack of support (sister far away and husband tells her to "go ahead and kill yourself");
- high suicide rate for age and cultural background;
- lack of life satisfaction (lack of purpose and motivation); and
- lack of fear of death (previous attempts).

We want to also demonstrate an alternative method for organizing Jan's case information: the Risk and Resource Interview Guide (Flemons and Gralnik, 2013, pp. 58–59), as shown in Table 11.2.

Given the involved and profoundly traumatic developmental history, it is not surprising that we find there to be more evidence of risks than resources, both within herself and also among her circle of social support. The picture painted by this analysis suggests someone who is indeed quite vulnerable and, in our opinion, at high risk for a suicide attempt. From

Table 11.2 Risk and Resource Interview Guide

Disruptions and Demands

	Client	*Client's Significant Others*
Risks	Strained marital relationship Financial stress	Husband is abusive
Resources	Historically was active in church	

Suffering

	Client	*Client's Significant Others*
Risks	Depressed and irritable Insomnia Nightmares Anxiety Rumination Trauma history	Husband taunts her to kill herself
Resources	Has called for help from sister Participating in counseling	One sister is supportive and sympathetic

Troubling Behaviors

	Client	*Client's Significant Others*
Risks	Zones out, withdraws from others Use of alcohol and marijuana to cope Weight loss	Husband also drinks
Resources	Attending counseling	

Desperation

	Client	*Client's Significant Others*
Risks	Helpless	Husband minimizes her plight
Resources	Committed to being a good mother Willingness to discuss her suicidality	Has a sister to whom she is close and has a good relationship

a broad developmental perspective, Jan might benefit over the long term by working on two aspects of her well-being: developing some internal skills for affective regulation and self-nurturance, and developing some external skills for establishing and maintaining healthy relationships with people who are stable and trustworthy. We will continue with a more detailed description of how we would make a dispositional decision about how to best help Jan in the immediate moment using the IS PATH WARM model.

One of the reasons suicide assessment differs from other assessment techniques, as mentioned earlier, is that the information gathering process itself can help support the clinician in choosing a course of intervention. Overall the clinical data clearly support a "high-risk" rating for Jan. Since it is difficult in a case study to relay all the potential nuances (e.g., the strength of therapeutic relationship, the client's nonverbal behavior, her progress in treatment, baseline of depression, etc.) of this clinical assessment, we will explore two potential outcomes: hospitalization of Jan and ongoing safety planning for her. In the event that the recommendation is for hospitalization, the specific policy/procedures at your work environment should be applied. Ongoing consultation with a clinical supervisor or colleague is imperative throughout this process. It is important that the client continue to be monitored (line of sight supervision) until transport to the hospital can be arranged. This may include transport by EMS, the police, and/or a family member. The clinician may be in contact with the hospital to provide information prior to the arrival or may follow the client to the ER. Once the client is admitted, it is imperative that coordination of the client's care occurs between the clinician and hospital staff for discharge planning of ongoing clinical treatment.

In the event that the client is evaluated by the ER and not hospitalized, a care plan/safety plan should be implemented. The plan should include: follow-up therapy appointments, steps to take should the SI increase, emergency contact numbers, and goals to decrease the level of ideation/plan. The following dialogue is an example of how we would have a discussion with Jan about safety.

Clinician:	I am concerned about your thoughts of "wanting to kill yourself" and want to keep you safe. You stated that you did not have the intention to kill yourself today. What gives you the strength at this time to do that when you are in so much pain?
Jan:	I keep thinking of my children . . . sometimes I think they would be better off without me . . . but I remember how it felt growing up without my mom there. I am not sure that I can do that to them. I also know that it would break my sister's heart.
Clinician:	Your love and connection with your children and sister provide you with the strength to cope.
Jan:	Yes, but it is still really hard . . . and I still think about it all the time.
Clinician:	Would it be less overwhelming if we focus on a commitment from you to keep yourself safe just for the next two days, until we can meet again and explore your thoughts/feelings further?
Jan:	Yes . . . I think I can stay safe for the next two days.
Clinician:	What kind of plan can we put into place to assist you in those times of struggle?
Jan:	I am not sure.
Clinician:	Are you willing to work with me on identifying some steps that you can use to deter those thoughts until we meet for our next session?
Jan:	Yes I think I can try.
Clinician:	That's great. We will write them down for you to take with you. Earlier you mentioned the importance of your children and sister. Are you able to talk to or spend some time with them to redirect your thoughts?

Jan: My kids are always around. Guess I just need to spend less time in my room and more time with them.

Clinician: So when the thoughts are really strong, you can come out of your room and spend time with your children?

Jan: Yes.

Clinician: How about your sister?

Jan: My sister is always busy.

Clinician: What if we called her and asked her to call you once a day to see how you are doing?

Jan: Ok [place call to sister to assist in monitoring].

Clinician: What about your husband, is he someone that can provide support?

Jan: No, in fact he stresses me out more and that makes the thoughts stronger.

Clinician: Then we will not consider him as part of the plan at this time. In addition to interacting with your family, what are things that you like to do that help you to refocus from your suicidal thoughts? For example, you tend to be playing a game on your cell phone when I come out to get you in the waiting room—does that help to distract you?

Jan: Yes I can spend hours focusing on getting to the next level.

Clinician: Is that something that we can add to your plan?

Jan: Yes.

Clinician: I know that you have also spoken about your spirituality in the past. Is prayer something that you rely on in times of stress?

Jan: I used to . . . I suppose I could try that again. It has helped before.

Clinician: Then let's add that to your plan. We have also talked about several mindfulness activities in session. Is there one that stands out for you?

Jan: I really enjoy coloring the mandalas. I have a workbook of them at home that I can use.

Clinician: Good. You now have activities and people in place to help you to refocus your thoughts. Now let's talk about instances in which the suicidal thoughts are too strong and you are not able to distract yourself from them. In those situations you can call me to discuss them. In the event that I do not get to your call immediately (i.e., after hours, in session) and it is urgent, I am also going to provide you with the crisis line number. The crisis line is available 24 hours per day. You can utilize this or simply go straight to the emergency room for an evaluation. Does this plan sound like something that you can make a commitment to until we meet in two days?

Jan: Yes.

Conveniently for us, in this case example, the client was compliant. However, there are times when clients will not be compliant regarding ensuring their safety. In those instances, the police and/or EMS (depending on your policies/procedures) may be utilized to assist you. When the assessment is complete, it is important to spend some time debriefing with your supervisor or other support staff, particularly if this is your first assessment. *Self-care cannot be emphasized enough.* In order for you to continue to assist others you need to be focused and grounded.

In summary, assessing clients for suicidal ideation is a complex process. Each client is an individual and each assessment must be individualized, even when you are relying on systematic procedures. Through this relational assessment the overarching goals are to ensure the safety of the client, instill hopefulness, and strengthen the therapeutic alliance for ongoing treatment.

Test Your Knowledge:

1. In the mnemonic IS PATH WARM, the "T" stands for:
   a. Truthfulness
   b. Tangential
   c. Trapped
   d. Tension

2. As an unlicensed clinician assessing a suicidal client, you should:
   a. Consult with your supervisor and/or a licensed clinician if your supervisor is not available
   b. Complete the assessment and make a decision regarding the client's care
   c. Follow your practice's or agency's policies and procedures regarding suicidal behavior
   d. Both A and C

3. Which of the following is NOT a risk factor for suicide?
   a. History of substance abuse
   b. History of mental illness
   c. First-born child
   d. Cognitive rigidity

4. Talking to a client about suicidal ideation is advisable because:
   a. There are few other ways to know someone is considering it
   b. There are implications for how the counselor submits insurance claims on that client if suicide is part of the picture
   c. It is not advisable; it could put ideas in a person's head
   d. None of the above are true

4. Even if a person has many risk factors, the presence of resources and assets can offset the negative impact of those risks.
   T or F?

5. If a person has had many previous "failed" suicide attempts, the likelihood he or she will actually complete a suicide is much lower than someone who has not previously attempted.
   T or F?

7. The diagnosis of Major Depression is always the appropriate diagnosis when suicidal ideation is part of the clinical picture.
   T or F?

8. One helpful place to focus discussion with a suicidal client is upon protective factors, existing coping strategies, and utilization of strengths.
   T or F?

9. It is imperative for a counselor to advise a client that he or she will absolutely not be permitted to kill him or herself; the counselor's job is to save them from making a huge mistake.
   T or F?

10. Suicide assessment should only be done if the client initiates the topic.
    T or F?

Discussion Questions/Prompts:

1. What is your reaction to the chapter discussion about the choice to live or die belonging to each of us?
2. How does this intersect with your beliefs about suicide?
3. What are your thoughts and feelings about involuntary hospitalization? What are the limitations of that strategy and how can those limitations be managed?
4. What are the local emergency resources in your area that you can access to assist you with a suicidal client (i.e., EMS, police, crisis line, inpatient unit at the hospital, etc.)? Create a list and/or index card with the names and contact information to utilize as a future resource.
5. You are working with a client who presents as very depressed. You ask the client if they are feeling suicidal. The client states "no." Your clinical observations and "gut response" tell you that they are not being truthful. What would be your next step?

12 Assessment in K–12 School Counseling

Trigg A. Even and Melanie A. Williams

It can be said that the counseling profession as we know it originated in part through the vocational assessment and guidance practices in what would become professional school counseling (Thompson, 2012; Wright, 2012). These early efforts to help young people overcome economic, educational, societal, and other challenges and inequalities attempted to match individualized student aptitudes with personal goals and vocational opportunities. This was a process of structured self-discovery, guided by a knowledgeable and trustworthy professional, and followed by an applied problem-solving, decision-making sequence. As you review this chapter, keep in mind that the practice and application of assessment in school counseling is, in a sense, a return to the foundational practices in the profession, rather than an addition to, or departure from, its current scope. Throughout this chapter, we have provided several citations of assessments used in school counseling practice. We encourage you to review these publications for more information on their uses and applications.

Introduction—A Composite Case Example

It was the middle of the grading period and the early alerts were streaming in. In response to the prior year needs assessment and campus improvement data, Ms. Rodriguez, the 9th grade counselor, had implemented a screening and identification process for the new school year. This process ensured that all teachers reported to the school counselor and administrator the names of freshman students at risk of failing the term, missing class more than 5% of the time, and/or showing signs of emotional or behavioral distress. So far, Ms. Rodriguez was pleased with the response to the in-service training she had provided teachers on what to watch for and how to support all students with classroom instructional strategies that keep students' social and emotional needs in mind. Ms. Rodriguez was also busy conducting whole-class guidance lessons in freshman classrooms to tell students what to expect from the upcoming standardized testing period and how the test results would be used. During these classroom guidance lessons, Ms. Rodriguez also invited students to voluntarily complete an informal screening survey. This survey contained a checklist of common concerns that students might have—in the personal, social, educational, and career development domains—and a placeholder for requesting a follow-up meeting with the counselor, should the student choose to do so. Although Ms. Rodriguez would compile and de-identify these screening data for program evaluation, the main purpose in the early part of the year was to encourage students who may need additional support to self-identify to the counselor.

Whether students completed the screening survey or not, she told students how to contact her and invited them to speak with her privately about personal concerns and/or standardized testing results. She also informed them of the upcoming parent night where she would explain to parents about the school counseling program services and how test scores can be interpreted and how they will be used, with other data, to inform instruction. Knowing that

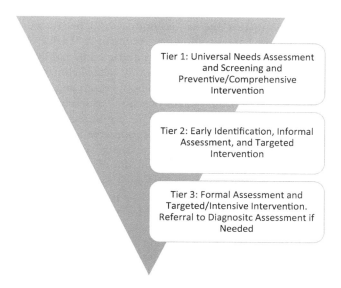

Figure 12.1 Data-driven Decision-Making Process

some students would be identified as needing additional support, Ms. Rodriguez was eager to begin approving students for various small group counseling programs.

Assessment is a dynamic process, not an event. This is especially true in school counseling. Assessment in the school setting naturally aligns with the spirit and rationale of comprehensive developmental programming, as organized and disseminated by the American School Counselor Association's National Model (ASCA, 2012). What this means is that, rather than focusing first on individual students, assessment practices are initiated at the universal, campus-wide level (Armistead, 2008; ASCA, 2014; Desrochers, 2015). Professional school counselors collaborate with other school professionals to administer, score, and interpret school-wide achievement and aptitude tests, disaggregate the assessment data to identify groups and individual students at risk of academic difficulty, and continue the assessment process to further isolate reasons for academic impairment. This process leads to decision-making about targeted follow-up responsive services and other educational, social, and behavioral supports that may benefit the student (please see Figure 12.1).

This chapter describes the process of assessment in K-12 school counseling and applies this process to the composite case of Evette, a high school freshman. Specifically, this chapter will focus on assessment as standard in the school counselor's scope of practice, the purposes and uses of assessment in school counseling, examples of assessments used in school counseling, and the decision-making process that accompanies assessment data.

Assessment and the School Counselor's Scope of Practice

Make no mistake about it, schools and the counselors they employ have one primary function: supporting students so they can learn (ASCA, 2012; Barna & Brott, 2013). The core business of education is teaching and learning, as measured by academic achievement gains (standardized test scores, GPA, adequate yearly progress, etc.). Increasingly, the profession of school counseling is being held accountable to produce empirical evidence that what it does works. Fortunately, there is increasing empirical evidence that students in schools with fully implemented, comprehensive developmental guidance and mental health services and programs show measurable gains in academic achievement (ASCA, 2016; Guzman et al., 2011; Lapan, 2012). Knowing that mental, emotional, and behavioral health conditions impact academic achievement (Armistead, 2008; Adelman & Taylor, 2006), and that students' academic achievement and mental health are impacted by family dynamics (Eppler & Weir, 2009; Unger, McLeod, Brown, & Tressel, 2000), school climate (Kramer, Watson, & Hodges, 2013; Thapa et al., 2012), access to the school counseling program services (Gruman, Marston, & Koon, 2013), and the quality of school counseling program implementation (ASCA, 2016), school counselors are in a unique position to positively affect academic achievement by intervening early and remaining accountable for the services and programs that are implemented to help students. All of these can be assisted with the use of assessment practices. School counselors need an efficient means of early identification, progress monitoring, and outcomes measurement, all of which can be implemented with careful planning, active engagement in a collaborative dynamic process, and embracing assessment as a standard practice (Erickson & Abel, 2013; Grier, Morris, & Taylor, 2001; Lyon et al., 2016).

Now known as the Association for Assessment and Research in Counseling, the Association for Assessment in Counseling and Education (AACE, 2003) published nine competencies in assessment that professional school counselors should demonstrate. By training, professional school counselors are recognized as having the knowledge and skill to ethically and responsibly select, evaluate, administer, score, interpret, and report assessments and assessment results, and to use these results to guide decision-making, program planning, and other accountability practices. Additionally, ASCA (2012) clearly established that cognitive, aptitude, and achievement testing is standard practice within the professional school counselor's scope.

Stop to Consider

A school counselor is advised by her Advisory Council to show evidence that her small group counseling program for students with social skill differences is both necessary and effective. Having already completed a needs assessment that relied on survey responses from students, teachers, and parents, the school counselor believes her program is a necessary intervention, and she can demonstrate that her decision to offer this group was data driven. She cites literature from the professional journals that shows a link between social skill competency and school performance, but she isn't sure that she can *prove* the group is effective at helping these students learn. Even though offering the group *feels* right, she wonders what kind of assessment data would help her ensure accountability to the school's core purpose of helping kids learn and show that these kids performed better academically as a result, in part, of participating in the group.

Purposes and Uses of Assessment in School Counseling

Professional school counselors, like counselors in community-based clinical mental health settings, use assessment for screening, admission and selection, identification of strengths and protective factors, problem identification and diagnostic support, placement and planning, progress monitoring, and outcomes measurement/accountability. Ideally, school counselors will approach assessment from a universal or Tier 1 angle first, followed by more targeted and specific assessments relative to identified needs and referral questions.

Screening

Used in the clinical sense, *screening* refers to the process of using assessment to guide decision-making about whether or not additional, more intensive assessment should be considered. In schools, screening might take the form of program needs assessment surveys (Thompson, Loesch, & Seraphine, 2003), testing for emotional problems (Erford, Butler, & Peacock, 2015), mood disorders (Prochaska, Le, Baillargeon, & Temple, 2016), even suicidal ideation questionnaires (Erickson & Abel, 2013). Students may also be screened for academic readiness (Stormont et al., 2015), learning differences (Hall, 2015), and advanced academics (Purcell & Eckert, 2006).

Admission and Selection

Because schools offer many academic and non-academic programs—both curricular and extracurricular—assessments may be used to inform decision-making about a student's suitability for a particular program or activity (Davis, Davis, & Mobley, 2013).

Identification of Assets and Opportunities for Growth

Comprehensive assessment considers strengths/protective factors as well as problems/risk factors. When using assessment to inform decision-making about how to support and help students, school counselors use assessment data to evaluate both the assets and liabilities with which students present (Nickerson & Fishman, 2013).

Diagnostic Support

Whether they are assessing school climate, program implementation, or individual student problems and concerns, school counselors use assessment practices to gather data for isolating the core areas of concern in order to develop or implement targeted responsive programs and interventions (Erford et al., 2015; Gruman et al., 2013). Note that, because training programs vary, some school counselors are trained to perform diagnosis of mental and behavioral health disorders while others are not.

Placement and Planning

Although school counselors rarely use the term *treatment planning* to describe the process of developing counseling action plans and goals, the use of assessment to inform this process is widely accepted as standard, expected practice. School counselors use assessment data to inform decision-making about placement of students in responsive services programs (i.e., individual counseling, small group counseling, referrals, etc.), general education and special education support programs, and to establish benchmarks for evaluating progress toward goals and objectives along the way (ASCA, 2014; Sprague & Walker, 2004).

Progress Monitoring

With a clear and well-operationalized counseling plan, school counselors can use assessment data collected at regular intervals to monitor progress toward the students' goals and objectives. Cooper, Stewart, Sparks, and Bunting (2013) and Murphy (2008) illustrated how counselors can use the Session Rating Scale and Outcome Rating Scale (Miller & Duncan, 2000) to monitor the progress of counseling.

Outcomes Measurement

Normally reserved for the program level, school counselors use aggregate and disaggregate assessment data to measure outcomes of programs relative to pre-determined objectives and desired outcomes. This process of using assessment, also referred to as program evaluation, allows the school counselor to justify continuation of programs and/or to revise programs as necessary in order to more effectively reach desired student-centered outcomes (Studer et al., 2006).

Stop to Consider

Mr. Chang is a new school counselor at a diverse urban high school. Although he will share the advising load through an alpha split among counselors, he is also tasked with being the identified at-risk counselor for all similarly identified students in grades 9–12. His administrator and the lead counselor meet with him during the first week of his new job to share the spreadsheet of all students who did not pass two or more core subject area standardized tests. Mr. Chang learns that his main job with these students will be to ensure that they pass all core subject area tests during the academic year.

Mr. Chang feels the pressure of high-stakes testing and wonders even where to begin. Besides the obvious standardized test scores, what assessment data should Mr. Chang consider as he begins formulating his plans to help these students?

Assessment Instruments Available for Use in School Counseling Practice

While many assessment instruments, tools, and practices exist that are applicable to the school counseling setting, we have chosen to highlight the use of just a few assessment instruments. Specifically, we will discuss and illustrate the use of student-informant and multirater-informant assessments for screening purposes, for evaluating mood and behavior, and for evaluating cognitive ability and achievement. Special consideration will be given to those assessment instruments that can be administered in groups and individually.

Assessment for Screening

Whether schools should screen students for mental health and other personal or social impediments to learning is controversial (Center for Mental Health in Schools at UCLA, n.d.). Nonetheless, there does appear to be some empirical evidence in support of the benefits to academic achievement and counselor availability resulting from structured screening processes (Grier et al., 2001; Gruman et al., 2013). While formal, standardized assessment tools for screening purposes do exist, the logistical and financial obligations to a school campus or district may make them use-prohibitive. School counselors who choose—with the approval of campus and district administration—to use screening assessment tools might find the resources of the Center for Mental Health in Schools at UCLA (2015) useful and informative. School counselors are also advised to comply with ASCA (2016) ethical standards related to the selection and administration of assessments for screening purpose and to carefully evaluate the need for informed consent against state, local, and district policy.

Assessment for Evaluating Mood and Behavior

The Behavior Assessment for Children, Third Edition (BASC-3, Reynolds & Kamphaus, 2015) is a package of self-report and multi-informant assessment tools designed to identify and differentiate the emotional, intrapersonal, interpersonal, and behavioral needs of school-aged youth. The various assessment products allow for structured behavioral observation, self-report, parent report, teacher report, triangulated multi-informant score reporting, and progress monitoring. In addition to convenient remote administration and online scoring and reporting, the BASC-3 score reports can be generated with recommendations for counselor-led interventions, making it a particularly comprehensive and efficient product for school counselors who have been afforded the autonomy to practice assessment within the scope of their training.

Packaged according to age ranges and developmental level from preschool (2–5), child (6–11), adolescent (12–21), and college (18–25), the three main questionnaire options include the self-report of personality (SRP for ages 8+), the parent rating scale (PRS up to age 21), and the teacher rating scale (TRS up to age 21). For younger children ages 6–7, the self-report of personality is administered by the counselor as a structured interview. The BASC-3 product also includes structured developmental history (SDH) and student observation system (SOS) forms should the counselor choose to triangulate the questionnaires with the data from these forms.

All of the rating scales and forms can be scored and reported separately, but a practical strength of the BASC-3 products is its functionality for multirater reporting. What this

Table 12.1 Behavior Assessment

Test	Strengths	Limitations	Intended Population	Typical Referral Questions	Qualification Level
Behavior Assessment System for Children (BASC-3)	Comprehensive self-report and multirater features Integrated with RtI Administration and scoring options including automatic online entry and scoring Easily scorable and interpretable with standardized T-score distribution Intervention plans can be generated Available in English and Spanish	School counselor schedules may not allow adequate time for administration and thorough interpretation Group administration not available except for the BASC-3 *Behavioral and Emotional Screening System* Software scoring and report generating option no longer available (as with BASC-2)	Multiple forms available for ages 2–25 Norms are available for both general and clinical sample populations US Census population represented in norm groups	Consider adaptive skills and strengths Differentiate internalizing and externalizing problems Identify specific executive function performance (Q-global version only)	B: Master's degree in related field—OR—license or certification—OR—formal, supervised, and subject-specific training

means for the counselor is that the various rating scales can be combined to form a comprehensive view of the student's profile, with particular consideration given to the subscales that are significantly correlated. When interpreting multirater score reports, counselors are encouraged to consider both the graphical pattern of the various score report profiles and the similarity/dissimilarity of subscale scores across raters.

Designed to help the counselor gain insight into the students' thoughts, feelings, and behaviors, the BASC-3 provides a standardized T-score distribution of scores across several subscales. While the subscales do differ between the rating scale versions, scores are reported across the various forms for internalizing (i.e., anxiety, depression), externalizing (i.e., hyperactivity, aggression), school problems (i.e., attention, learning problems), emotional or behavioral symptoms index (i.e., withdrawal, social stress, sense of inadequacy), and adaptive skills/personal adjustment (i.e., interpersonal relations, self-esteem, leadership, activities of daily living). Standardized T-scores between 40–59 generally indicate observations in the normal range. Scores between T = 60–69 indicate observations in the at-risk range. Scores at or above T = 70 generally indicate observations in the clinically significant range. While school counselors typically do not use assessment to diagnose mental health conditions or emotional disturbances, the BASC-3 product allows a school counselor to differentiate between those behavioral, emotional, interpersonal, or executive functioning factors that may be contributing to academic underachievement. Interpretation of standard scores should consider the particular norm group referenced and the confidence level selected. A special consideration for school district decision-makers and policymakers would be informed consent that must be signed by parents prior to administration, that explicitly states that the school counselor's use of the instrument is solely as a screening tool for planning short-term interventions that target the behaviors most in need of intervention and aim to increase student achievement. Counselors who use the instrument should be educated on district policies regarding refraining from making diagnoses or using language that implies that clinical or diagnostic decisions are being made.

Assessment for Evaluating Cognitive Ability

The Cognitive Abilities Test, or CogAT (Lohman, 2012a), measures students' learned verbal, quantitative, and nonverbal reasoning abilities and is designed to portray how students solve problems they have not been directly taught (Lohman, 2014) (see Table 12.2). Instructional strategies are provided based upon students' ability profiles (Lohman, 2013b). When academic achievement significantly differs from a student's CogAT scores, school counselors may investigate the cause in order to design the most effective interventions.

All levels of the test, which correspond to kindergarten through 12th grade, have three batteries with three subtests each. The verbal battery consists of picture/verbal analogies, sentence completion, and picture/verbal classification. The quantitative battery includes number analogies, number puzzles, and number series, and the nonverbal battery includes figure matrices, paper folding, and figure classification (Lohman, 2014). Actual administration time varies before Level 9 because the administrator paces the test, and each of the nine subtests for Levels 9 and higher are fixed at 10 minutes each (Lohman, 2014). The test can be administered in group or individual settings. All questions are in multiple choice format.

No special training in educational testing is required, but the developers recommend that the test administrator is someone who is familiar with the students (Lohman, 2014). School counselors in charge of testing procedures should educate test administrators so that they understand and adhere to standardized procedures, as well as understand how to handle accommodations for students with special needs. In schools, this usually involves training to inform staff of what is permissible during testing and what is not, as well as how to store

Table 12.2 Cognitive Assessment

Test	Strengths	Limitations	Intended Population	Typical Referral Questions	Qualification Level
Cognitive Abilities Test Form 7	Measures reasoning abilities in three cognitive domains Reports are available in multiple formats, and for different purposes Reasonable amount of time Online or paper-based administration Out-of-level testing is possible Can be administered in group or individual settings Scores can inform instruction and program placement decisions	Results are not intended to represent a full measure of IQ If scoring by hand, scores are subject to human error	K–12 students	Need for special programming or interventions Understand current cognitive abilities	No special training in educational testing is required, but the developers recommend that the test administrator is someone who is familiar with the students (Lohman, 2014) Houghton Mifflin Harcourt requires test purchasers to submit a Test Purchaser Qualification Form

and transport materials. Schools that choose paper administration over online administration have the option of ordering pre-coded labels so that students and teachers are not required to complete demographic information by hand (Lohman, 2013a). The paper-based CogAT can be hand-scored, sent to Riverside Scoring Service for scoring, or answer documents can be scanned locally and transmitted to the scoring service.

Every item has been evaluated for bias by a panel of minority educators, in addition to the test author and publisher (Lohman, 2013b). Spanish directions for administration are available, and directions can be administered in another language if the administrator uses common words and simple sentences (Lohman, 2014). For English-language learners who take Levels 5/6, 7, or 8 (which correspond to kindergarten, 1st, and 2nd grade), the sentence completion subtest in the verbal battery can be omitted. A large-print version of the test is available for students with visual impairments.

A best practice in school counseling is to notify parents of the tests their children will be taking as well as purposes for the testing, and parent permission should be obtained before testing students for special programming. When discussing the results of the CogAT with parents, school counselors should be aware that scores are not long-range predictors of academic achievement (ASCA, 2016; Lohman, 2013b).

Assessment for Evaluating Achievement

The Iowa Assessments (The University of Iowa, 2012a) are achievement tests, available for students in grades kindergarten through 12, that measure students' skills in reading, language, mathematics, social studies, and science (see Table 12.3). They can be used in addition to teacher observations and other classroom assessments to identify students' academic strengths and weaknesses in different content areas, monitor academic growth, help schools make judgments about past and future instruction, and inform placement decisions in special programs (The University of Iowa, 2012c).

Assessments are available in the version of a complete battery, which includes all content areas. A core battery that omits science and social studies, and a survey battery that consists of the language or written expression test and select questions from the reading and mathematics tests, is available for certain levels (The University of Iowa, 2014b). Administration time for the complete battery is between 2 hours 30 minutes and 5 hours 40 minutes, depending upon the level of the test and whether optional tests within the battery are administered. The core battery can be administered between 3 hours 20 minutes and 4 hours 30 minutes, depending upon the level of the assessment, and the survey battery takes approximately 1 hour 40 minutes. All questions are in multiple choice format. A Braille edition is available, and a large-print edition is available in Levels 7–17/18 for students with visual impairments.

English-language learners can take the Iowa Assessments, and depending upon the level of English-language proficiency, students may benefit from the use of accommodations. For Spanish-speaking students, Logramos is an achievement test that parallels the scope and sequence of the Iowa Assessments in grades kindergarten through 8th, with science and social studies beginning in 1st grade (The Riverside Publishing Company, 2014).

The same observance of standardized testing procedures and test administrator training used for CogAT is to be used with administration of the Iowa Assessments. Hand-scoring

Table 12.3 Achievement Assessment

Test	Strengths	Limitations	Intended Population	Typical Referral Questions	Qualification Level
Iowa Assessments Form E	Measures strength in different content areas Can be administered in group or individual setting Can be administered outside grade level Reports in multiple formats, for parents, school, and district data analysis Complete, core, and survey batteries available, depending upon level Online or paper-based administration Scores can inform instruction	If hand-scoring, subject to scorer error in grading and norming	K-12 students	Current level of academic performance Progress monitoring Need for specialized instruction or programming	Houghton Mifflin Harcourt requires first-time test purchasers to submit a Test Purchaser Qualification Form The test can be administered by trained school staff members (The University of Iowa, 2014a)

and scoring service portions are available, as well. The Iowa Assessments Score Interpretation Guide (The University of Iowa, 2012c) recommends that those who interpret scores to parents and students use simple, everyday language and give equal time to discussing strengths and weaknesses. The Student Profile Narrative offers the score profile and graph, and a description of score ranges.

Application of Assessment in School Counseling

At the same time she was generating aggregate reports on the recent standardized tests, Ms. Rodriguez was reviewing the student surveys and early alerts she used to screen for students in need of additional support. In collaboration with the other school counselors and two student interns from a local university, Ms. Rodriguez would soon be starting small groups to help students with personal, social, or academic support needs. As she and one of the interns reviewed the student surveys and early alerts, they created a spreadsheet of presenting areas of concern (checklists) in order to track themes and patterns in these self-referral data for program evaluation, but also to begin selecting students for specific small groups. Part of the task involved using the available assessment data to help decide which students might benefit from a study skills group for academic needs only, versus those students who might need a small group to help with interpersonal and social skills, emotional, or behavioral concerns, and which students may not be appropriate for small group counseling. Ms. Rodriguez hoped to have all these data analyzed before the parent night in case parents came with questions about counseling help for their students, so she could explain to parents the support her colleagues and she would be able to provide. For privacy and confidentiality reasons, parents would be encouraged to schedule conferences with Ms. Rodriguez if they had questions pertaining to their children's individual concerns.

One student in particular caught her attention. Evette, a freshman, was new to the district. Ms. Rodriguez had already been in contact with Evette and her mother, Lydia, when they came to enroll just before school started, and again when Lydia called Ms. Rodriguez to ask about the test results. Ms. Rodriguez felt a greater sense of urgency now, seeing that Evette also asked to meet with Ms. Rodriguez because of grade and friendship issues.

Ms. Rodriguez recalled learning that Evette excelled academically and socially in elementary school and most of middle school, but for the previous year had been showing less interest in coursework with a slight decline in grades. Ms. Rodriguez had noted that Evette described how she loves art and feels the happiest after her twice-weekly private after-school art class.

Review of Screening Assessment Data

Ms. Rodriguez decides to review the early alert documentation from Evette's teachers. Her English teacher reported that Evette listens well, seems to understand and apply concepts fairly easily in class, and that her social behaviors in class are appropriate. Her art teacher described her as very talented and a joy to work with. Evette's biology and algebra teachers, however, reported that while she does not tend to disrupt the class, she at times appears to not pay close attention, does not take notes, does not complete homework, and has been disrespectful when asked to participate in class discussions.

At this time, Evette's grades are 75 in English, 40 in algebra, 55 in biology, 62 in world geography, 95 in art, and 92 in dance. Ms. Rodriguez recognized that something is helping Evette to excel in art and dance and maintain passing grades in English; however, Evette's failing grades in algebra, biology, and world geography warrant further consideration.

Initial Referral Question and Decision-Making Process

Although Evette has already received school counseling help in the form of classroom guidance, her current grades, the early alert system, and her self-identification on the screening survey indicate that she may need additional support. At this point, Ms. Rodriguez is most interested in making sure Evette is transitioning to the new district and high school campus sufficiently and that she is fully utilizing the academic supports that are available to her. Ms. Rodriguez decides to take a closer look at Evette's recent standardized test scores to ascertain to what degree her cognitive ability/aptitude aligns with her academic achievement and performance. Consistencies and discrepancies will help guide Ms. Rodriguez's investigation and decision-making process.

Review of CogAT Score Report

In preparation for a follow-up advising meeting with Evette, Ms. Rodriguez reviews Evette's CogAT score report and sees that Evette has a Verbal (V) standard age score of 118, a Quantitative (Q) score of 98, a Nonverbal (N) score of 110, and a VQN composite score of 110. For the fall of 9th grade, her verbal score is at the 87th percentile or 7th stanine, placing her current verbal reasoning in the above-average range (Lohman, 2012b; Lohman, 2013b). Her quantitative score is at the 43rd percentile or 5th stanine, placing her quantitative reasoning within the average range, and her nonverbal score is at the 72nd percentile or 6th stanine, placing her nonverbal reasoning ability also in the average range. Her composite standard age score of 110 is at the 72nd percentile or 6th stanine for 9th grade, also within the average range (see Table 12.4). Ms. Rodriguez refers to the CogAT Score Interpretation Guide to determine which feedback will be the most important to share with Evette and her mother, Lydia. Houghton Mifflin Harcourt (2017) also offers a public online application, that does not require the creation of an account, to help school staff and parents interpret students' ability score profiles.

Evette's median age stanine of six indicates an average level of reasoning ability (Lohman, 2013b). Her scores show a contrast in verbal and quantitative reasoning, with a relative strength in verbal ability and relative weakness in quantitative ability. Ms. Rodriguez sees that students of Evette's age with these tendencies typically have higher scores on verbal subtests of achievement tests and lower scores on math subtests. It is possible that Evette will need more help with procedures and structure in algebra than in English or biology; however, Ms. Rodriguez knows that she can gather additional information from sources such as achievement test scores, grades in class, teacher observations, parent consultation, and Evette's self-report to inform the interpretation and feedback process.

Table 12.4 Intelligence Assessment Using the Cognitive Abilities Test, Form 7, Level 15/16

	Universal Scale Score	Standard Age Score, Age 14 Years, 3 Months	Fall 9th Grade Percentile Rank	Stanine	Qualitative Descriptor
Verbal Reasoning	262	118	87	7	Above Average
Quantitative Reasoning	218	98	43	5	Average
Nonverbal Reasoning	225	110	72	6	Average
VQN Composite	235	110	72	6	Average
Ability Profile 6C (V+ Q-)					

Source: Lohman (2012b)

Review of Iowa Assessment Student Profile

Before talking with Evette or her mother, Ms. Rodriguez also reads Evette's current Iowa Assessments Student Profile Narrative, which reports scores in multiple formats and provides additional information that may help guide discussions with Evette and Lydia.

She sees an English language arts total with a national percentile ranking (NPR) of 82 and grade equivalent (GE) of 13+, which comprises a Reading NPR of 80 and GE of 13+, Written Expression NPR of 74 and GE of 13+, and Vocabulary NPR of 82 and GE of 12.8 (The University of Iowa, 2012b). Evette's English language arts total is in the above-average range, and an NPR of 82 indicates that she performed as well as or better than 82% of students in a nationally representative sample. The GE of 13+ describes Evette's score location on an achievement continuum in terms of grade level; however, it does not necessarily indicate that Evette is ready to complete work at the college freshman level (The University of Iowa, 2012c).

Ms. Rodriguez also sees that Evette has a mathematics composite score with an NPR of 43 and GE of 8.4, which includes a mathematics NPR of 41 and GE of 8.1, and a computation NPR of 46 and GE of 8.8. Her mathematics scores are within the average range, slightly below the 50th percentile, with a slightly higher score in computation than in the mathematics test that required understanding of concepts, relationships, visual representations, and problem-solving (The University of Iowa, 2014b). Evette's core composite consists of language arts and mathematics totals and shows an NPR of 62 and GE of 10.5.

Evette's science NPR is 47 with a GE of 8.8, and her social studies NPR is 54 with a GE of 9.7. Evette's scores indicate that she is performing within the average range in both content areas. She also knows that the complete composite NPR of 58 and GE of 10.2 is not an average of all tests Evette took, rather a score derived from a formula that weighs some tests more heavily than others (The University of Iowa, 2012b).

Overall, Evette's Iowa Assessments percentile rankings show she may have a relative strength in English language arts and a relative weakness in mathematics, although her mathematics percentile ranking is within the average range. When Ms. Rodriguez compares Evette's CogAT and Iowa Assessments data, she notices that the relative strength in verbal ability seems to be reflected in language arts achievement scores, and that the relative weakness in quantitative ability is reflected in mathematics achievement scores. When she compares Evette's current achievement scores to her scores from previous years, she can see that Evette's percentile rankings for language arts are higher than they have ever been before,

Table 12.5 Standardized Intelligence Assessment using the *Iowa Assessments, Form E, Level 15*

	Standard Score	National Percentile Rank, Fall 9th Grade	Stanine	Grade Equivalent	Qualitative Descriptor
Reading	289	80	7	13+	Above Average
Written Expression	285	74	6	13+	Average
Vocabulary	280	82	7	12.8	Above Average
ELA Total	**286**	**82**	7	**13+**	Above Average
Mathematics	243	41	5	8.1	Average
Computation	250	46	5	8.8	Average
Mathematics Total	**245**	**43**	5	**8.4**	Average
Core Composite	**266**	**62**	6	**10.5**	Average
Social Studies	259	54	5	9.7	Average
Science	250	47	5	8.8	Average
Complete Composite	**262**	**58**	5	10.2	Average

Source: The University of Iowa (2012b)

science and social studies are about the same, and math is considerably lower than in previous years. While percentile rankings are not always as reliable for measuring student growth as standard age scores or grade equivalents, if they are the only form of achievement data available to Ms. Rodriguez, she may choose to take note of the trend, but focus on current scores when providing feedback.

Summary of Initial Referral Question and Decision-Making Process

With achievement scores in the average range in math, science, and social studies, it is not easy for Ms. Rodriguez to ascertain whether Evette should be passing her respective courses; however, Evette's relative weakness in math achievement and quantitative reasoning ability will likely be a support target, and if Evette can identify skills that are helping her succeed in art, dance, and English, she may be able to apply the same or a similar approach in other subjects. Ms. Rodriguez will keep in mind that when students with average reasoning abilities learn something new or complex, they may need strategies for understanding and remembering the information (Lohman, 2013b). At first it may look like the coursework is too challenging in some subjects because Evette has higher grades in subjects of interest and lower grades in the subjects she dislikes or finds tedious, which is the same pattern as last year when grades started to decline. Achievement scores have historically shown she was achieving consistently at a satisfactory level, but grades in classes were dropping. Work in art and other classes of interest require less time and energy from her than other subjects, and since school had been relatively easy for her until the last year, she may not have developed the skills to deal with challenges.

Based on her review of the CogAT and Iowa Assessment results, Ms. Rodriguez was able to answer initial referral questions: how can Ms. Rodriguez design appropriate interventions to facilitate Evette's academic and social-emotional development? What should the first steps be, and how might Lydia support Evette at home? It appears as though Evette's skill levels reported in standardized test results may not completely match current grades and performance in class. With reasoning skills in the average range, Evette may benefit from strategies for learning. The norm-referenced test results show how she compares to other students, but grades in classes do not. Course grades provide some information about content knowledge; however, they are also influenced by behaviors that affect success in school, such as those associated with study skills, organizational skills, and time management. Because ability and academic achievement can be influenced by school success skills (Brigman, Webb, & Campbell, 2007; Topping & Trickey, 2007), Ms. Rodriguez determines that an appropriate intervention would be to include Evette in a once-weekly, six-week academic support/study skills small group. She contacts Lydia to follow up and request parental consent for participation in group skillstreaming.

Follow-Up Assessment Referral Question

Because she knows that establishing rapport with Evette will be important to the counseling relationship (Sharpley & Heyne, 1993), Ms. Rodriguez explains at the beginning of small group counseling that she and the students will work together to find ways to help them reach their goals. Evette explains that her main academic goal is to pass her courses, and her presenting concern is that she does not know how she will pass algebra and biology. She also seems to be seeking support but is unsure how or where to obtain it.

Ms. Rodriguez asked the students to think about their personal and academic strengths over the next week and told them that they would talk about these strengths in relation to the strengths identified by standardized test results. They would plan together which skills are already strong, so that they might be used to overcome challenges. Ms. Rodriguez told the students that she would also provide tips for time management, organizational skills, and study skills.

Over the course of next six weeks, Ms. Rodriguez tracks the academic performance of each student in the small group. She notes that Evette's grades have steadily increased in most classes, but Ms. Rodriguez continues to receive correspondence from teachers about problematic behavior in some classes and appearance of distress in others. It appears that Evette continues to underperform in core subject areas. Could it be that Evette is experiencing emotional distress or some other mental health or behavioral condition? Ms. Rodriguez decides to request a parent consultation with Evette's mother, Lydia, to discuss Evette's academic progress relative to her course grades, standardized test scores, completion of the small group, and recent teacher feedback.

During this consultation, Ms. Rodriguez secures informed consent from Lydia, explaining the nature and purpose of the BASC-3 assessment, its inherent strengths and limitations, and the ways that results will be used to guide further decision-making about helping Evette. Ms. Rodriguez explains that even though she has the training to interpret the BASC-3, she will not be using it to diagnose clinical conditions. Furthermore, she explains to Lydia that she will provide a list of community referrals that other parents have found helpful should Lydia perceive the results of the BASC-3 to indicate the need for specialized counseling support outside the school.

After securing signed written consent from Lydia, Ms. Rodriguez administered the BASC-3 self-report, parent rating scale, and teacher rating scale tools using a secure remote online administration feature that allowed each respondent to complete the assessment in the privacy of her or his home, office, or at a private testing computer in the counseling center. Once Evette, her mother, and her teacher completed their respective assessments, Ms. Rodriguez was immediately able to generate both individual and multirater score reports.

Ms. Rodriguez began her review of the BASC-3 score reports by examining the validity indices and response patterns. There are two ways to do this: 1) the BASC-3 score reports return an interpretation of several validity indices, and 2) by visual inspection of multirater profile patterns. All validity indices were categorized as acceptable, and Ms. Rodriguez proceeded to visually inspect the score profiles. She saw that the score profiles followed a similar pattern, more or less, even if the scores were not exactly the same. The BASC-3 uses a standardized T-score distribution having a mean of 50 and standard deviation of 10. Knowing this, Ms. Rodriguez understood that any T-scores between 40–59 would fall in the average range, relative to the norm group; in Evette's case, gender-specific general, non-clinical norms. She also paid attention to subscale scores in the at-risk range of $T = 60–69$ and in the clinical range of $T = 70$ and above.

Ms. Rodriguez also reviewed the adaptive skill profile for each rater, paying particular attention to any subscale score that fell within the at-risk range of $T = 31–40$ or the clinically significant range of $T = 30$ and below.

Because Ms. Rodriguez was not able to embed the self-report data on the multirater teacher and parent report, she reviewed Evette's self-report as an individual score report first. She noted that, in comparison to non-clinical female adolescents, Evette rated herself in the average range for all subscales except *Attitude to Teachers* ($T = 66$, At Risk), *Sense of Inadequacy* ($T = 60$, At Risk), *Self-Esteem* ($T = 37$, At Risk), *Relations with Parents* ($T = 32$, At Risk), *Interpersonal Relations* ($T = 28$, Clinically Significant), *Self-Reliance* ($T = 21$, Clinically Significant), and *Personal Adjustment* ($T = 24$, Clinically Significant). The BASC-3 administration protocol recommends that follow-up with a student on any subscale scored in the at-risk range may be necessary. For subscale scores in the clinically significant range, the BASC-3 administration protocol recommends that follow-up is usually warranted. On the remaining

Table 12.6 Parent and Teacher Assessment of Students using the *Behavior Assessment System for Children* (BASC-3)

	Validity Index Summary	School Problems T-Score/%	Internalizing Problems	Externalizing Problems	Emotional Symptoms Index	Behavioral Symptoms Index	Adaptive Skills/Personal Adjustment
Self-Report (SRP)	All Acceptable	T = 55/70th	T = 47/50th **		T = 58/81st **		T = 24/1st ★
Parent Report (PRS)	All Acceptable **		T = 55/78th	T = 58/86th **		T = 58/84th	T = 35/9th ★
Teacher Report (TRS)	All Acceptable	T = 62/88th ★	T = 49/64th	T = 52/74th **		T = 53/75th	T = 38/14th ★

Source: Reynolds & Kamphaus (2015)

 ★ These scores fall in the at-risk or clinically significant range
★★ These subscale scores are not available for the particular rating scale

subscales used to assess mood and other internalizing factors, Evette rated herself in the average range and no follow-up is explicitly advised.

Next, Ms. Rodriguez examines the parent and teacher multirater score report, and overlays corresponding subscale scores from Evette's self-report for consideration.

By visual inspection of a composite clinical profile, Ms. Rodriguez identifies a generally consistent pattern in the profiles, meaning the direction of scores from one data point to the next proceeds in the same general direction (higher or lower). When clear discrepancies exist, the clinical profiles suggest that the raters may not have similar experiences with the same student, and/or that the response pattern of one or more respondents is not congruent with how things are actually. When this occurs, the validity indexes should confirm the counselor's interpretation.

Next, Ms. Rodriguez examines the data points that converge for all raters. She does this by visually inspecting the score profiles and reviewing the *Multirater Report T-Score Summary*, a feature of the online scoring option that indicates whether the difference between subscale ratings is statistically significant or not at p < .05. By making these comparisons, Ms. Rodriguez is able to efficiently identify those subscales where all the raters agree, paying particular attention to those consensus scores reported by the BASC-3 scoring feature as falling within the at-risk or clinically significant range. While some of the PRS and TRS ratings individually reached the at-risk range, none of the consensus ratings did so. When considered separately, Evette was rated at risk for *Hyperactivity* (T = 61, Parent), *Attention Problems* (T = 64, Teacher), *School Problems* (T = 62, Teacher), and *Withdrawal* (T = 66, Parent). Similarly, Evette's adaptive skill profile indicated some at-risk subscale scores for *Social Skills* (T = 35, Parent; T = 40, Teacher), *Leadership* (T = 30, Parent; T = 38, Teacher), *Functional Communication* (T = 36, Parent), and general *Adaptive Skills* (T = 38, Teacher; T = 35, Parent).

When using the online scoring option of the Parent and Teacher Rating Scales, the BASC-3 now includes Content Scale and Probability Index T-Score Profiles. Of particular interest to Ms. Rodriguez was the finding that Evette was rated by both parent and teacher in the high average to at-risk range for *Emotional Self-Control* (T = 59, Teacher; T = 57 Parent), *Executive Functioning* (T = 64, Teacher; T = 62, Parent), and *Negative Emotionality* (T = 61, Teacher, T = 64, Parent) content scales. In addition, Ms. Rodriguez noted that Evette was profiled as at risk for the *ADHD Probability* (T = 64, T = 62) index and the Functional Impairment probability index (T = 61, T = 60).

Summary of Follow-Up Referral Questions and Decision-Making Process

Per the results of the BASC-3 self-report and multirater parent and teacher reports, Ms. Rodriguez wonders if Evette's apparent difficulty with executive function and her tendency to respond with negative emotion explains her apparent lack of motivation to perform in certain courses, particularly those in which she struggles, and her tendency to display intolerance toward distress and frustration in academic work and classroom behavioral expectations. Incorporating this information with what Ms. Rodriguez knows about Evette's current cognitive ability profile from the CogAT and achievement assessed in the Iowa Assessments, Ms. Rodriguez's initial decision to provide Evette with Tier II academic and study skills support was further affirmed, and she had new evidence that Evette may benefit from more personalized interventions.

Recommendations and Next Steps

All of the individual BASC-3 rating scales can be generated with recommendations for interventions. Based on Evette's SRP ratings, the recommended primary and secondary improvement areas include self-reliance, social skills, attitude to teachers, self-esteem, and sense of inadequacy. From the TRS, it is recommended that counseling help Evette improve study skills and other academic attentiveness skills. From the PRS, it is recommended that Evette receive support to improve compliance with rules and structure, avoiding isolation and withdrawal, and communicating her thoughts, feelings, and needs clearly. The BASC-3 products include numerous lists of recommended interventions.

Ms. Rodriguez infers, from both support materials provided by assessment publishers and her knowledge of school counseling strategies, that Evette may use her strength in verbal ability to become more successful in algebra and biology by using verbal statements to make sense of symbols, rules, and relationships, and she may produce sketches of problems and label what she knows and what she does not yet know. She may also benefit from working in small, diverse, structured groups in class or tutoring where she can participate in discussions that may facilitate her understanding (Lohman, 2013b).

Ms. Rodriguez also reads that when students with average reasoning abilities learn something new or complex, they may be learning at the limit of their working memory (Lohman, 2013b). Evette's teachers may help her reduce this burden by including graphic organizers or concept maps in instruction so that information is presented in one location. They may also offer frequent feedback on her progress, and her English teacher may find ways to recognize her strengths in language arts, which could increase Evette's sense of encouragement.

Ms. Rodriguez may want to discuss the use of strategies with Evette, on more than one occasion, to increase her awareness and ability to monitor what works best for her while she learns. She may need help realizing when a specific strategy is not working and a new approach is in order, and Ms. Rodriguez may choose to model or practice this skill with Evette. It would be important for Ms. Rodriguez to provide feedback as Evette practices the skills, so that Evette's self-monitoring would be scaffolded.

With Evette's academic history, self-report, teacher and parent observations, and current assessment data, Ms. Rodriguez forms a plan for working with Evette. Feedback and interventions for Evette include:

- Continue activities in passion area of art to encourage expression and sense of accomplishment (Tier I)
- Identify verbal reasoning ability, art class performance, dance class performance, and the language arts subject area as strengths (Tier I)

- Recommend setting aside time at home each afternoon or evening to practice her strategies with homework assignments, in a quiet space with organized materials (Tier I)
- Speak with Evette to help her see that while she is failing algebra, biology, and world geography, her math, science, and social studies achievement scores are not below average. Scores from standardized assessments would indicate that she has the ability to understand the content but may need strategies for learning the new information (Tier II)
- Work together with Evette to develop strategies that use her verbal strengths to learn new information, especially in algebra and biology (Tier II), such as:

  - Using oral statements to make sense of symbols, rules, and relationships
  - Participating in class discussions by asking questions
  - Producing sketches of problems and labeling the parts as "known" and "unknown." Asking a study partner or parent to help formulate the "unknowns" into questions to ask the teacher during class or tutorials
  - Drawing flow charts of procedures or steps. Listening for teachers' clue words, such as "first" and "next"
  - Verbalizing which strategies she uses to be successful in English class and how she practices resilience when confronted with a challenge in that subject

- Continue to teach strategies for simple note-taking in outline form and sketching graphic organizers, and provide immediate feedback to her as she practices (Tier II)
- Reframe the purpose of homework from getting better homework grades (which are not heavily weighed in the gradebook) to a way to practice the strategies that will lead to increased understanding of new concepts, which will increase confidence as well as grades on assignments and assessments in class (Tier II)
- Inform Evette's algebra, biology, and world geography teachers that she may benefit from instruction that includes visual aids, cooperative groups so she can verbalize her understandings and listen to peers' interpretations, and give positive feedback when appropriate to increase encouragement (Tier II)
- Assess progress by asking Evette which strategies are working for her and which are not as helpful (All Tiers)
- Address social skills, including avoiding isolation and withdrawal; attitude to teachers; and communicating thoughts, feelings, and needs clearly, in group or individual counseling or skillstreaming (Tier III)
- Address self-esteem, sense of inadequacy, compliance with rules and structure, and self-monitoring, in individual and/or group counseling, and in collaboration with her mother Lydia (Tier III)

Summary

Difficulties with academic achievement are not always due to the ability to understand content. Social, emotional, cognitive, and environmental factors at home, in the school, and in the community influence student growth and achievement, and professional school counselors can help students identify unmet needs and target discrepancies between the student's current situation and what he or she needs to be successful in school and life.

Students' perceptions of their abilities and school performance influence their self-concept and motivation to achieve. Because the ongoing interactions between cognitive ability, emotional well-being, behavior, skills for success, and relationships with peers and significant adults influence a student's thinking, feelings, and behaviors, effective school counselors acknowledge this reciprocal interaction and use tools and strategies to facilitate changes that will help students solve problems by enhancing and applying strengths to current challenges and future growth opportunities.

Assessment is a logical and necessary extension of the professional school counselor's scope of practice. Assessment in school counseling practice is used to observe and measure students' well-being, social functioning, ability to learn, and current performance, as well as to make comparisons to known population norms. Using multiple points of data, school counselors are able to make informed decisions about where to focus efforts and strategies to help all students with evidence-based and well-planned interventions. Finally, school counselors use assessment to monitor progress that invites direct feedback from those most receptive and responsive to the process of change. With appropriate understanding of assessment purposes and uses, the professional school counselor can help clients move from positions of need to positions of growth.

Test Your Knowledge:

1. Cognitive ability scores provide a holistic view of students' ability to achieve.
   a.   True
   b.   False (achievement, performance in class, and other factors contribute to a more holistic view)

2. Which type of assessment is not within the school counselor's scope of practice?
   a.   Achievement
   b.   Cognitive ability
   c.   Aptitude
   d.   Projective

3. According to the Association for Assessment and Research in Counseling, which of the following are assessment competencies that professional school counselors demonstrate?
   a.   Select assessments for school use
   b.   Interpret assessment results to students and parents
   c.   Use assessment results for program planning
   d.   All of the above
   e.   None of the above

4. Which is a recommended approach for school counselors?
   a.   Regarding assessment practices, focus first on individual students, then initiate assessment practices at the school-wide level
   b.   Before collaborating with other professionals, disaggregate assessment data
   c.   Use assessment data to make program decisions at the end of the school year
   d.   Assist with referral to diagnostic assessment, if needed

5. The primary function of school counseling is to:
   a.   Provide long-term personal and family counseling
   b.   Support students so that they can learn
   c.   Guide students through course selection and post-secondary education options
   d.   Serve as the campus testing coordinator

6. School counselors need efficient means of:
   a.   Early identification of at-risk students
   b.   Progress monitoring
   c.   Outcomes measurement
   d.   A and B only
   e.   All of the above

7. Which is one purpose of assessment in clinical mental health counseling that differs from school counselor practice?
   a.   Assessment is used for differential diagnosis in clinical mental health counseling
   b.   Assessment is used for progress monitoring in clinical mental health counseling
   c.   Assessment guides decision-making and treatment planning in clinical mental health counseling
   d.   Assessment is used for screening purposes in clinical mental health counseling

8. When assessing students' social, emotional, and academic needs, school counselors should first focus on risk factors?
   a.   True
   b.   False (focus on strengths and protective factors, as well)

9. When selecting assessment instruments for use in K-12 schools, counselors should:
   a.   Use only standardized, norm-referenced instruments
   b.   Comply with ASCA ethical standards related to the selection of assessments
   c.   Comply with school district and state policies related to the selection of assessments
   d.   A and C only
   e.   B and C only (school counselors also use informal assessment)

10. Cognitive ability is relatively fixed throughout development, but achievement may be facilitated by effective school counseling interventions.
    a.   True
    b.   False (cognitive ability is not fixed and can be nurtured for growth)

Concluding Thoughts

Jim McHenry

At this juncture in the book, I am assuming that you possess at least a beginning understanding of appraisal instrumentation and techniques. You also have an expanded grasp of major assessments used in your particular field (school counseling, rehabilitation counseling, etc.), coupled with an understanding of the major statistical concepts (normal curve, standard deviation, standard error, and the like) necessary to understand and interpret data, either individual or group.

So at this point I have but one question for you.

"So what?"

Exactly what do you, professional that you either are or are in the process of becoming . . . just what is it that you plan to do with this newly gained knowledge?

Well, may I suggest that your work be anchored on an *analysis of the individual* basis. May I suggest that your *primary goal*, to every degree possible, be focused on helping each of your clients/students better understanding their developing selves, no matter what her/his age or situation.

Labeling Versus Truly Honoring Client/Student Uniqueness

Now pause for a moment and reflect on your own life—your personal history as it were. Can you think of anyone, anyone at all, who has gone through all the same personal experiences you have? Even if you are an identical twin, equally equipped genetically with your sibling, each of you has not stepped in each other's footprints exactly (and certainly not simultaneously), even though you may have learned to walk at almost exactly the same time. So let us take as a given that each and every one of the 7 or 8 billion human beings on planet earth is experiencing life in a somewhat different way. And here we are not even considering that each and every one of us brings an ever-changing internal potential that we use to shape our own personal history. You are indeed *unique*, as is each and every one of your clients/students.

Let's also agree, of course, that the dynamic life history of any person is shaped by only two factors: (1) what is inside (DNA, soul, id, ego, superego, pick your own description) and (2) what is outside (all the "out there" matters, from economic resources to societal and personal advantages and disadvantages and the like).

Therefore, while you might generally hypothesize some theories from a thumbnail sketch of a client/student, I suggest you be very, very careful before drawing any firm conclusions. Take your author, for example. I was born in a coalminer's shanty that featured, among other amenities, a dirt floor. Further, shortly after I arrived on this planet, my mother divorced my father, making me the son of a single mother, statistically a two-year product of a broken home. That's starting out early with two strikes in the game of life. Nonetheless, thanks to a National Defense Education Act Fellowship (thank you Sputnik!), I was eventually able to attend and earn a doctorate from The George Washington University, one of the most expensive universities in the United States. That trip, from dirt floor shanty to George's university was filled with some very unique, though not really unusual, occurrences, as were the trips of my two sisters, each of whom earned master's degrees and became teachers, and my brother, who also earned a master's and became a teacher. And indeed, many of our childhood classmates, many sons and daughters of coal miners and such, were able to become teachers, nurses, accountants, physicians, successful entrepreneurs, and successes in many avenues of life. Suffice to say then, attending any 30-, 40-, or 50-year reunion will reveal many surprises. People, unique as they are, have a way of confounding our predictions.

So where does that leave us?

Well before you answer, consider the following conversation, still indelibly etched in my mind, which occurred early in my public school teaching career (the 1960s, actually).

A fellow-teacher and I were walking down a hall. It was early in the school year near the end of the first grading period.

Fellow-teacher:	I need to get over to the main office and get a list of my students' IQs.
Me:	Why?
F.T.:	Well, I can't give a low grade to any of the smart kids.

Even in those neophyte teaching days, I recognized the folly of this use of assessment.

Fast forward a bit. After teaching at the junior-senior high school level for five years and having completed my master's at Penn State in secondary school counseling, I surveyed the possibilities of becoming a counselor in that system (very bleak; they did not add any new positions for over 10 years). So I took a junior high school position at Painted Post (NY) Junior High School, part of the Corning-Painted Post School District.

Corning turned out to be a fortunate choice. First, the district had an outstanding administration, a very solid faculty, and a forward-looking counseling staff distributed across the two high schools and three junior highs. Second, my school, where I was the entire counseling department starting on day one of my arrival, was run by one of the brightest, most creative educators I had ever come across in my travels, Ernst Auerbacher. Further, upon my arrival, Ernie gave me a really fine gift that I probably didn't really appreciate fully at the time. He said, "We have your recommendations from Penn State, and we know you know what you are doing" (or words to that effect) "so you are in charge. As long as it makes sense, I'll support your program." What a gift. And, even though I really was not all that confident that I knew what I was doing, I did take him up on that challenge (and, true to his words, Ernie did support and augment my efforts).

Now, of course, based on my five years of public school teaching, I actually did have a number of ideas regarding how counseling services should operate in the junior high, and over the three years I was there, I implemented as many as I could. For purposes of this effort, however, I will focus on the appraisal area.

Again, some background. The two public schools I had previously taught in were fond of homogeneous grouping. And so was Painted Post Junior High. When I arrived there, each grade 7 through 9 had five tracks labeled as follows: 1 (top track), 2 (middle three tracks), and 3 (bottom track). Not really very imaginative. When you consider labeling 12- to 15-year-olds this way, human beings emerging from Freud's latency period as it were, you better be absolutely sure you are correct. Run that certainty around your newfound understanding of appraisal statistics and add a dash of human development, adolescent and pubescent changes and the like, sorting and relegating 12–13-year-olds into convenient piles ("I need to know their IQs") may really be actually quite *un*scientific. Part of my anathema for this type of labeling had grown from my earlier experience in public school teaching. In one school, the administration decreed that they would label the sections with letters, in this case A through M, and vary the letters in each grade (i.e., the top section in 7th grade might be section D; in 8th, L; in 9th, G; and so on). Many students, of course, would do a quick survey of their classmates on opening day and quickly conclude their standing accordingly ("still in with the dummies").

So, back to Painted Post, where a splendiferous event occurred. During my first year there, someone in the administration loosened some money that enabled the counseling staff to go to Schenectady, New York to learn how to access a mainframe computer for our student scheduling. Now back in those primitive days, the 1960s, people didn't yet have computers in their pockets. If memory serves me right, the computer that we utilized took up most of the space in a rather large building. You probably have more computing power on your wrist than we utilized, but this mainframe was sufficient for our purposes. Nonetheless, following a three-day training period, we counselors learned how to input data for our respective schools and student schedules.

And of course, upon my return, our school was still the same size, so we still had three grades and five tracks: a 1, three 2s, and a 3.

However, based on my understanding of what the phrase "analysis of individual differences" really means and my *extreme dislike of labeling*, which often results in *mislabeling*, I sensed an opportunity. In my counseling education, I had come to appreciate that if we are really interested in working with individuals, as counselors we really need to focus primarily on those differences that exist *within the individual* rather than spending our time always trying to sort them into convenient piles. Further, we need to be very careful with our labeling. In my experience, our instruments were (and are) still only rough approximations, measures made at a given time and not numbers etched in concrete.

With these ideas in mind, I made a deal with Ernie, my principal. By accessing the wizardry of the computer, we could now break up the block scheduling. Block scheduling resulted in students being relegated to one group as a solid unit for the entire day. A Track 1 student took all his/her classes with all the other Track 1 students. Each of the Track 2 sections stayed intact and separate from the other four groups. The Track 3 group also was separate from the others.

The changed model that Ernie agreed upon was as follows: students could take core group classes (English, science, mathematics, social studies, reading) at more than one level. Further, we decided, rather arbitrarily really, that *no student would be placed in Track 3 in all his/her core classes*. One of my duties then was to find at least one section 2 core class for every student formerly relegated to Track 3 in all classes. What core class (or classes) was (were) each student's strongest? This I was able to do utilizing teacher recommendations, grades, and yes, testing data, etc. Of course, if indicated, our top students in each class were able to stay in Track 1 in all their core classes. Nonetheless, quite a number of students ended up with split schedules (taking English and social studies in Track 1, and mathematics and science in Track 2, for example). Here again, of course, I relied on grades, assessment data, and teacher recommendations to sort a lot of this out during the summer. (NOTE: Since my contract ran through the summer, I was able to work on the schedule during that time.) Also, since our 7th grade students came to us from several feeder schools, I needed to meet with 6th grade teachers during the spring to get some of the data needed. So another significant added benefit here was that I got to know more about both our incoming students and their teachers. Still another major benefit of this shattering of our block scheduling, I think, was that more of our students got to mix with more of their peers, especially in the special areas such as art, phys. ed., and the like.

Issues arose because of the change, of course. For example, one 8th grade student came to my office to request that he be put back in all Track 3 classes. I asked him why and he allowed that unlike in section 3, in section 2 teachers "gave homework." I quizzed him on whether he could do the homework, and he allowed that he could. I recommended that he stay with it a bit longer, and he agreed. He finished up the year successfully where he was. There were, of course, a number of individual student course modifications needed, but about the same number as the previous year. Also, when such modifications were needed, while a move in the earlier (block schedule) model meant moving a student out of all his/her core classes, a major disruption in an adolescent's life, the new model often entailed a move of only one class (his/her math class, for example).

This example then represented our attempt, using various assessments and measures, to enrich and broaden the school experience and opportunities for each of our individual students.

Different Level, Different Use

Later in my career, I served as a counselor education professor at Edinboro University of Pennsylvania. During several summers, our chairperson, Dr. Salene Cowher, sought and received funding for a week-long on-campus summer experience designed for rural high school students who had limited access to higher education possibilities. The program offered as much of an exposure to the college experience as possible, and my summer graduate appraisal class members were utilized in an exercise designed not so much to evaluate and measure the participant's abilities as such, but to open their eyes to both their greater potential and available possibilities. Utilizing instruments that were admittedly "quick and dirty" due to the shortness of the program (primarily Myers–Briggs and the like), I was able to match my students-in-training with the program participants. This facet of the program culminated with a counselor-trainee–student-participant, one-on-one sharing of the appraisal data, often resulting in a real reconsideration/modification of the high school students' aims, attitudes, and goals. We took part in this summer experience for a number of summers, and Dr. Cower did conduct some follow-up indicating that (of students responding) (1) everyone had completed high school, and (2) over 90% had gone on to either higher education, technical training, or the military.

Additionally, both the students in my appraisal class and program participants viewed the experience as a truly worthwhile and exciting educational experience. Dr. Cowher's follow-up data also indicated that program participants gave the counselor-appraisal experience outstanding ratings.

This example represented our attempt to further participants' understanding of self and introduce and broaden their worldviews.

Static Versus Dynamic Development

The examples in this chapter suggest that we temper our tendency to label our students/clients too quickly . . . too broadly. Consider, for example, if you, or I, are charged with some sort of incredibly heinous act and brought to court; chances are both the prosecuting and defense lawyers will bring expert psychiatric witnesses that will declare us sane on the one side and insane on the other (that is, of course, if we had enough money . . . economic factors have a way of affecting each individual's life).

And, while the United States is a strong and wonderful country, we are still often remiss in fostering opportunities for the development of many of our citizens. For example, most of the population in our penal system are undereducated, but to the extent that we warehouse and punish them instead of educating and rehabilitating them, we do them no favor. Labeling and forgetting them does society no favor either since 80–90% of these human beings will eventually be released back into the greater society.

Exactitude versus Fluid Approximation

Well then, what exactly should we be doing?

This is where the true concept regarding *analysis of individual difference* fits. And let us marry it to one of the most basic principles championed by experts in the field of rehabilitation—*coping*.

Today, the rehabilitation field is truly blessed with many practitioners who are able to take the clients they are serving and help them utilize their abilities, their strengths, their talents, their *whatever*, and build on that. So a man with one leg climbs Mt. Everest, men and women in wheelchairs compete at the university level in basketball. Less famously, slight, relatively inexpensive modifications enable thousands of less-able-bodied people to earn their meaningful living in the nation's economy. Many of these modifications are based, of course, on both assessment techniques and a skillful matching of the individual's skills and potential and the event or job requirements. *Such actions, I suggest, are the result of the true and effective analysis of a given individual's differences.*

So where does all this leave us?

Sorter Versus True Change Agent

Well, now recall my 1960s teacher-friend in the hall (a really nice, kind, fine person, incidentally). She was sure that "IQ" was somehow a key to successfully grading her students. The IQ label was a simple number, good enough for her. With 12- and 13-year-olds. Further, in those days, the IQ score as such was generally believed to possess more exactitude than it does today.

So what?

So, this.

You can decide to become a sorter, a labeler, a go-to person who determines (possibly limits) the opportunities ("I'm in the dummy class. I must be a dummy. After all the school must know what it's doing").

Or, in consultation with the client/student, you can take as careful a look as possible at her/his *ideas*, *interests*, *hopes*, and *strengths* (and *weaker areas*) and help match and utilize them in as developmental a way as possible.

As a professionally educated counselor/therapist, you will play an extremely important role in our society.

Sorter or change agent, the choice is yours.

Concluding Thoughts

1. Every last one of us is unique.
2. Every last one of us is a dynamically changing human being existing and constantly interacting with a changing, often challenging environment.
3. Gaining insight into our own developing uniqueness can be life-changing in a positive way.
4. Counselors/therapists can assist us in gaining insight in many ways, *often through the effective and timely use of appraisal tools and techniques.*
5. *When used effectively, such tools and techniques* can assist each of us to take steps to help clients/students in their journeys through the life-long process of becoming.

References

Abidin, R. R. (2012). *Parenting Stress Index* (4th ed.). Lutz, FL: PAR.

Achenbach, T. M. (2009). *The Achenbach System of Empirically Based Assessment (ASEBA): Development, Findings, Theory, and Applications*. Burlington, VT: University of Vermont, Research Center for Children, Youth, & Families.

Achenbach, T. M. (2014). *DSM-Oriented Guide for the Achenbach System of Empirically Based Assessment (ASEBA)*. Burlington, VT: University of Vermont Research Center for Children, Youth, and Families.

Achenbach, T. M., & Rescorla, L. A. (2001). *Manual for the ASEBA School-Age Forms and Profiles*. Burlington, VT: University of Vermont, Research Center for Children, Youth, and Families.

Achenbach, T. M., & Rescorla, L. A. (2007). *Multicultural Supplement to the Manual for the ASEBA School-Age Forms & Profiles*. Burlington, VT: University of Vermont, Research Center for Children, Youth and Families.

Achenbach, T. M., & Rescorla, L.A. (2015). *Mental Health Practitioners' Guide for the Achenbach System of Empirically Based Assessment (ASEBA)* (9th ed.). Burlington, VT: University of Vermont, Research Center for Children, Youth, and Families.

Adelman, H. S., & Taylor, L. (2006). Mental health in schools and public health. *Public Health Reports*, *121*(3), 294–298.

Allen, J. P. (2003). Assessment of alcohol problems: An overview. In J. P. Allen & V. B. Wilson (Eds.), *Assessing Alcohol Problems: A Guide for Clinicians and Researchers* (2nd ed.). Washington, DC: U.S. Department of Health and Human Services.

American Counseling Association (ACA). (2014). *ACA Code of Ethics*. Alexandria, VA: Author.

American Counseling Association (2014). *Standards for Qualifications of Test Users*. Alexandria, VA: Author.

American Educational Research Administration (AERA), American Psychological Association (APA), and National Council on Measurement in Education (NCME). (2011). *Standards for Educational & Psychological Testing*. Washington, DC: AERA.

American Psychiatric Association (APA). (2013). *Diagnostic and Statistical Manual of Mental Disorders*. Arlington, VA: American Psychiatric Publishing.

American School Counselor Association (ASCA). (2012). *The ASCA National Model: A Framework for School Counseling Programs* (3rd ed.). Alexandria, VA: Author.

American School Counselor Association (ASCA). (2014). *The school counselor and multitiered system of supports*. Retrieved from www.schoolcounselor.org

American School Counselor Association (ASCA). (2016). *ASCA Ethical standards for school counselors*. Alexandria, VA. Retrieved from www.schoolcounselor.org

American Society on Addiction Medicine (ASAM). (2001). *Resources*. Retrieved from: https://www.asam.org/resources/definition-of-addiction

Americans with Disabilities Act of 1990, Pub. L. No. 101–336, 104 Stat. 328 (1990).

Anastasi, A., & Urbina, S. (1997). *Psychological Testing* (7th ed.). Upper Saddle River, NJ: Prentice Hall.

Armistead, R. J. (2008, March). *School-based mental health services promote academic success*. School Board News "Viewpoint." National Association of School Psychologists, Bethesda, MD.

Association for Assessment and Reseach in Counseling and International Association of Addiction and Offender Counselors (2010). *Standards for Assessment in Substance Abuse Counseling*. Authors.

Association for Assessment in Counseling and Education (AACE). (2003). *Competencies in Assessment and Evaluation for School Counselors*. Alexandria, VA: Author. Retrieved from www.aac.ncat.edu

Association for Assessment in Counseling and Education (AACE) & International Association of Marriage and Family Counselors (IAMFC). (2010). *Marriage, couple and family counseling assessment competencies*. Retrieved from http://aarc-counseling.org/resources

Association for Assessment in Counseling and Education (AACE) & National Career Development Association (NCDA). (2010). *Career counselor assessment and evaluation competencies*. Retrieved from http://aarc-counseling.org/resources

Association for Assessment and Research in Counseling (AARC). (2003). *Responsibilities of Users of Standardized Tests* (RUST). Alexandria, VA: Author. Retrieved from http://aarc-counseling.org/resources

Association for Assessment in Counseling and Education (AACE). (2012). *Standards for multicultural assessment*. Retrieved from: http://aarc-counseling.org/assets/cms/uploads/files/Research_Resource_List.pdf

Association for Assessment and Research in Counseling (AARC). (2014). *Standards for Multicultural Assessment*. Alexandria, VA: Author. Retrieved from http://aarc-counseling.org/resources

Association for Assessment and Research in Counseling (AARC). (2017). *Resources*. Retrieved from http://aarc-counseling.org/resources

Association for Assessment in Counseling and Education (AARC) & American Mental Health Counseling Association (AMHCA). (2010). *Standards for assessment in mental health counseling*. Retrieved from http://aarc-counseling.org/resources

Association for Assessment in Counseling and Education (AARC) & American School Counseling Association (ASCA). (1998). *Competencies in assessment and evaluation for school counselors*. Retrieved from http://aarc-counseling.org/resources

Association for Assessment in Counseling and Education (AARC) & International Association of Addictions and Offenders Counselors (IAAOC). (2010). *Standards for assessment in substance abuse counseling*. Retrieved from http://aarc-counseling.org/resources

Bakke v. Regents of the University of California, 438 U.S. 265 (1978).

Bandelow, B. (1999). *Panic and Agoraphobia Scale (PAS)*. Göttengin, Germany: Hogrefe & Huber Publishers.

Barbor, T. F., de la Fuente, J. R., Saunders, J., and Grant, M. (1992). AUDIT. *The Alcohol Use Disorders Identification Test. Guidelines for use in primary health care*. Geneva, Switzerland: World Health Organization.

Barna, J. S., & Brott, P. E. (2013). Making the grade: The importance of academic enablers in the elementary school counseling program. *Professional School Counseling, 17*(1), 97–110.

Beck, A. (1979). *Cognitive therapy of depression*. New York: Guilford Press.

Beck, A. T., Kovacs, M., & Weissman, A. (1979). Assessment of suicidal intention: The scale for suicide ideation. *Journal of Consulting and Clinical Psychology, 47*(2), 343–352.

Beck, A. & Steer, R. (1991). *Beck scale for suicide ideation*. San Antonio, TX: Pearson.

Beck, A. T., & Steer, R. A. (1993). *Beck Anxiety Inventory Manual*. San Antonio, TX: The Psychological Corporation.

Beck, A. T., Steer, R. A., & Brown, G. K. (1996). *Manual for the Beck Depression Inventory* (2nd ed.). San Antonio, TX: The Psychological Corporation.

Begle, A. M., & Dumas, J. E. (2011). Child and parental outcomes following involvement in a preventative intervention: Efficacy of the PACE program. *Journal of Primary Prevention, 32*, 67–81. doi: 10.1007/s10935-010-0232-6

Benson, N. (2014). Test review of Wechsler Intelligence Scale for Children – Fifth Edition. In J. F. Carlson, K. F. Geisinger, & J. L. Jonson (Eds.), *The Nineteenth Mental Measurements Yearbook*. Retrieved from http://web.b.ebscohost.com

Betters, C. J., & Sligar, S. R. (2015). The tools of the trade: A national study on tool utilization in vocational evaluation. [Special issue]. *Vocational Evaluation and Work Adjustment Association Journal and Vocational Evaluation and Career Assessment Journal*, 8–16.

Bobby. C. (2013). The evolution of specialties in the CACREP standards: CACREP's role in unifying the profession. *Journal of Counseling & Development, 91*(1), 35–43. doi: 10-1002/j.1556–6676.2013.0068.x

Bram, A. (2015). To resume a stalled psychotherapy? Psychological testing to understand an impasse and reevaluate treatment options. *Journal of Personality Assessment, 97*(3).

Briere, J. (1995). *Trauma Symptom Inventory Professional Manual*. Odessa, FL: Psychological Assessment Resources.

Brigman, G. A., Webb, L. D., & Campbell, C. (2007). Building skills for school success: Improving the academic and social competence of students. *Professional School Counseling, 10*(3), 279–288.

Brooks, F., & McHenry, B. (2009). *A Contemporary Approach to Substance Abuse and Addiction Counseling*. Alexandria, VA: American Counseling Association.

Buber, M. (1970). *I and Thou.* New York: Charles Scribner.

Camara, W. (2014). Issues facing testing organizations in using the standards for educational and psychological testing. *Educational Measurement: Issues and Practice, 33*(4).

Canivez, G. L., & Watkins, M. W. (2010). Investigation of the factor structure of the Wechsler Adult Intelligence Scale—Fourth Edition (WAIS–IV): Exploratory and higher order factor analyses. *Psychological Assessment, 22*(4), 827–836. doi:10.1037/a0020429

Cappa, K. A., Begle, A. M., Conger, J. C., Dumas, J. E., & Conger, A. J. (2011). Bidirectional relationships between parenting stress and child coping competence: Findings from the pace study. *Journal of Child and Family Studies, 20,* 334–342. doi: 10.1007/s10826-010 9397-0.

Carballo, J. J., Serrano-Drozdowskyj, E., Nieto, R. G., Jeeira-Herando, M. D., Perez-Fominaya, M., Molina-Pizarro, C. A., De Leon-Martinez, V., & Baca-Garcia, E. (2014). Prevalence and correlates of psychopathology in children and adolescents evaluated with strengths and difficulties questionnaire dysregulation profile in clinical settings. *Psychopathology, 47,* 303–311. doi:10.1159/000360822

Carl D. Perkins Vocational and Applied Technology Education Act, 20 U.S.C. §2301 *et seq.* (2006).

Carlson, J. F., Geisinger, K. F., & Jonson, J. L. (Eds.). (2014). *The Nineteenth Mental Measurements Yearbook.* Lincoln, NE: Buros Center for Testing.

Cattell, J. (1890). Mental tests and measurements. *Mind, 15,* 373–381.

Center for Mental Health in Schools at UCLA. (2015). *Screening/assessing students: indicators and tools.* Retrieved from http://smhp.psych.ucla.edu/pdfdocs/assessment/assessment.pdf

Center for Mental Health in Schools at UCLA. (n.d.). *Screening Mental Health Problems in Schools.* Los Angeles, CA: Center for Mental Health in Schools. Retrieved from http://smhp.psych.ucla.edu.

Center for Substance Abuse Treatment (CSAT). (2006). *Addiction Counseling Competencies: The Knowledge, Skills, and Attitudes of Professional Practice* (Technical assistant publication (TAP) series 21). Rockville, MD: Substance Abuse and Mental Health Services Administration. (DHHS Publication No. [SMA] 08–4171).

Chiu, E. (2014). Psychological testing in child custody evaluations with ethnically diverse families: Ethical concerns and practice recommendations. *Journal of Child Custody, 11,* 107–127.

Choe, D. E., Olson, S. L., & Sameroff, A. J. (2013). Effects of early maternal distress and parenting on the development of children's self-regulation and externalizing behavior. *Development and Psychopathology, 25,* 437–453. doi:10.1017/S0954579412001162

Connors, G. J., & Volk, R. J. (2003). Self-report screening for alcohol problems among adults. In J. P. Allen & V. B. Wilson (Eds.), *Assessing Alcohol Problems: A Guide for Clinicians and Researchers* (2nd ed.). Bethesda, MD: National Institute on Alcohol Abuse and Alcoholism.

Cooper, M., Stewart, D., Sparks, J., & Bunting, L. (2013). School-based counseling using systematic feedback: A cohort study evaluating outcomes and predictors of change. *Psychotherapy Research, 23*(4), 474–488.

Costa, P., & McCrae, R. (2010). *NEO-PI-3.* London: Sigma Assessment Systems.

CPP. (2017). *Strong Interest Inventory ® Manual.* Retrieved from www.cpp.com/en/strongitems.aspx?ic=8410

Craig, R. J. (2004). *Counseling the Alcohol and Drug Dependent Client: A Practical Approach.* Boston, MA: Allen and Bacon.

Crippa, J., Sanches, R., Hallak, J., Loureiro, S., & Zuardi, A. (2001). A structured interview guide increases Brief Psychiatric Rating Scale reliability in raters with low clinical experience. *Acta Psychiatrica Scandinavica, 103*(6), 465–470.

Davis, P., Davis, M. P., & Mobley, J. A. (2013). The school counselor's role in addressing the advanced placement equity and excellence gap for African American students. *Professional School Counseling, 17*(1), 32–39.

Derogatis, L.R. (1983). *SCL–90–R: Administration, Scoring, and Procedures Manual II.* Baltimore: Clinical Psychometric Research.

Derogatis, L.R. (1994). *Symptom Checklist 90–R: Administration, Scoring, and Procedures Manual* (3rd ed.). Minneapolis, MN: National Computer Systems.

Desrochers, J. E. (2015, October). RX for mental health. *Educational Leadership, 73*(2), 46–50.

Diana v. California State Board of Education, CA 70 RFT (N.D. Cal. 1970).

Doll, B. J., Furlong, M. J., & Wood, M. (1998). Child behavior checklist. In J. C. Impara & B. S. Placke (Eds.), *The Thirteenth Mental Measurements Yearbook.* Retrieved May 24, 2017 from Ebscohost databases

Donovan, D. M. (2013). Evidence-based assessment: Strategies and measures in addictive behaviors. In B. S. McCardy & E. E. Epstein (Eds.), *Addictions: A Comprehensive Guidebook* (2nd ed., pp. 311–351). New York, NY: Oxford University Press.

Doweiko, H. E. (2015). *Concepts of Chemical Dependency.* Belmont, CA: Brooks/Cole.

Dozier, V. C., Sampson, J. P., Lenz, J. L., Peterson, G. W., & Reardon, R. C. (2015). The impact of the self-directed search form R Internet Version on counselor-free career exploration. *Journal of Career Assessment*, *23*, 210–224.

Drummond, R., & Jones, K. (2010). *Assessment Procedures for Counselor and Helping Professionals* (7th ed.). Boston: Pearson.

Drummond, R. J., Sheperis, C. J., & Jones, K. D. (2016). *Assessment Procedures for Counselors and Helping Professionals* (8th ed.). Boston: Pearson.

Dumont, R., & Willis, J. O. (2003). Issues regarding the supervision of assessment. *The Clinical Supervisor*, *22*, 159–176.

Durand, D., Strassnig, M., Sabbag, S., Gould, F., Twamley, E. W., Patterson, T. L., & Harvey, P. D. (2015). Factors influencing self-assessment of cognition and functioning in schizophrenia: Implications for treatment studies. *European Neuropsychopharmacology*, *25*(2), 185–191. doi:10.1016/j.euroneuro.2014.07.008

Eppler, C., & Weir, S. (2009). Family assessment in K-12 settings: Understanding family systems to provide effective, collaborative services. *Psychology in the Schools*, *46*(6), 501–514.

Erford, B. T., Butler, C., & Peacock, E. (2015). The Screening Test for Emotional Problems—Teacher report version (STEP-T): Studies of reliability and validity. *Measurement and Evaluation in Counseling and Development*, *48*(2), 152–160.

Erickson, A., & Abel, N. R. (2013). A high school counselor's leadership in providing school-wide screenings for depression and enhancing suicide awareness. *Professional School Counseling*, *16*(5), 283–289.

Ethics Code Task Force (ECTF). (2001). *Ethics code revision*. Retrieved from www.apa.org/ethics.

Evans, F. B., & Finn, S. E. (2016). Training and consultation in psychological assessment for professional psychologists. *Journal of Personality Assessment*, *98*, 785–798.

Ewing, J. A. (1984). Detecting alcoholism: The CAGE questionnaire. *Journal of the American Medical Association*, *252*, 1905–1907.

Family Educational Rights and Privacy Act of 1974, 20 U.S.C. § 1232g (1974).

Farreras, I. (2014). Clara Harrison Town and the origins of the first institutional commitment law for the "feebleminded": Psychologist as expert diagnostician. *History of Psychology*, *17*(4), 271–281. doi:10.1037/a0036123

Fiellin, D. A., Reid, M. C., & O'Connor, P. G. (2000). Screening for alcohol problems in primary care: Systemic review. *Journal of General Internal Medicine*, *15*(1), 65–66.

Finkelstein, H., & Tuckman, A. (1997). Supervision of psychological assessment: A developmental model. *Professional Psychology: Research & Practice*, *28*, 92–95.

Flemons, D., & Gralnik, L. M. (2013). *Relational Suicide Assessment: Risks, Resources, and Possibilities for Safety*. New York: W.W. Norton & Company.

Foa, E. B., Keane, T. M., Friedman, M. J., & Cohen, J. A. (2008). *Effective Treatments for PTSD: Practice Guidelines from the International Society for Traumatic Stress Studies*. New York, NY: Guilford Press.

Folstein, M. F., Folstein, S. E., & McHugh, P. R. (1975). 'Mini-mental status'. A practical method for grading the cognitive state of patients for the clinician. *Journal of Psychiatric Research*, *12*(3), 189–198.

Fouad, N. A. (1993). Cross-cultural vocational assessment. *Career Development Quarterly*, *42*(1), 4.

Garner, D. M. (2004). *The Eating Disorder Inventory-3: Professional manual*. Odessa, FL: Psychological Assessment Resources, Inc.

Geldard, K., Geldard, D., & Yin Foo, R. (2013). *Counseling Children: A Practical Introduction* (4th ed.). Los Angeles, LA: Sage.

Georgia Vocational Rehabilitation Agency. (2014). *Client Services Policy Manual*. Atlanta, GA: Author.

Gladwell, M. (2008). *Outliers*. New York: Little, Brown and Company. ISBN: 978-0-316-01792-3.

Gomez, R., Vance, A., & Gomez, R. M. (2014). Analysis of convergent and discriminant validity of the CBCL, TRF, and YSR in a clinc-referred sample. *Journal of Abnormal Child Psychology*, *42*, 1413–1425. doi:10.1007/s10802-014-9879-4

Good, M. J., James, C., Good, B. J., & Becker, A. E. (2003). The culture of medicine and racial, ethnic, and class disparities in health care. In B. D. Smedley, A. Y. Stith, & A. R. Nelson (Eds.), *Unequal Treatment: Confronting Racial and Ethnic Disparities in Health Care*. Washington, DC: National Academies Press.

Granello, D. G. (2010). The process of suicide risk assessment: Twelve core principles. *Journal of Counseling and Development*, *88*(3), 363–371.

Grasso, E., Jitendra, A. K., Browder, D. M., & Harp, T. (2004). Effects of ecological and standardized vocational assessments on office of vocational rehabilitation counselors perceptions regarding individuals with developmental disabilities. *Journal of Developmental and Physical Disabilities*, *16*(1), 17–31. doi:10.1023/b:jodd.0000010037.17733.52

Greenfield, S. F., & Hennessy, G. (2008). Assessment of the patient. In M. Galanter & H. D. Kleber (Eds.), *Textbook of Substance Abuse Treatment* (4th ed.). Washington, DC: American Psychiatric Press, Inc.

Gregory, P. (2013). *Psychological Testing: History, Principles, and Applications* (7th ed.). Upper Saddle River, NJ: Pearson.

Grier, R., Morris, L., & Taylor, L. (2001). Assessment strategies for school-based mental health counseling. *Journal of School Health*, 71(9), 467–469.

Griffs v. Duke Power Company, 401 U.S. 424 (1971).

Gruman, D. H., Marston, T., & Koon, H. (2013). Bringing mental health needs into focus through school counseling program transformation. *Professional School Counseling*, 16(5), 333–341.

Guzman, M. P., Jellinek, M., George, M., Hartley, M., Squicciarini, A. M., Canenguez, K. M., . . . Murphy, J. M. (2011). Mental health matters in elementary school: First-grade screening predicts fourth grade achievement test scores. *European Child & Adolescent Psychiatry*, 20(8), 401–411.

Gysbers, N., Heppner, M., & Johnston, J. (2009). *Career Counseling: Contexts, Processes, and Techniques*. Alexandria, VA: American Counseling Association.

Haack, L. M., Kapke, T. L., & Gerdes, A. C. (2016). Rates, associations, and predictors of psychopathology in a convenience sample of school-aged Latino youth: Identifying areas for mental health outreach. *Journal of Child and Family Studies*, 25, 2315–2326. doi:10.1007/s10826-016-0404-y

Hale, J. B., Fiorello, C. A., Kavanagh, J. A., Holdnack, J. A., & Aloe, A. M. (2007). Is the demise of IQ justified? A response to special issues authors. *Applied Neuropsychology*, 14, 37–51. doi:10.1080/09084280701280445

Hall, J. G. (2015). The school counselor and special education: Aligning training with practice. *The Professional Counselor*, 5(2), 217–224.

Hamilton, M. (1959). The assessment of anxiety states by rating. *British Journal Medical Psychology*, 32, 50–55.

Hays, D. G. (2013). *Assessment in Counseling: A Guide to the Use of Psychological Assessment Procedures* (5th ed.). Alexandria, VA: American Counseling Association.

Henriksen, R. C., Nelson, J., & Watts, R. E. (2010). Specialty training in counselor education programs: An exploratory study. *Journal of Professional Counseling: Practice, Theory, and Research*, 38(1), 39–51.

Hirschfeld, R. M., Williams, J. B., Spitzer, R. L., Calabrese, J. R., Flynn, L., Keck, P. E., . . . Russell, J. M. (2000). Development and validation of a screening instrument for bipolar spectrum disorder: the Mood Disorder Questionnaire. *American Journal of Psychiatry*, 157(11), 1873–1875. https://doi.org/10.1176/appi.ajp.157.11.1873.

Holland, J., & Messer, M. (2013). *John Holland's Self-Directed Search Fast Guide*. Lutz, FL: Psychological Assessment Resources, Inc.

Hood, A., & Johnson, R. (2007). *Assessment in Counseling*. (4th ed.). Alexandria, VA: American Counseling Association.

Hopwood, C. J., & Richard, D. S. (2005). Graduate student WAIS-III scoring accuracy is a function of full scale IQ and complexity of examiner tasks. *Assessment*, 12(4), 445–454.

Houghton Mifflin Harcourt. (2017). *Cognitive abilities test form 6 and form 7 interactive ability profile interpretation system* [Web application]. Retrieved from www.hmhco.com/cogat/cogatprofile

Hubble, M. A., Duncan, B. L., Miller, S. D., & Wampold, B. E. (2010). Introduction. In B. L. Duncan, S. D. Miller, B. E. Wampold, & M. A. Hubble (Eds.), *The Heart & Soul of Change: Delivering What Works in Therapy* (2nd ed., pp. 23–46). Washington DC: American Psychological Association.

Individuals with Disabilities Education Improvement Act of 2004, Pub L. No. 108–446, 118 Stat. 2647 (2004).

Ivey, A. E., & Ivey, M. B. (2007). *Intentional Interviewing and Counseling* (6th ed.). Belmont, CA: Thomson Brooks/Cole.

Iwanicki, S., & Peterson, C. (2017). An exploratory study examining current assessment supervisory practices in professional psychology. *Journal of Personality Assessment*, 99(2), 165–174.

Joyce, P., & Sills, C. (2010). *Skills in Gestalt Counselling & Psychotherapy* (2nd ed., pp. 3–16). London: Sage Publications.

Juhnke, G. A. (2002). *Substance Abuse Assessment and Diagnosis*. New York: Brunner-Routledge.

Juhnke, G. A., Granello, P. F., & Lebron-Striker, M. A. (2007). IS PATH WARM? *A Suicide Assessment Mnemonic for Counselors (ACAPCD-03)*. Alexandria, VA: American Counseling Association. Retrieved from www.counseling.org/resources/library/ACA Digests/ACAPCD-03.pdf

Kaplan, R. M., & Saccuzzo, D. P. (2001). *Psychological Testing: Principles, Applications, and Issues* (5th ed.). Belmont, CA: Wadsworth.

Karch, D. L., Dahlberg, L. L., & Patel, N. (2010). Surveillance for violent deaths national violent death reporting system, 16 states, 2007. *Morbidity and Mortality Weekly Report, 59*, 1–50.

Kaufman, A. S. (1994). *Intelligent Testing with the WISC-III*. New York: John Wiley & Sons.

Kerr, E. N., & Blackwell, M. C. (2015). Near-transfer effects following working memory intervention (Cogmed) in children with symptomatic epilepsy: An open randomized clinical trial. *Epilepsia, 56*(11), 1784–1792. doi:10.1111/epi.13195.

Kilts, C. (2004). Neurobiology of substance use disorders. In A. F. Schatzberg & C. B. Numeroff (Eds.), *Textbook of Psychopharmacology* (3rd ed.). Washington, DC: American Psychiatric Publishing.

Konold, T. R. (2017). Review of the behavior assessment system for children. In J. F. Carlson, K. F. Geisinger, & J. L. Jonson (Eds.), *The Twentieth Mental Measurements Yearbook*. Lincoln, NE: Buros Institute of Mental Measurements. Retrieved from Mental Measurements Yearbook with Tests in Print database

Koocher, G. P., & Rey-Casserly, C. M. (2003). Ethical issues in psychological assessment. In J. R. Graham & J. A. Naglieri (Eds.), *Handbook of Psychology: Volume 10: Assessment Psychology*. Hoboken, NJ: Wiley.

Kramer, D. A., Watson, M., & Hodges, J. (2013, August). *School Climate and the CCPRI*. Atlanta, GA: Georgia Department of Education. Retrieved from www.gadoe.org

Lambert, M. J., Morton, J. J., Hatfield, D., Harmon, C., Hamilton, S., Reid, R. C., Shimokawa, K., . . . Burlingame, G. M. (2004). *Administration and Scoring Manual for the Outcome Questionnaire-45*. Salt Lake City, UT: OQMeasures.

Lapan, R. T. (2012). Comprehensive school counseling programs: In some schools for some students but not in all schools for all students. *Professional School Counseling, 16*(2), 84–88.

Larry P. v. Riles, 502 F.2d 963 (N.D. Cal. 1974).

Lawson, T. G. (2007). Ask the expert. (B. M. McDowell, Ed.). *Journal for Specialists in Pediatric Nursing, 12*(1). doi:10.1111/j.1744–6155.2007.00088.x

Leahy, M. J. & Szymanski, E. M. (1995) Rehabilitation counseling: Evolution and current status. Journal of Counseling and Development. 74, 2. https://scholars.opb.msu.edu/en/persons/michael-j-leahy-2/publications/

Leamon, M. H., Wright, T. M., & Myrick, H. (2008). Substance related disorders. In R. E. Hales, S. C. Yudofsky, & G. O. Gabbard (Eds.), *The American Psychiatric Publishing Textbook of Psychiatry* (5th ed.). Washington, DC: American Psychiatric Publishing Inc.

Lee, E., & Ditchman, N. (2012). Assessment. In F. Chan, M. Bishop, J. Chronister, & C. Chiu (Eds.), *Certified Rehabilitation Counselor Examination Preparation* (pp 135–154). New York, NY: Springer.

Lewis, T. (2014). *Substance Abuse Treatment: Practical Application of Counseling Theory*. Upper Saddle River, NJ: Pearson Education, Inc.

Lewis, C., & Sabedra, C. (2001). *When assessments fail: Using alternative approaches to career exploration*. Retrieved from ERIC database: https://eric.ed.gov/?id=ED458490

Linehan, M., Goodstein, J., Nielsen, S., & Chiles, J. (1983). Reasons for staying alive when you are thinking of killing yourself: The reasons for living inventory. *Journal of Consulting and Clinical Psychology, 51*, 276–286.

Lohman, D. F. (2012a). *Cognitive Abilities Test Form 7* [Assessment Instrument]. Rolling Meadows, IL: The Riverside Publishing Company.

Lohman, D. F. (2012b). *Cognitive Abilities Test Form 7 Norms and Score Conversions Guide* (V. 2). Rolling Meadows, IL: The Riverside Publishing Company.

Lohman, D. F. (2013a). *Cognitive Abilities Test Form 7 Planning and Implementation Guide* (V. 4). Rolling Meadows, IL: The Riverside Publishing Company.

Lohman, D. F. (2013b). *Cognitive Abilities Test Form 7 Score Interpretation Guide* (V. 2). Rolling Meadows, IL: The Riverside Publishing Company.

Lohman, D. F. (2014). *Cognitive Abilities Test Form 7 Product Guide*. Rolling Meadows, IL: The Riverside Publishing Company.

Luft, J. (1969). *Of Human Interaction*. Palo Alto, CA: National Press.

Luft, J., & Ingham, H. (1955). *The Johari Window: A Graphic Model for Interpersonal Relations*. University of California Western Training Lab.

Lyon, A. R., Wasse, J. K., Hendrix, E., Ludwig, K., Bergstrom, A., & McCauley, E. (2016). Determinants and functions of standardized assessment use among school mental health clinicians: A mixed methods evaluation. *Administration & Policy in Mental Health & Mental Health Services Research, 43*, 122–134.

MacCluskie, K. C., Welfel, E. R., & Toman, S. T. (2002). *Using Test Data in Clinical Practice: A Handbook for Mental Health Professionals*. Thousand Oaks, CA: Sage.

Mackewn, J. (1997). *Developing Gestalt Counselling: A Field Theoretical and Relational Model of Contemporary Gestalt Counselling and Psychotherapy*. London: Sage.

Marcia, J. E. (1980). Identity in adolescence. *Handbook of Adolescent Psychology, 9*(11), 159–187.

Mayfiled, D., McLeod, G., & Hall, P. (1974). The CAGE questionnaire: Validation of new alcoholism instrument. *Journal of Psychiatry, 131*, 1121–1123.

McGoldrick, M., Gerson, R., & Petry, S. (2008). *Genograms: Assessment and Intervention.* New York, NY: W.W. Norton & Company.

Mignon, S. I. (2015). *Substance Abuse Treatment: Options, Challenges, & Effectiveness.* New York, NY: Springer Publishing Company.

Miller, C. J., Johnson, S. L., & Eisner, L. (2009). Assessment tools for adult bipolar disorder. *Clinical Psychology: Science and Practice, 16*, 188–201. doi:10.1111/j.1468-2850.2009.01158.x

Miller, G. (1997). *Substance abuse subtle screening inventory.* Springville, IN: SASSI Institute.

Miller, F. G., Lazowski, L. E. (2001). The Adolescent Substance Abuse Subtle Screening Inventory A2 (SASSI-A2). Manual. Springville, IN: The SASSI Institute.

Miller, S. D., & Duncan, B. L. (2000). *The Outcome Rating Scale.* Chicago: Author.

Morgen, K. (2017). *Substance Use Disorders and Addictions.* Thousand Oaks, CA: Sage Publication, Inc.

Moriarty, J. B., Minton, E. B., & Spann, V. (1981). *Preliminary Diagnostic Questionnaire: Module 3 and 4: Administration, feedback, and interpretation.* Dunbar, WV: WV Rehabilitation Research and Training Center.

Morrow, M. T., Lee, H., Bartoli, E., & Gillem, A. R. (2017). Advancing counselor education in evidence-based practice. *International Journal for the Advancement of Counselling, 39*(2), 149–163. doi:10.1007/s10447-017-9288-9

Murphy, J. J. (2008). *Solution-focused counseling in schools.* A paper presented to the ACA Annual Conference and Exhibition. Retrieved from www.counseling.org

Myers, I. B. (1998). *Introduction to Type.* Mountainview, CA: CPP Inc.

National Archives. U.S. Equal Opportunity of Employment Opportunity Commission: Title VII of the Civil Rights Act of 1964, 1972, 1978, 1991.

National Board for Certified Counselors (NBCC). (2016). *NBCC code of ethics.* Retrieved from www.nbcc.org/Ethics

National Center for O*NET Development. Food Preparation and Serving Related Occupations. *O*NET code connector.* Retrieved May 18, 2017, from www.onetcodeconnector.org/find/family/title?s=35

National Institute on Drug Abuse (NIDA). (2012a). *Principles of Drug Addiction Treatment: A Research Based Guide* (3rd ed.). Bethesda, MD: Author.

National Institute on Drug Abuse (NIDA). (2012b). *Resources guide: Screening for drug use in general medical settings.* Retrieved May 23, 2017 from www.drugabuse.gov/publication/resource-guide/nida-quick-screen

Naugle, K. A. (2009). Counseling and testing: What counselors need to know about state laws on assessment and testing. *Measurement and Evaluation in Counseling and Development, 42*(1), 31–45.

Neukrug, E., & Fawcett, R. C. (2015). *The Essentials of Testing and Assessment: A Practical Guide to Counselors, Social Workers, and Psychologists* (3rd ed.). Stamford, CT: Cengage.

Nickerson, A. B., & Fishman, C. E. (2013). Promoting mental health and resilience through strengths-based assessment in US schools. *Educational & Child Psychology, 30*(4), 7–17.

No Child Left Behind Act of 2001, Pub. L. No 107–110. 20 U.S.S. 6301 *et seq.* (2002).

The Normal Distribution. Retrieved from https://commons.wikimedia.org/wiki/File:The_Normal_Distribution.svg

Paniagua, F. A. (2005). *Assessing and Treating Culturally Diverse Clients: A Practical Guide* (3rd ed.). Thousand Oaks, CA: Sage.

Parrott, D. J., & Giancola, P. R. (2006). The effect of past-year heavy drinking on alcohol related aggression. *Journal of Studies on Alcohol, 67*, 122–130.

Pearson Clinical. (n.d.). *Wechsler Intelligence Scale for Children-Fifth Edition.* Retrieved from www.pearsonclinical.com/psychology/products/100000771/wechsler-intelligence-scale-for-childrensupsupfifth-edition—wisc-v.html#tab-scoring

Peterson, C. H., Lomas, G. I., Neukrug, E. S., & Bonner, M. W. (2014). Assessment use by counselors in the United States: Implications for policy and practice. *Journal of Counseling and Development, 92*, 90–98. doi:10.1002/j.1556–6676.2014.00134.x

Phelps, L. L. (2013). *Intervention, Treatment, & Recovery: A Practical Guide to the TAP 21 Addiction Counseling Competencies.* Dubuque, IA: Kendall Hunt Publishing.

Piazza, N. J., Martin, N., & Dildine, R. J. (2000). Screening instrument for alcohol and other drug problems. *Journal of Mental Health Counseling, 22*(3), 218–227.

Piper, B. J., Gray, H. M., Raber, J., & Birkett, M. A. (2014). Reliability and validity of brief problem monitor, an abbreviated form of the Child Behavior Checklist. *Psychiatry and Clinical Neurosciences, 68*, 759–767. doi:10.1111/pcn.12188

Pokorny, A. D. (1983). Prediction of suicide in psychiatric patients: Report of a prospective study. *Archives of General Psychiatry, 40*, 249–257.

Power, P. W. (2013). *A Guide to Vocational Assessment* (5th ed.). Austin, TX: PRO-ED.

Prochaska, J., Le, V., Baillargeon, J., & Temple, J. (2016). Utilization of professional mental health services related to population-level screening for anxiety, depression, and post-traumatic stress disorder among public high school students. *Community Mental Health Journal, 52*(6), 691–700.

Purcell, J., & Eckert, R. (2006). *Designing Services and Programs for High-Ability Learners*. National Association for Gifted Children. Thousand Oaks, CA: Corwin Press.

Rawlins-Alderman, L. A., Dock, R. E., Steele, M., & Wofford, L. (2015). Current vocational assessment methods. [Special issue]. *Vocational Evaluation and Work Adjustment Association Journal and Vocational Evaluation and Career Assessment Journal*, 18–36.

Read, K. L., Settipani, C. A., Peterman, J., Kendall, P. C., Compton, S., Piacentini, J., . . . March, J. (2015). Predicting anxiety diagnosis and severity with the CBCL-A: Improvement relative to other CBCL scales. *Journal of Psychopathological Behavior and Assessment*, (37), 100–111. doi:10.107/s10862-014-9439-9

Regehr, C., Bogo, M., LeBlanc, V. R., Baird, S., Paterson, J., & Birze, A. (2016). Suicide risk assessment: Clinicians' confidence in their professional judgment. *Journal of Loss and Trauma, 21*(1), 30–46. doi:10.10 80/15325024.2015.1072012

Reynolds, C. R., & Kamphaus, R. W. (2015). *Behavioral Assessment System for Children* (3rd ed.). San Antonio, TX: Pearson.

Reynolds, W. (1988). *Adult suicide ideation questionnaire*. Ann Arbor, MI: Ann Arbor Press.

The Riverside Publishing Company. (2014). *Logramos Tercera Edición Product Guide*. Orlando, FL: Houghton Mifflin Harcourt.

Rogers, C. R. (1961). *On Becoming a Person: A Therapist's View of Psychotherapy*. New York: Houghton Mifflin Company.

Rogers, J., & Alexander, R. (1994). Development and psychometric analysis of the Suicide Assessment Checklist. *Journal of Mental Health Counseling, 16*, 352–368.

Rubin, S. E., & Roessler, R. T. (2008). *Foundations of the Vocational Rehabilitation Process* (4th ed.). Austin, TX: PRO-ED.

Rudd, D. M. (2014). Core competencies, warning signs, and a framework for suicide risk assessment in clinical practice. In M. K. Nock (Ed.), *The Oxford Handbook of Suicide and Self-Injury* (pp. 323–336). New York: Oxford University Press.

Sartor, T. A., McHenry, B., & McHenry, J. (2017). Ethics of working with children, adolescents, and their parents. In T. A. Sartor, B. McHenry, & J. McHenry (Eds.), *Ethical and Legal Issues in Counseling Children and Adolescents*. New York, NY: Routledge. ISBN: 9781138948006

Schoppe-Sullivan, S. J., Schermerhorn, A. C., & Cummings, E. M. (2007). Marital conflict and children's adjustment: Evaluation of the parenting process. *Journal of Marriage and Family, 69*, 1118–1134.

Scott, J. C., & Marcotte, T. D. (2010). Everbody impact of HIV-associated neurocognitive disorders. In T. D. Marcotte & I. Grant (Eds.), *Neuropsychology of Everyday Functioning*. New York: Guilford Press.

Seppala, M. D. (2004). Dilemmas in diagnosing and treating co-occurring disorders: An addiction professional's perspective. *Behavioral Healthcare Tomorrow, 13*(4), 42–47.

Shapiro, D. (2012). Theoretical value of psychological testing. *Journal of Personality Assessment, 94*(6).

Sharif v. New York State Educational Development, 709 F. Supp. 345 (S.D.N.Y. 1989).

Sharpley, C. F., & Heyne, D. A. (1993). Counsellor communicative control and client-perceived rapport. *Counselling Psychology Quarterly, 6*(3), 171–182.

Shem, S. (1978). *The House of God*. New York: Dell Publishing Co.

Simon, R. I. (2002). Suicide risk assessment: What is the standard of care? *The Journal of the American Academy of Psychiatry and the Law, 30*, 340–344.

Smedema, S. M., Ruiz, D., & Mohr, M. (2017). Psychometric validation of the world health organization disability assessment schedule 2.0- twelve-item version in persons with spinal cord injuries. *Rehabilitation Research, Policy, and Education, 31*(1), 7–20.

Soltis, K., Davidson, T. M., Moreland, A., Felton, J., & Dumas, J. (2015). Associations among parental stress, child competence, and school-readiness: Findings from the PACE study. *Journal of Child and Family Studies, 24,* 649–657. doi: 10.1007/s10826-013-9875-2

Spearman, C. (1904). "General intelligence": Objectively determined and measured. *American Journal of Psychology, 15,* 201–293.

Spielberger, C. D., Gorsuch, R. L., Lushene, R., Vagg, P. R., & Jacobs, G. A. (1983). *Manual for the State-Trait Anxiety Inventory.* Palo Alto, CA: Consulting Psychologists Press.

Sprague, J. R., & Walker, H. M. (2004). *Safe and Healthy Schools: Practical Prevention Strategies.* New York, NY: Guilford Press.

Stormont, M., Herman, K. C., Reinke, W. M., King, K. R., & Owens, S. (2015). The Kindergarten academic and behavior readiness screener: The utility of single-item teacher ratings of kindergarten readiness. *School Psychology Quarterly, 30*(2), 212–228. doi:10.1037/spq0000089

Studer, J. R., Oberman, A. H., & Womack, R. H. (2006). Producing evidence to show counseling effectiveness in schools. *Professional School Counseling, 9*(5), 385–391.

Substance Abuse and Mental Health Services Administration (SAMHSA). (2014). *Improving cultural competence.* Retrieved from https://www.samhsa.gov/capt/applying-strategic-prevention/cultural-competence.

Substance Abuse and Mental Health Services Administration (SAMHSA). (2015). *Suicidal thoughts and behavior among adults: Results from the 2015 National Survey on Drug Use and Health.* Retrieved from www.samhsa.gov/data/sites/default/files/NSDUH-DR-FFR3-2015/NSDUH-DR-FFR3-2015.htm

Sullivan, G. R., & Bongar, B. (2006). Psychological testing in suicide risk management. In R. I. Simon & R. E. Hales (Eds.), *The American Psychiatric Publishing Textbook of Suicide Assessment and Management* (pp. 177–196). Washington, DC: American Psychiatric Publishing.

Tarter, R. E. (2011). Psychological evaluation of substance use disorder in adolescents and adults. In R. J. Frances, S. I. Miller, & A. H. Mack (Eds.), *Clinical Textbook of Addictive Disorders* (3rd ed.). New York, NY: Guilford Press.

Tavassolie, T., Dudding, S., Madingan, A. L., Thorvardarson, E., & Winsler, A., (2016). Differences in perceived parenting style between mothers and fathers: Implications for child outcomes and marital conflict. *Journal of Child and Family Studies, 25,* 2055 2068. doi: 10.1007/s10826-016-0376-y

Thapa, A., Cohen, J., Higgins-D'Alessandro, A., & Guffey, S. (2012, August). *School Climate Research Summary.* National School Climate Center. Retrieved from www.schoolclimate.org.

Thompson, D. W., Loesch, L., & Seraphine, A. (2003). Development of an instrument to assess the counseling needs of elementary school students. *Professional School Counseling, 7*(1), 35–39.

Thompson, R. A. (2012). *Professional School Counseling: Best Practices for Working in the Schools* (3rd ed.). New York, NY: Routledge/Taylor & Francis.

Thorndike, R. M. (1997). *Measurement and Evaluation in Psychology and Education* (6th ed.). Upper Saddle River, NJ: Prentice Hall.

Topping, K. J., & Trickey, S. (2007). Collaborative philosophical enquiry for school children: Cognitive effects at 10–12 years. *British Journal of Educational Psychology, 77*(2), 271–288. doi:10.1348/000709906X05328

U.S. Department of Health & Human Services (DHHS). (1987). Confidentiality of alcohol and drug abuse patient records: Final rule. *Federal Register, 52*(10), 21796–21814.

Unger, D. G., McLeod, L. E., Brown, M. B., & Tressell, P. A. (2000, June). The role of family support in interparental conflict and adolescent academic achievement. *Journal of Child and Family Studies, 9,* 191–202. http://dx.doi.org/1062-1024/00/0600-0191$18.00/0

United States. (1996). *The Health Insurance Portability and Accountability Act (HIPAA).*

The University of Iowa. (2012a). *Iowa Assessments Form E* [Assessment Instrument]. Orlando, FL: Houghton Mifflin Harcourt Publishing Company.

The University of Iowa. (2012b). *Iowa Assessments Forms E & F Complete Levels 15–17/18 Norms and Score Conversions Guide with School Norms* (V. 3). Orlando, FL: Houghton Mifflin Harcourt Publishing Company.

The University of Iowa. (2012c). *Iowa Assessments Forms E & F Levels 15–17/18 Score Interpretation Guide* (V. 2). Orlando, FL: Houghton Mifflin Harcourt Publishing Company.

The University of Iowa. (2014a). *Iowa Assessments Forms E & F Planning and Implementation Guide* (V. 4). Orlando, FL: Houghton Mifflin Harcourt Publishing Company.

The University of Iowa. (2014b). *Iowa Assessments Forms E & F Product Guide* (V. 4). Orlando, FL: Houghton Mifflin Harcourt Publishing Company.

van der Ende, J.,Verhulst, F. C., & Tiemeier, H. (2016).The bidirectional pathways between internalizing and externalizing problems and academic performance from 6 to 18 years. *Development and Psychopathology, 28*, p. 855–867. doi: 10.1017/S0954579416000353

van der Gaag, M., Hoffman, T., Remijsen, M., Hijman, R., de Haan, L., van Meijel, B., . . . Wiersma, D. (2006). The five-factor model of the Positive and Negative Syndrome Scale II: A ten-fold cross-validation of a revised model. *Schizophrenia Research, 85*, 280–287.

van der Veen-Mulders, L., Nauta, M. H., Timmerman, M. E., van den Hoffdakker, B. J., & Hoekstra, P. J. (2017). Predictors of discrepancies between fathers and mothers in rating behaviors of preschool children with and without ADHD. *European Child and Adolescent Psychiatry, 26*, 365–376. doi:10.1007/s00787-016-0897-3

Ventura, J., Lukoff, D., Nuechterlein, K. H., Liberman, R. P., Green, M., & Shaner, A. (1993). Brief Psychiatric Rating Scale (BPRS) expanded version (4.0) scales, anchor points and administration manual. *International Journal of Methods in Psychiatric Research, 3*, 227–244.

Veen-Mulders, van der, L., Nauta, M. H., Timmerman, M. E., van den Hoofdakker, B. J., & Hoekstra, P. J. (2017). Predictors of discrepancies between fathers and mothers in rating behaviors of preschool children with and without ADHD. *European Child & Adolescent Psychiatry, 26*(3), 365–376.

Wechsler, D. (1940). Non-intellective factors in general intelligence. *Psychological Bulletin, 37*, 444–445.

Wechsler, D. (2008). *Wechsler Adult Intelligence Scale* (4th ed.). San Antonio, TX: Pearson.

Wechsler, D. (2012). *Wechsler Preschool and Primary Scale of Intelligence* (4th ed.). San Antonio, TX: Pearson.

Wechsler, D., Raiford, S. E., & Holdnack, J. A. (2014). *Wechsler Intelligence Scale for Children – Fifth Edition: Technical and Interpretive Manual*. Bloomington, MN: Pearson.

Weed, R. O., & Hill, J. A. (2008). *CRC Exam Guide to Success* (9th ed.). Athens, GA: Elliott & Fitzpatrick.

Weiss, L. G., Saklofske, D. H., Holdnack, J. A., & Prifitera, A. (2016). *WISC-V Assessment and Interpretation: Scientist-Practitioner Perspectives*. San Diego, CA: Elsevier.

West, S. L., Armstrong, A. J., & Ryan, K. A. (2005). An assessment of institutional publication productivity in rehabilitation counseling. *Rehabilitation Counseling Bulletin, 49*(1), 51–54.

Whiston, S. C. (2009). *Principles and Applications of Assessment in Counseling*. Australia: Brooks/Cole, Cengage Learning.

Whiston, S. C. (2012). *Principles and Applications of Assessment in Counseling* (4th ed.). Belmont, CA: Brooks/Cole.

Whiston, S. C. (2017). *Principles and Applications of Assessment in Counseling* (5th ed.). Boston, MA: Cengage Learning.

Winerman, L. (2013). Breaking free from addiction. *Monitor on Psychology, 44*(6), 30–34.

Wong, P. (2015). Meaning therapy: Assessments and interventions. *Existential Analysis, 26*(1).

World Health Organization (WHO). (2014). *WHO disability assessment schedule 2.0 [Measurement instrument]*. Retrieved from www.who.int/classifications/icf/more_whodas/en/

Wright, R. J. (2012). *Introduction to School Counseling*. Thousand Oaks, CA: Sage.

Yan, H., & Chen, J. (2011). The broad prospects of the clinical applications of drawing art therapy. *Medicine and Philosophy, 10*, 56–57.

Zunker, V. (2015). *Career Counseling: Applied Concepts of Life Planning* (6th ed.). Pacific Grove, CA: Brooks Cole.

Answer Key to End-of-Chapter Test Your Knowledge Questions

Chapter										
1	D	D	C	B	A	C	D	C	D	D
2	B	A	C	D	D	A	C	B	B	B
3	B	D	C	C	D	B	D	D	D	A
4	B	C	A	C	F	T	F	F	F	F
5	C	A	D	A	A	B	D	D	T	F
6	D	C	T	A	B	D	C	F	F	F
7	C	B	D	T	C	D	D	T	T	T
8	B	C	D	F	A	C	B	C	A	T
9	B	C	C	A	C	A	A	D	A	B
10	B	C	D	D	B	A	B	C	B	A
11	C	D	C	A	T	F	F	T	F	F
12	F	D	D	D	B	E	A	F	E	F

Index